40 DATES
& 40 NIGHTS

40 DATES & 40 NIGHTS

THE TRUE DATING ADVENTURES OF AMY MAIN

ADAPTIVE BOOKS

AN IMPRINT OF ADAPTIVE STUDIOS
CULVER CITY, CA

Throughout this book, I have attempted to re-create stories, conversations, events, and locations as accurately and faithfully as possible. Nonetheless, in many cases I have changed the names of individuals and places in order to maintain appropriate anonymity; in addition, in some cases I have changed identifying characteristics and details such as physical attributes, occupations, and places of residence.

Copyright © 2016 Adaptive Studios
All rights reserved. No part of the publication may be reproduced, distributed, or transmitted in any form or by any means, including photocopying, recording, or other electronic or mechanical methods, without the prior written permission of the publisher, except in the case of brief quotations embodied in critical reviews and certain other noncommercial uses permitted by copyright law.

Visit us on the web at www.adaptivestudios.com

Library of Congress Cataloging-in-Publication Number: 2015950712
ISBN 978-0-9864484-7-8
eBook ISBN 978-0-9964887-0-9

Printed in the USA.
Designed by Mallory Grigg.

Adaptive Books
3578 Hayden Avenue, Suite 6
Culver City, CA 90232

10 9 8 7 6 5 4 3 2 1

This book is dedicated to all of the hopeful romantics and dreamers. Never give up!

The Girl who Cried Romeo

You know that friend of yours who's always way too excited about the person she's dating? They've only been out twice, but already it's "he's totally perfect for me" or "I've never met a guy who's made me laugh this much" or "we even joked about getting married at the bar"? And all you can think is, *Oh boy, here we go again. How many days till we're hitting the old-fashioneds and blowing through boxes of Kleenex?* And often it's two weeks, occasionally it's three months, and once it was two years, but it always ends exactly the same—with said friend being single? Well, that friend is me.

I never plan to fall in love so fast. I know it makes me seem crazy. One week it was Jarred, the next it was Greg, then Liam, John, Nick, Kal. I could see the look in my girlfriends' eyes when I began gushing about the latest beau, their glances to each other as I recited his poetic text messages. I tried to slow myself down, to stop being so charmed, to remind my biological clock to shut the hell up. But it didn't seem to help. I still forgot to check for the parachute before I jumped out of the plane. Which is precisely what happened with James.

I had just returned from a spectacular month in Europe. I'd drunk rosé in Saint-Tropez, sung "Edelweiss" on a *Sound of Music* tour in Salzburg, ridden a rental bike through the rain-streaked *rues* of Paris, and managed to fall hard for only two beautiful men (both Londoners living in Shoreditch, one a hard-bodied Jewish financier, the other an ultrahip creative exec at a top ad agency—*swoon*). In short, I was primed for love.

I've never understood why people get so weird about saying that they met someone online, as if the only people trolling the Internet for partners are actual trolls. They're not. Prior to James, my veritable Prince Charming, I'd met perhaps a dozen non-trolls through OkCupid and Match.com. I found the quality higher on the latter, but both sites had produced perfectly normal human beings. And that's how I found James.

Or rather, he found me. I was on a train from San Diego to Los Angeles when he reached out. It was love at first email. His perfect balance of compliments ("you're the most interesting person I've had the pleasure to come across recently") and humble brags (he worked for an NGO in Kenya, NBD), his use of vocab words like "eloquent," "brevity," and "crepuscular" (okay, he didn't write that last one, but I'm sure he has at some point), his offer of coffee, dinner, or a screening of a Sundance darling—I was done for.

Next thing I knew, James met me that evening at Union Station. In retrospect, this was a horrible idea—trusting a complete stranger to pick me up in downtown LA?—but at the time it seemed impossibly romantic, a story for the grandchildren. That's how certain I felt from a few well-chosen photos and text messages.

My instincts were right. By the end of our first date, I knew James was my soul mate. How could he not be? Adorable, athletic, Mensa brilliant, world traveler, ridiculously well read, empathetic, humanitarian, fantastic kisser, winsome dimples—game over. James was everything I'd ever wanted. And remarkably, he seemed to feel the same way about me. Somehow we just *knew*.

Our second date, a staycation at his parents' beautiful home in the Palisades (they no longer lived there), lasted twelve hours. We listened to Sigur Rós, watched *This Is the End*, ate Ben & Jerry's, drank a bottle of pinot noir, had sex.

Yeah, I know. Sex on the second date. *Whoops.* We talked about it beforehand, and both figured it might not be the best idea. But then again, we were going to be together forever, right? What difference did it make if we waited one date or twenty? Besides, I'd been sexually liberated over the last year through pole dancing. I could handle it.

And so I fell in love. Truly, madly, deeply, blindly. With each passing day, I climbed higher and higher, paying no attention to the thousand sharp spears that would impale me if I fell. I didn't care—the world became so much brighter with

James by my side. It was as if he'd delivered some payload to the sun and all this crazy light and energy had burst into the universe and magnificently illuminated everything. He had lit this fuse inside of me that was maddening and overwhelming but also so exciting, I hoped it never exploded, unless that explosion was some sort of genius aha moment in which I discovered the secret of the universe. (Spoiler alert: this book will not reveal the secret of the universe.)

"This is it," I told my friends, my coworkers, anyone who would listen to a hopelessly lovesick twenty-eight-year-old. "This has to be it. This time it's real. I've found my true Romeo!"

♥

But as any die-hard Leonardo DiCaprio fan will tell you, the story of Juliet and her sweet Romeo does not end well. In fact, it ends horribly. It ends in twin suicides—pretty much the most tragic ending imaginable. Luckily the story of Amy and James ends better than that. No one commits suicide. No one dies. There's not even a slap or the slamming of a door.

Although, for me, it did feel like a death. Maybe because when I'd jumped out of the plane I hadn't even bothered to put on the backpack with the parachute. There was nothing to break my free fall except those thousand heart-puncturing spears I had ignored. Well, I couldn't ignore them now, as they bled me out in the form of fat, ugly tears on my UCLA sweats. *You win, spears, you win.*

"So what on earth happened?" you ask. "How did you guys go from one hundred to zero so fast?"

Well, it's complicated. But long story short, there *was* an explosion—of his career. And not the good kind, like when a celebrity "blows up," but the bad kind—"good-bye job." Which would be hard enough for any new romance, but coupled with his severe, lifelong struggle with OCD, it spelled the end of our world. And while he thought I was "amazing," exactly the girl he had always hoped to find—his Juliet—he had to end our relationship and put back together the pieces of his life.

"I won't ask you to wait, because that would be selfish," he told me as he held me in his perfect arms. "But I hope maybe someday we can try this again. When the timing is right."

After the initial sucker punch that defines any heartbreak (sobbing in the car to Celine Dion; sobbing on the phone to my best friend, Ashley; sobbing in bed to Teddy, my teddy bear), I managed to convince myself that James and I were simply on a break. Sure, he hadn't asked me to wait, but he had totally implied that I should, right? I mean, "hope," "try again," "timing"—those words just *screamed* three-week break, no? James would find a new career, his OCD and insomnia would subside, I would do a spa weekend in Palm Springs and write the romantic comedy version of *Romeo and Juliet*, and by October we'd be back together! (Hey, I'd been acting for two decades; at this point I was capable of believing anything.)

The illusion lasted a week. Then it got ugly. I contracted the flu and spent several miserable days in bed. I reached out to James once a day for four days, but was met with silence. *Maybe he actually did die*, I worried. *Maybe this is more Shakespearean than I thought.* Finally I received a hurried call from him. He had been in the hospital (!!!), some sort of ear infection; he had to go, but he'd call me back later. And that was it. I never heard from him again. The truth sank in.

My physical health returned, but I continued to stay in bed, comforting myself with sad, dark Nordic artists and Costco-sized bags of Dark Chocolate M&M's (bonus guilt: I dip them in peanut butter). For two weeks, I did nothing but plow through Karl Ove Knausgaard's *My Struggle* and a six-pack of Kleenex. I ignored phone calls from friends. I binge-watched Lars von Trier films. I stopped wearing clothes (my pink polka dot robe is so soft). In short, I was depressed.

After a month came and went without a single text from James, not one "I miss you" or "I'm thinking of you" or even "I have a new girlfriend, bitch, so get over it," I decided it was finally time to take a serious look in the mirror.

And it was terrifying. My roots had grown in an inch, I'd put on several pounds, my eyes were in a state of permapuff—I needed to reevaluate my life.

REEVALUATION OF MY LIFE (from my journal)

My name is Amy Main. I am a twenty-eight-year-old single white female living in Los Angeles. I have a very good life, at least on paper. For one, I make a decent living as an actress. Well, sort of. Most of my income comes from doing commercial background and standing in for the Wendy's girl, so it's not exactly acting or in any way artistically fulfilling, but I don't have to wait tables between real gigs anymore. HUGE victory. It also provides me with enough time and money to do things like go to Europe for a month and write. Which is what I really want to do. Write. But I'm too scared. Anyways ...

I've been financially independent and living on my own since I was nineteen. I rent a comfortable bungalow that my mom helped me decorate. I bought my car outright with money I saved, which was awesome, and I have no student loans, also awesome. I don't really use my degree in art history from UCLA, but that's okay, because I loved my studies. I'm pretty and healthy and intelligent. Compared to so many people in this world, struggling with poverty and war and illness, my life is a bed of roses. Yet I cry every day. Why?

Because I am lonely.

Ah, there was the rub. After a month without James, I felt deeply, utterly, profoundly lonely. And I needed to do something about it, because my current strategy—waiting around crying Romeo—wasn't working. Nope, it was slowly sucking away my life. My one beautiful, blessed, incredible, magical life. And perhaps James wasn't ready for a relationship right now, or a marriage, or a family, but I was. And I could either waste my days in bed or go out and get it.

From Tinder to OkCupid

Tinder. I'd avoided the app in the past, because hey, it's only for hookups, amiright? But after talking to male friends who advocated for it—decent, relationship-worthy guys—I wanted to see what all the fuss was about.

I signed up and performed my first swipe left at approximately 5:25 p.m. For those of you who have no idea what I'm talking about, let me explain. It's the easiest game you'll ever play.

HOW TO PLAY TINDER
1. Open up the app.
2. Set your parameters (age range and distance).
3. Evaluate a profile. (You will be shown a picture,

along with name, age, number of mutual friends, and common interests.)
4. Press the X for "no," the ♥ for "yes," OR drag your finger across the picture to the left for "hasta la vista," right for "come to mama" (this will save 0.34 seconds in drag time).

That's it! And if you swipe right, and the other person swipes right, then you WIN! A screen pops up, congratulating you on your match, and then you have the option to either begin chatting or keep playing. Thrilling, right?

And addicting. My first hour using Tinder reminded me of my first day of high school. For five years I'd been in class with the same eleven or twelve guys at Catholic school, holding hands with Tyler and then Alex and then Tyler again, and then Jacob and then Alex and then Tyler, and then suddenly there were *eight hundred dudes* to choose from. Holy testosterone overload! Sure, I only wanted to make out with a handful of them (how many guys are on a football team?), but the point is, there were just *so many frickin' boys*. Way more than enough to temporarily distract me from thinking of James.

And then fate intervened. A girlfriend called me mid-swipe to invite me to a comedy show at the Upright Citizens Brigade—*The OkCupid Show*, where one person goes on three live online dates in a row. I agreed to meet her there in an hour.

Over the course of the show, I watched as the hosts coached the awkward contestant through each of his dates. He had zero (possibly negative) game at the outset, but by the third date, he'd actually—remarkably—improved. He transformed from

Eeyore to adjusted male suitor in just over an hour, thanks to the feedback he'd received from his consecutive dates.

And that's when it hit me, like some sort of insanely twisted arrow had been launched in my direction by a mischievous Cupid: if this dorky cartoon editor could learn that much about dating in three back-to-back dates, what could I learn in three dates? Ten dates? Twenty? The wheels were churning. I had an idea. One as crazy as love at first sight.

MY CRAZY IDEA

I was going to go on forty dates in forty days and blog about it. If that sounds like a lot of work to you, well, yeah. It's practically a full-time job. But I was serious about this dating business, so serious I was ready to take it on as my second career.

I had it all worked out: I would write my blog under a pen name, Jamy Madison, to protect my identity and allow for greater vulnerability in my writing. I would also change the names of my suitors and leave out incriminating details to spare the innocent. And I would do the whole thing through Tinder. It seemed like the perfect way to rid myself of James, gain a better perspective, find a new man, and solve the mysteries of dating.

In prepping for my Lenten period of dating, I felt a mix of excitement and apprehension, the sort of nervous anticipation I usually reserved for international travel. (I'm one of those people who books a trip spontaneously after three glasses of wine, packs the day of, and uses any spare time at the airport to google-research the destination.) I had a start and end date for my adventure, but there was no telling what might happen in between. Would I meet a Brazilian mad scientist and stay up all night talking about particle physics on his air mattress, like I had in Zurich? Or have an unexpected rooftop rendezvous with a guy I hadn't seen since sixth grade, à la my night in Phnom Penh? Or maybe I'd wake up on the floor of a sketchy pharmacy, having been knocked out cold for two hours from a mystery shot to the derriere. *When in Rome* ...

My friends and family had polarized feelings about my mission. Obviously, my parents worried for my safety and questioned the merits of Tinder. I drove out to Palm Springs the day after *The OkCupid Show* to celebrate their thirtieth anniversary with them. They were leaving for Europe on Wednesday, the same day I was planning to start my project. They both looked slightly appalled when I told them my crazy idea.

"Isn't it used for gay sex?" my dad asked, mistaking Tinder for Grindr.

I reassured them this would not be *Fifty Shades of Tinder*.

"Well, whatever you want to do, sweetie, it's your life," my mom said, giving her blessing and opinion in a single statement. For better or worse, she had always let my brother and I make our own decisions, whether it came to fashion, school, career, or dating. I loved her for this.

All of my girlfriends jumped on board with the idea immediately. They knew that my intentions were pure; plus, they were sick of me falling in love so fast. If this could help cure me of some of my bad dating habits, then Tinder away! But my male friends seemed less than enthused.

"Are you looking for a real man or a movie deal?" my friend Garrett needled me. I flinched.

"A man," I replied sheepishly.

"Then don't turn your life into a romantic comedy," he cautioned. "And anyway, aren't you already busy with some other project? Your pole dancing thing or whatever?"

I was producing a short film with two of my girlfriends, "Why I Dance." I'd come up with the idea in the spring: a simple piece showcasing the beauty of the women I witnessed each week in our studio. Five months and one successful Kickstarter campaign later, we were still struggling to figure out our shoot dates. I needed to do something *now*.

But Garrett had a point. Feeling suddenly unsure of what I was signing myself up for with *40 Dates*, I created a list of pros and cons:

Pros
-Meet a bunch of new people outside the Hollywood circle
-Could find my husband
-Get over James
-Improve my dating skills
-Creative outlet for writing

Cons
-Ethically questionable
-Could be a ton of weirdos
-Likely to take up all of my time
-Could suffer exhaustion, pass out, and bang my head on corner of desk like Arianna Huffington but not be as lucky as her and die
-Could end up in Dumpster of sketchy pharmacy

It was a no-brainer. I had to do it. I bought a domain and posted the first entry, committing myself to forty dates in as many days. Sure, I could quit at some point if I needed to, if I ended up desperately in love with, say, Date #23, or in a hospital. But barring those two extremes, I was going to do this.

Time to swipe right!

THE Rules

June 19, 2015, 12:31 PM

1. A date a day for 40 days.

2. A blog a day for each date.

3. All dates from Tinder.

4. Maximum of 3 dates with any one guy.

5. No sex till monogamy - courtesy Patty Stanger

1. **A date a day for forty days.**
   Why?
   - To get my mind off James and open me up to other possibilities
   - To really experience what's out there
   - It's a nice biblical number

2. **A blog a day for each date.**
   Why?
   - To fully reflect on my experiences and learn from them
   - To give others insight into the dating process

3. **All dates from Tinder.**
   Why?
   - The Triple Fs: fast, facile, free
   - It's hugely popular

4. **Maximum of three dates with any one suitor.**
   Why?
   - To keep myself from falling in love with every guy just because he likes me and takes me on two dates
   - To slow myself down and figure out what I really want from a partner

5. **No sex till monogamy—courtesy Patti Stanger.**
   Why?
   - Casual sex can make you fall in or out of love way too fast
   - Pregnancy and STDs
   - Sex is better with someone you really know and have built intimacy with

DATE No. 1

The Tall Prince

WEST HOLLYWOOD

My Tinder marathon got off to a rough start. Actually, more like a false start, as my first suitor canceled on me due to work ten hours before go time. I could have used the same excuse not to go on a date that night—I had been booked on a background job for a pharmaceutical company—but the prospect of breaking my own arbitrary rules horrified me.

"You are seriously addicted to that thing, aren't you?" one of the camera guys asked me as I frantically pulled out my phone and typed away in between takes.

"I, uh...yeah. Obsessed with Instagram," I lied, not wanting to reveal my true actions: compulsively messaging dozens of guys, "Busy tonight?" I suddenly flashed back to my clubbing days in my early twenties, when I used to text my entire phone book looking for the "best party," and immediately regretted this mud-against-the-wall approach. *What if all of them are free? What will I say then? And how desperate do I sound, fishing for a date at ten a.m.?* This was not good form.

The responses trickled in, and as luck would have it, only one was available: Jordan. The others all seemed flattered enough that I was (not so subtly) hinting at a date, and thus I only felt mildly pathetic.

JORDAN:

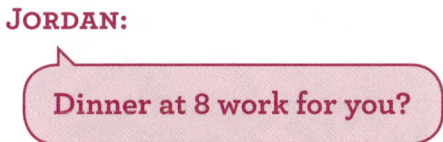

Dinner at 8 work for you?

I studied his profile.

JORDAN, 33
Singer/guitar player, Day Trader, Chef Extraordinaire, Comedy writer, wildlife

Wildlife? That seemed like an odd fifth profession. But hey, I'm from the Northwest, my dad's degree is in forestry—I can hang with a Paul Bunyan.

ME:

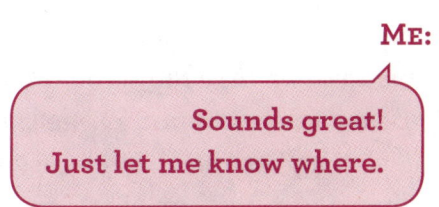

Sounds great! Just let me know where.

Jordan:

Harlowe

Me:

I put away my phone and began to relax—until Dustin approached. He was the drunk uncle of background acting, that guy you once found cool, until you realized he was just an alcoholic.

"Hey, Amy! Ashley told me about this crazy blog you started. Please tell me you're going out with all sorts of guys."

"Yeah, everyone except actors," I replied. I didn't want Dustin thinking he had a chance; plus, I'd been seriously burned by enough actors to know not to put my hand in that fire.

"Sweet! So you've been matching with super-fat Asian guys and seventy-year-old grandfathers, right?" he asked devilishly.

"Uh, no, Dustin. I actually am looking for someone to be in a relationship with, not just a good blog write-up."

I escaped to the craft service table, annoyed. *That's not what this is about*, I thought, grabbing a handful of cashews. *Not that super-fat Asian guys and seventy-year-old men don't deserve love, or that they would inherently make for a good blog post, but they're not for me ... right?* I was beginning to feel like an ageist, racist Tinderer.

I opened up the app. The very first profile was a slightly

chubby Asian guy on a yacht holding a cocktail. I clicked on the picture.

DAVID, 33
Sushi lover, dog lover, cat lover, yacht lover, Muay Thai lover, zoo lover. My friends call me Panda.

Should I give David a chance? I wondered. I mean, he did have a rather nice smile. And I liked pandas. *No, Amy, what the hell are you thinking? You're not even remotely attracted to this guy! And that's okay, because there are billions of guys out there, and you don't have to be attracted to all of them. Dustin is a douche—swipe left.*

I did as I told myself, and finished my cashews. *And stop being so easily swayed by others' opinions. This isn't about anybody but you, and the forty guys you are going to go out with. So just chill the eff out.*

We wrapped at 5:45 p.m., and I had plenty of time to get home, freshen up my makeup, and pick out an outfit. I sent a photo of my short black skirt, silver sparkly top, and five-inch heels to Ashley. I'd been out of the dating game for a few months now, and wasn't quite sure what to wear.

ASHLEY:

> **WAY too fancy.**
> **jeans, cute t-shirt, and heels to dress it up a tad.**
> **don't make it look like you're trying too hard**

I heeded her advice, and threw on exactly that. Satisfied with the ensemble, I headed out the door.

I got to Harlowe at 7:55. The expired meter blinked ominously at me: *Stop. Do not pass go.* My nerves began to rise to the occasion, bundling up like a van Gogh haystack. *Why am I freaking out at the eleventh hour?* "I'm a terrible person," I confided to the steering wheel. "This is a horrible idea." The steering wheel stared back at me. "Yeah, you're right," I said. "I've been on hundreds of dates; this one's no different..."

"Except it's totally different! It's the first of forty in a row! Through Tinder! I'm an insane person! I'm actually crazy!"

My hands started sweating, ready to spin the wheel away from the curb. My phone buzzed in my lap; he was at the bar. I relaxed my grip. *Get it together, Amy.* I took a deep, cleansing breath. *You're just looking for love. And your blood sugar's low.* The red flashing stopped, and I stepped out of my car.

Jordan was actually more attractive than his pictures, with the sort of ethnically ambiguous look they're always clamoring for in casting. We hugged awkwardly—because what else do you do when you're meeting someone for the first time from Tinder?—and then sat down.

Within twenty seconds a server hurried up. "Have you guys been waiting a long time?" she asked, concerned.

"Twenty-five minutes, and we're pissed," I said, straight-faced. Jordan laughed. *Yes!* "We just need a few minutes, thanks." I smiled and she walked away.

The conversation sputtered around for the first half hour or so, stuck in Smalltalkland, but what did one expect with a complete stranger? An in-depth discussion of *War and Peace*? Our thoughts on US military action against ISIS? My crippling need for validation and love? No. How long we'd been in LA and our favorite sushi spots worked just fine to thaw the ice.

As the whiskey tickled my mind and the brussels sprouts and prosciutto flatbread placated my stomach, we began unearthing some more interesting ground. He was 100 percent Egyptian, with family still in Cairo, and I asked him ten thousand questions about the time he spent there (I was obsessed with ancient Egyptian art history at UCLA). He revealed to me the source of his multiple hats, from day-trading to wildlife-ing: ADD. Self-diagnosed, but it seemed plausible enough. And he showed me his Halloween costume, which apparently he prepares all October for: Prince. Or the symbol. Or the Artist Formerly Known As. Or whatever. He looked just like him in the photo, only taller.

In true Amy fashion, any lulls in the evening I attempted to fill with facial contortions and weird voices. This was a habit I'd developed somewhere back in elementary school to deal with discomfort, and I was painfully aware of it. He, however, seemed to enjoy it, and attributed it to my comedy prowess. I assured him I was very bad at improv, somehow always making things sexual and gross, but he didn't believe me. Which was okay, because I had a hard time believing him too when he said he was a sketch comedy writer—until he showed me an insanely dirty scene he'd written. I thought of what my acting teacher had told us the night before: "Our true selves are more revealed in our art than our real lives." *Great. So he wants to insert his celery stick into my tomato juice.*

Overall, I found Jordan quite wonderful. He was handsome, thoughtful, interesting, motivated, kind; there was nothing objectionable about him at all. Except maybe the double ear piercing, and the velvet blazer, but these could be forgiven. I mean, he was a musician. And preparing to be Prince.

He paid the check, I thanked him, and he walked me to my car. It had been a nice evening, but I felt tired and ready to go home. We stood there awkwardly, coming full circle, and he leaned in to kiss me. The angle was off and I stumbled into him, laughing uncomfortably. He kissed me gently for a few moments, and we said good night.

Back home, as I was brushing my teeth, my phone buzzed.

Jordan:

> **Let's plan something soon. It was great meeting you.**

I smiled. It had been nice meeting Jordan. I'd really enjoyed his company. But deep down, I knew the chemistry just wasn't really there.

I could still give it a shot, I thought optimistically. *I mean, he seems like a pretty great guy.* But then I remembered the times in the past when I'd tried this, going on three, four, even ten dates with someone I didn't really have chemistry with. It always ended more or less painfully, and I inevitably felt like a fraud, trying to push my square-pegged self into a beautiful, if not perfect, circle.

> **ME:**
> It was great meeting you, too. Thanks for a nice night.

I turned my phone off. A brief wave of sadness washed over me. Jordan was going to make a wonderful Prince Charming for some girl out there, but I knew it wasn't me. *Oh well,* I sighed inwardly, *the wave riding out into the distance. That's just the way dating goes.*

DATE N.º 2

Lovers and Friends

STUDIO CITY

It felt good to be busy again. In addition to my new writing and dating responsibilities, I also had a feature film audition that afternoon, my first in months. As I excitedly imagined being Allison, a slutty sorority girl who gets murdered, my phone buzzed. It was Sascha, my coproducer for the dance film. I picked up, figuring she wanted to discuss shooting dates.

"Amy, he sounds so great! Why are you dismissing him so quickly?" she lamented. Apparently she'd read about Jordan on my blog.

"I don't know," I replied. "I mean, he was great, but I just didn't feel that intense connection, you know?"

"You mean you didn't feel what you felt with James," she

said. This felt like a reprimand, but I'm sure that had more to do with my interpretation than her actual intention.

"Well, no. I mean, yes, but it also was pretty awkward. Oh god, that kiss! Falling into him, the forced nature of it. It wasn't good, Sasch, I'm telling you."

"I still think you should give him another chance. Think about it at least. And promise me you're going to stay open," she said.

"I promise. In the meantime, I have thirty-nine more dates to prepare for. And this horror flick role I'm going to crush. Love you, bye!"

♥

I wouldn't say I crushed it so much as gently squashed it. Or dutifully massaged it. You'd think after fourteen years of being an actress, I'd strut into auditions with nothing but Kanye West-like confidence. But no. I still got nervous before almost every one, even when I'd put in the work. *What if they don't like me? If I'm too fat, or say something wrong, or cry when I'm supposed to laugh?* Totally inappropriate thoughts to be having when playing a bitchy sorostitute.

It was not unlike the nervousness I felt going into Tinder Date #2. Ten years in the dating field and already I had anxiety at six o'clock, more than an hour before I was meeting him at Aroma Café. *Will he like me? Will he laugh at my jokes, or find me annoying, or peg me as a bitchy sorostitute?* Thank goodness I had time to mull over the important questions.

My audition was less than a mile from our date spot, so I decided to pop into a Starbucks. I strolled up to the counter, eager for my first wintry latte of the endless SoCal summer season.

"Let's see, I'll have a ..." *Oh man, pumpkin spice or salted caramel mocha? Tough one ...* I reached into my purse to buy myself seven more seconds of decision making and realized I'd left my wallet in my clutch the night before. "Ice water."

There definitely wasn't time to go home in rush-hour LA traffic, so I sat at a table outside with my water and a library book. Inside, a guy on his MacBook kept glancing at me. *I wonder if he's on Tinder ... and wants to buy me a pumpkin spice latte.*

I cracked open the book, and stared at the first page for twenty minutes. I couldn't concentrate; all I could think about was dating. *Tinder, Jordan, the guy with the Mac, James ...* My mind was flooded. I closed the book and opted for a walk instead.

It was nearly dark when I got to Aroma at seven fifteen. I waited for John on a bench out front, staring once again at page one of my book. I'd finally made it to page two when he arrived at exactly seven thirty. He was taller than I'd pictured. And more cherublike.

"I've been waiting since six," I said, poker-faced.

"You have?" His doe eyes registered fear.

"No. Well, yes." I laughed and explained to him the whole boring story while we waited in line to order, sparing no snooze-worthy detail. He half-smiled.

"So, uh, yeah. I'm sorry, but you're definitely going to have to pick this one up," I joked. Except it wasn't a joke. I cringed.

"She'll have a water," he said to the guy taking our order. I groaned, but I deserved it. "Totally kidding. She'll have whatever she likes." I grinned. He was cute.

After making Obvious Tinder Dating Mistake #1: Leaving Wallet at Home (I realize for some women this may actually be helpful advice, but not if you appreciate little things like escape plans), it took about three minutes before I made Obvious Tinder Dating Mistake #2: Not Reviewing Profile before Meeting (Especially When Talking to Thirty-Five People). No sooner had we sat down than I revealed just how little attention I'd been paying.

"So, you work in hotels?" I asked.

He looked confused. "Uh, no. Where'd you get that?"

I tried to save face. "I, uh, thought it said that in your profile. Hospitality?"

He shook his head. "I work on a ship for the merchant marine." I swallowed hard. Definitely the wrong guy, and this was only Date #2. I made a mental note to double up on ginkgo biloba.

I'd never been on a date with a merchant marine before, let alone knew what that meant, so he explained. "I spend four months a year on a ship, making sure it doesn't hit things." *Huh, they should've had more of these guys on the* Titanic.

"And the other eight months?" I asked, remembering how depressed I got not seeing James for a week.

"Paid vacation," he responded. *Sweet!* "But it's actually not as cool as it sounds. I get jealous of my friends with their nine-to-fives." *Not so sweet. Water's always bluer, I guess.*

I probed a little further, and John told me he'd found his calling senior year of high school at a college fair. He'd been a bit of a problem child—"you haven't lived until you've been on the verge of straight D-pluses" (I've never even come close to living; straight-A student for life, or, uh ... death?)—and felt he needed some correctional guidance. He went past the khaki-and-plaid Ivy Leaguers and became a stoic, Sylvester Stallone–looking badass (my interpretation). Four years of academy training later, he was off sailing the world, and twelve years after that, he was homeless.

"Homeless?" My jaw dropped, and I quickly picked it back up, not wanting to be rude, further regretting my missing wallet.

"Well, not actually. I own the home where I'm staying until I build a new one on this property I just got in Woodland Hills. But I bought it for my mom, and now that she passed, my stepdad lives there. I just don't like to say I live with my parents."

Whoa. This was a lot of information.

"You bought your mom a house?" I asked gingerly, careful not to push too far.

"Isn't that the dream?" he replied. I nodded. He was sweet.

We talked about reading and writing, *Game of Thrones* spoilers, and the article he'd had published in a motorcycle magazine. I told him about some of the things I had acted in, and a different blog I had, *An Actress Muses* (random personal essays). He told me about all of his toys: trucks, dirt bikes, motorcycles, four-wheelers, eight-wheelers (I may have made that last one up, but if it does exist, he owns it). He divulged his love for building things, getting lost in the creation of a cabinet or the fixing of a car the way I get lost in characters and sentences. He reminded me a bit of my dad.

"Let's get dessert!" he exclaimed after we finished eating.

"Okay!" I said, justifying this decision with the salad I'd

ordered for dinner. "Good thing I didn't have pasta!" I'd been using this sort of logic since I'd learned the true meaning of a carb upon moving to California.

Over chocolate cheesecake and berry cobbler the topic of Tinder came up.

"Ten years," he informed me when I asked how long he'd been on dating sites.

"Seriously?!" I was shocked. Ten years ago I was still AIMing boys in high school.

"How else am I going to meet girls when I'm always around dudes?" Touché.

He asked if I'd had any bad experiences so far (I said I hadn't), and then he told me about a couple of his.

"One girl didn't have an arm and a leg. That was pretty weird. Not that she was missing them, but that she didn't mention it, you know?" Uh, yeah, I did know. That would definitely be ... pretty weird.

"And then this other girl got really drunk at sushi and started naming our children. And kept using her name with my last name." *Yikes!* No wonder he had looked scared when I told him I'd waited for an hour and a half. "But mostly it's been positive. I've met some of my best friends from online dating." I smiled. I could definitely see that.

The nine cups of water I drank were running through me, and I excused myself to the bathroom. I checked my phone.

ASHLEY:

> Still breathing?

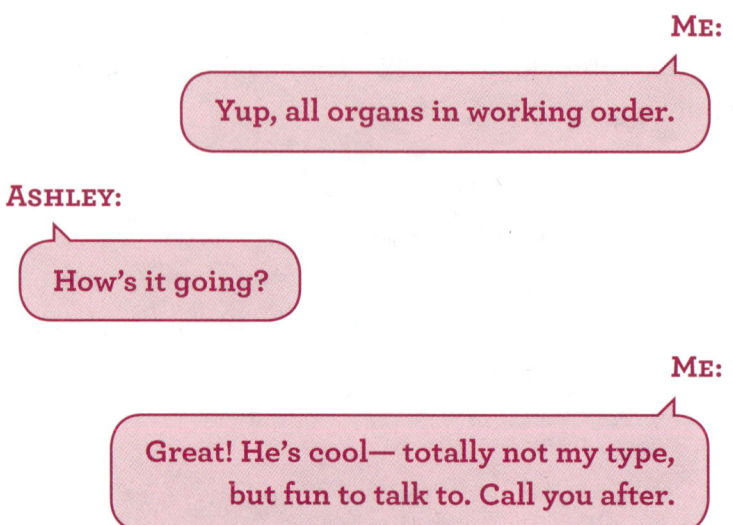

I washed my hands and returned to the table.

"You're making me miss the Angels, you know that?" John teased. I stared at him. *Is this a really bad pickup line?* "It's the playoffs. My buddy just texted me asking where I was."

I laughed. *Baseball.* "I'm sorry! We could have gone to a sports bar!" I pretty much hate sports bars, but there was no need to tell him that.

"Nah, it's cool. I've enjoyed hanging out with you."

"Me too." I smiled. I took one last bite of my cheesecake and boxed it up.

John walked me to my car and gave me a hug. It was neither awkward nor sexual, just casual and comfortable.

"We should do this again sometime," he said, putting to rest all my pre-date worries. I nodded, happy he had mentioned meeting friends online. I could tell we weren't well matched as partners, but it was refreshing to be out with a guy who had such a different energy than I was used to.

"For sure," I said, reaching for my keys. "But next time I'll bring my wallet."

For the record...

TYPES OF GUYS I WAS USED TO GOING OUT WITH:

1. Actors who show you the world for three weeks, then lose all interest after you have sex with them.

2. Actors who show you the world for three weeks, then leave you for the next best thing, aka a prettier actress.

3. Actors who show you the world sporadically for a year, but only when it's convenient for them and fits between their hectic shooting schedule and sleeping with another actress.

4. Waiters and bartenders who are also actors, who show you the world but don't want a relationship because they're too busy trying to get their careers off the ground.

5. Broke writers who borrow money from you and never pay it back.

6. Broke writers who are emotionally abusive and give you panic attacks.

7. Not-so-broke real estate brokers.

Date No 3

Great Expectations

HOLLYWOOD

I started the day on a high, feeling the best I had in a month. *Cheesecake for breakfast, a 2/2 record in the fun date department, a great pole workout?* There was a lot to thank God for beyond it being Friday.

It was actually my first time at S Factor, my pole studio, since the James Explosion. I'd been avoiding dance because I'd felt the polar opposite of sexy the past month (and was afraid of what the M&M's had done to my thighs), but not today. Today I felt invigorated and strong, swinging around that cool piece of metal, flipping upside down into Descending Angels and Superwomans (pole tricks have great names). I was back!

I spent the rest of the day writing, researching Parisian apartments on Airbnb, and anticipating my date that evening with Gordon. Since we matched the previous Friday, Gordon had been the guy I had most been looking forward to meeting: a twenty-nine-year-old TV writer from my hometown, with Clooney-esque salt-and-pepper hair and bone structure and aspirations to be an English bulldog owner. *Swoon.* Plus, he was a regular Cyrano de Bergerac when it came to texting:

GORDON:
This Friday!! So close!

ME:
Yet so far away. Like, 5 days. #impatient

GORDON:
#goodthingscometothosewhowait #usuallydontusehashtagsintexts

ME:
#ilovehashtags #imlearningthevirtue

GORDON:
I hope you are as adorable in person!

See what I mean? How could one not fall prematurely in love? But alas, our drinks date started off on a disappointing note. Not because Gordon was missing limbs, or asked me to marry him, or demonstrated obvious signs of psychopathy. No, he was affable, funny, easy on the eyes, a good conversationalist—the kind of guy you'd feel comfortable taking home to Mom and Dad. So what was the problem?

Me. And my absurdly high expectations (Obvious Tinder Dating Mistake #3: Don't Fall for an Idea of Someone before You Get to Know Them). All that adorable text message banter, the common Portland ground that had created an instant bridge between us (at least in my head), his love of Jenga and coffee brewing—I had worked up some major Tinderthusiasm.

So when he walked into the Library Bar at the Hollywood Roosevelt Hotel, not quite as tall or Henry Cavill-physiqued as I'd imagined, somehow different from his photos and yet looking just like them, my heart sank. Not like a plummet, more of a gentle slump, but a definite change in elevation. I immediately felt guilty, the fault entirely mine, for not recognizing the distance between the page and the world, between my fantasies and his very real self. It was not the first time I'd projected on someone.

He gave me a quick hug, and dashed straight to the bar. I wondered if he wasn't feeling some disappointment in me, too … or maybe he just really needed a drink. We ordered, and he asked the bartender for the billiard balls (pool had been one of our many text convos).

"Oh, you want to jump in just like that!" I exclaimed. He looked nervous, and I didn't want him to be. "I mean, I figured we could talk a little bit first, is all."

He smiled, loosening up. "Yeah, no, of course."

We found two empty leather chairs and sat down. I took a long pull of sauvignon blanc, and made the conscious decision to be as open and present as possible. *We're just getting to know each other, Amy; that's what you do on a first date. No big deal.* I took one more pull, and the small talk began.

We covered the usual bases: how long we'd been in Los Angeles, how we liked the city, what we thought of Tinder. And then, suddenly, the conversation took a dramatic turn. Somewhere between favorite libations and complaints about the weather, we veered into Serioustopicville, and things got interesting. We examined mortality, discussed the responsibility of the artist, psychoanalyzed my ex-boyfriend Phil, whom he had attended high school with. Pretty soon we'd emptied our glasses and needed a refill.

We managed to squeeze in one game of pool before I needed to move my car, which was parked at a two-hour meter. He absolutely schooled me on the felt; then we walked together down the streets of Hollywood, the warm night air and happy buzz compelling me to dance to the various sounds floating from the bars and restaurants.

"You want to grab one more drink?" he asked, clearly enjoying my moves.

"Sure, why not?" I said, wishing there was a pole nearby I could throw my body onto. (One of the dangers of taking pole dancing classes and drinking: no street sign or tentpole is safe.)

We grabbed a couple of beers at a local dive, and continued to share more about ourselves. We talked about scripts we were writing and projects we had shot, exchanging website addresses to our work. (Industry talk is almost impossible to avoid in La-La Land.)

I learned he had no sense of smell (tragic!), he learned about my near-death experience in a horrible car wreck (also tragic!), and we both learned about our shared preference for Blue Moon (delicious!).

The night wound down, and I offered to drive him back to his place (he lived only a couple of blocks away and had walked). I parked on the street, and he kissed me good night. It was nice, but I couldn't help feeling something was missing.

"All right, I'm gonna go in, make some coffee, and check out your stuff." He smiled and got out.

"Yup, me too!" I yelled after him.

Except I didn't. I drove home and sat in my driveway and cried. Partly it was the alcohol, partly it was PMS, and partly it was just the sheer overwhelming nature of dating. Gordon had ended up being a great guy, like the Tall Prince and the Merchant Marine. But he wasn't James. Nobody had ever been James.

When I got inside, I went straight for the cupboards, then my laptop. I should have made two more rules when I'd started my adventure—#6: No Late-Night Binge-Eating and #7: No Facebook-Stalking Exes—but I hadn't. Now it was too late. I'd put back too many drinks to stop this train from wrecking.

I chomped on tear-soaked cheese puffs, scrolling through photos, torturing myself with James's newsfeed. It had been so intense when we'd met, so perfect. And I'd known that very first instant. *Why did things fall apart? Aghhh, I miss him so much!* I reached for my phone.

ME:

> It's taking everything in me right now...

ASHLEY:

> Aww, don't. The least sexy thing is a drunk sad girl texting you after 1am.

I stopped crying. *Oh god, that's what I am! A drunk, sad girl! A drunk, sad twenty-eight-year-old binge-eating and looking at Facebook!* I quickly closed out the tab and threw the bag of cheese puffs across the table. *You are stronger than this, Amy. You are better than this.*

I reached for my phone again, pulled up my conversation with Gordon, and browsed through a few of the exchanges. I smiled, typed the YouTube link he'd sent me into my computer, and pressed "play."

"All right, Gordon, let's see what you got."

He might not be James—in fact, he most definitely wasn't James—but maybe that wasn't such a bad thing.

DATE N⁰ 4

The Cab Driver

DOWNTOWN LOS ANGELES

Need to go somewhere? A friend's house, a fancy restaurant, New York? Just swipe right on Colin, the best taxi driver on both sides of the Mississippi! But hurry up, because a guy this good won't be on the streets long!

♡

I barely slept. Even though I managed to stop the waterworks, I couldn't shut off my brain. I tossed and turned until six in the morning, when the sunlight started peeking through the curtains. Finally I gave up and reached for my computer. I was hungover, exhausted, and once again puffy-eyed.

I somehow powered through my morning, writing and

working out before forcing myself to go to my improv class. I dreaded trying to be funny while feeling like death, but when I looked around the classroom, I realized the universe was giving me a reassuring sign that I was on the right track, in spite of last night's breakdown: twelve men, one woman.

"Looks like the set of *The Bachelorette*," I remarked. The boys laughed. I almost asked who was on Tinder but refrained.

The class went remarkably well, considering the circumstances, but by the time it ended at three, I felt sick to the point of throwing up. *Should I cancel my date tonight?* I pondered on my drive home. I mean, I did feel really awful, and I didn't want to have another mental collapse. *No, I'll just take a nap and stick to the rules.* Plus, I wanted to meet Colin.

Like Gordon, Colin and I had matched on my first day of Tinder. He'd been a bit of an outlier, a right swipe based mostly on his About Me section. In fact, his pictures had my finger *thisclose* to dragging the other way: one normal photo, one weird, ugly monkey photo, one of him making a terrifying pig face (seriously, the stuff of bad horror films), and a bearded Archer screenshot. No, he won me over with this:

COLIN, 36

I'm looking for a slightly damaged, emotionally distant, and attractive woman who likes to live her life one odd choice at a time. Please own a pair of red sunglasses.

I had recently acquired just such a pair of shades—red heart Guess ones from a music festival—and took this as a good omen. *Swipe right.*

Colin came out of the gate doing everything right. First, he started our Tinder chat with both humor and a compliment:

COLIN:

> Amy, you may be beautiful but you do not appear to own any red sunglasses.

I quickly contradicted him, snapping a photo #nomakeup for confirmation.

Second, it took a mere five exchanges for him to ask me to dinner, and to let me choose the restaurant. *Don't mind if I do.* And third, his philosophy on life deeply resonated with me: "If I can't afford the cost or time to go to Detroit or Amsterdam for a weekend bash, I'm doing something wrong." *Hell yeah! Party in Detroit!*

I chose Orsa & Winston, a new omakase-style restaurant downtown. We both arrived precisely at seven, and both proceeded to excuse ourselves to the bathroom (I don't know about him, but I *really* had to pee).

As I sat at the table, perusing the only two options on the menu—five or eight courses, sixty-five or ninety dollars per person—I felt a twinge of guilt at my cheeky foodie tastes. But that quickly passed as my mouth watered over the night's offerings. *Kanpachi crudo with persimmon and anchovy jus? Koshihikari rice with uni and pecorino cream? Yes, please!*

"You're still here." He eased into his seat.

"Did you think I was going to leave?" I laughed, studying his face. He was cute in an intense sort of way, like a cross between Shane West and Michael Shannon.

"I have a confession to make," he said gravely. *Oh no*, I thought. *Has he forgotten his wallet? Are the fate gods paying me back for Date Two?* "I'm a vegetarian."

I looked back at the menu: pork, black cod, pancetta, salmon roe. *Well, shit…*

A waiter flew in like a spy drone. "Dietary restrictions?" I glanced around, half-expecting to spot a hidden camera in our tea light. "We can do a fully vegetarian menu for you, sir. Not a problem." *Fiasco aborted, fine dining experience saved!*

Colin was just as funny and candid in person as he was over text. He jumped right in, asking me about my Tinder experiences, requesting details on each date, analyzing my profile and first impressions (apparently I'm intimidating in my nerdy hotness).

"How many people are you matched with?" he asked. I hesitated. "I've got two hundred twenty," he said bluntly.

I sighed, relieved. "I'm only at sixty-two."

He launched into his temporary obsession with the app, explaining his strategy, the lines that worked in his profile to earn a right swipe and those that didn't. I suddenly didn't feel so bad about my blog.

The courses started coming out, each complex and exquisite, interesting and highly unusual, not unlike the conversation. He told me about his job in finance, which required extensive travel (150,000 miles covered last year).

"You're good with computers and tech, right?" he asked when I inquired further into what he actually did.

"I mean, I can email," I responded, and then attempted to follow as he elaborated on his position as account executive for several hedge funds.

"Basically, I get to travel the world for free and have freedom from corporate slavery, while preserving my expectations for a high quality of life," he stated. "But if I'm being real, I'd prefer to be a stand-up comic."

This led to a discussion of favorite comedians, which naturally progressed to the topic of death (his are all deceased), and pretty soon we were comparing notes on generalized anxiety disorder.

Him: "Mine started when I was twenty-seven."

Me: "Mine too!"

Other similarities included exes with borderline personality disorder, our lead feet (he once averaged ninety-three miles per hour from San Diego to San Francisco; I had managed a cool three-hour drive between here and Vegas), and a strong distaste for one-night stands. We both dreamed of visiting India in the near future, and I got jealous when he told me he used to watch Animal Planet with Ravi Shankar.

When the check came three hours later, it felt like no time had passed.

"I'm a time traveler," he joked, giving the waiter his card. Then he looked at me, serious. "Okay, I have a question to ask."

"Shoot."

"Do you leave twenty percent before tax or after?"

I grinned. "You've obviously never been a waiter before."

He shook his head. "Nope, but I was a cab driver for three months."

"What?" I laughed. "When? Tell me everything!"

And he did. Apparently he had done it not for the

money (he had been in real estate at the time) but simply for the experience, to see the world in a different light. He'd been good at it, too, sussing out what type of music customers would want to listen to, always bringing a good attitude.

"I got awesome tips." His eyes shone, and he pulled out cash to leave for the gratuity.

As we walked to my car, my dress kept riding up. I pulled it down, embarrassed.

"Sorry I wore such a short dress," I apologized.

"Yeah," he said stonily, "that dress shows *way* too much leg ... said no guy ever." I laughed, and we reached my Jetta. There was an awkward pause, the first of the night.

"So, we cool?" he said, studying me. My face contorted—*we cool?* "I just mean we don't have to put any pressure on this, like we have to kiss because it's the end of the date. I don't like those sort of expectations."

For a second I stood there stunned. *Well, this was different! But kind of...awesome.*

"Yeah, no, totally. That's actually pretty cool." I gave him a hug.

"I only kiss a girl at the end if I know there isn't going to be a second date," he admitted. "Like a sort of good-night, good-bye kiss."

I smiled. "Well, then we're definitely not kissing." I opened my door. "Good night!"

DATE Nº 5

All About Me
BRENTWOOD

After four nights of going out for dinner and drinks, I was grateful for the change of pace on Sunday: a brunch date. I wasn't scheduled to meet Jon in Brentwood until eleven thirty, so I went for a long, leisurely run through my neighborhood. It felt great—sun shining, Lumineers on my Pandora, the memory of the Cab Driver still lingering.

I showed up to Le Pain Quotidien a few minutes late. Luckily there was an empty space right in front. I did a quick check in the rearview mirror, made sure my silk romper was buttoned and not revealing any bra, and got out of the car. My phone buzzed.

Jon:

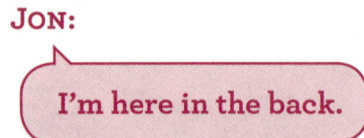
I'm here in the back.

I walked through the restaurant to the patio and did a quick scan. No young single men. *Maybe he came from the back, so he really means the front?* I pivoted and reversed through the restaurant, eyeing every nook and cranny for a cute boy with curly brown hair, but saw none that fit his profile. *Hmm.*

I scanned through our messages to make sure I was in the right place. We had indeed agreed upon the San Vicente location, but when I clicked on the pin he had dropped me, it directed me to Barrington. A simple, annoying case of miscommunication. *Oh well. At least it's only ten minutes away and not another city over.*

He was waiting for me at a table by the window. I slipped into the empty seat and apologized for the misunderstanding.

"That's okay. I digne haoisk fleaid," he mumbled.

I stared at him. "I'm sorry, what?"

"It's not a umerd blissten." *Is he Russian? Polish? Kazakh?* I could barely understand a thing he was saying. And yet he looked as American as apple pie. In fact, I knew he was as American as apple pie from his profile. It said he was a Santa Barbara native.

Juan, our waiter, came over promptly to greet me, and I ordered a coffee, wondering if I didn't just have a really bad four-day hangover. But the coffee changed nothing. It all sounded like gibberish.

"So what do you do for a living?" I asked.

"I work glumsid otitba Century City aplins ertchie junior agent." It wasn't a speech impediment or a learning disability; he just talked lower than Kramer's girlfriend Leslie. And I had notoriously bad hearing. This was not good.

After the ninth or tenth time asking "what?" I finally gave up and took over the reins. (Plus, the coffee ended up being strong enough to kill a horse.)

"So yeah, I grew up in Portland but then moved here right after I graduated high school. My first summer, I lived in a Jewish fraternity at USC. It was *awful*. Then I spent freshman year as a Trojan, but I was an absolute mess, burning the bridge at every end, hostessing at a restaurant four nights a week, taking acting classes in the Valley and assisting my coach the other three, all the while trying not to feel like a fat, broke loser next to the son of John Landis and the ninety-pound daughter of Larry Charles and that blond guy from *Seventh Heaven*. It was pretty rough—like high school, only on steroids, where the popular kids were now famous and actual royalty and point-zero-one-percenters. It was just like, *kill me*. Actually, I honestly believe I would have died if I had stayed there. UCLA was much more my speed."

I took a deep breath, tired of hearing myself talk, and he smiled at me blankly. I was clearly not a romantic match for him either. I thought about canceling my order and leaving, but it just seemed too rude. We were already here, and he was cute and sweet, if not a little young (twenty-six, to be exact).

"So, where do you live?" I tried to ask generic questions, so I could nod and smile when in doubt about his response.

"Brentwood. With five guys."

"I'm sorry, what?"

Clearly I must have heard this wrong. But I hadn't. Jon repeated himself. *Five guys.* That's right, count 'em. One, two, three, four, five. Six dudes in one house. That qualified as a frat in my book, and I'd already been there, done that. I was beginning to remember why I had almost exclusively dated older guys since moving to LA.

He went on to tell me that he did want to get out of the house and live alone, which was encouraging, but then he dropped this: "I mean, glosten ippos losteim flaggor, right?" he said assuredly.

"I'm sorry, can you repeat that?"

"Who knows at our age if they want kids or not, right?" He grinned.

I stared at him in disbelief. I wanted to scream, "Wrong! Dead wrong! I want kids, and preferably by the time I'm thirty-five! So yeah, I have a seven-year plan, and it sounds like you have a maybe-never plan, and this is never going to work! Cancel my order, Juan!" But instead I smiled politely, and replied, "Actually, I do want kids. But let's talk about something else. What's your favorite TV show?"

Thankfully, we were able to move past our totally incongruous views on baby-making and shift into less controversial topics: *Arrested Development*, sci-fi authors, Palm Springs. It ended up being mostly a soliloquy, with me expounding at length on Philip K. Dick's experience of God in a goldfish necklace on LSD, my mom's several marriage proposals, and, of course, pole dancing.

"Pole dancing?" Jon clarified nervously.

"Yeah, I started a year ago, when I got cast in this play

as an ex-stripper. I was at a real low in my life then, dealing with some really bad anxiety, and pole was like this magical space I could just be me. And it totally helped me with my body dysmorphia. I finally stopped judging my body against Victoria's Secret models, and started loving it for what it was, this powerful miracle, ya know?"

He nodded. "I went to a strip club once. A couple of girls took me for my birthday and got me a lap dance. I didn't really like it, though; she smelled like orsten gahben own."

"Like what?"

"Other men's cologne."

I smiled. Kind of adorable, if not a bit...innocent.

By the time we paid the check (yes, I definitely split this one), I actually felt quite fond of Jon—mumbling, family goals, and all. In a land of sharks like the entertainment industry, he was a genuinely nice guy, and I appreciated his gentleness. (Of course, he could have been talking about killing kittens and drinking blood for all I really know.) He walked me to my car; we hugged, exchanged a couple of niceties, and parted ways. Probably forever. *Godspeed, Young Jon.*

I turned on my car and pulled away, reflecting on the past couple of hours to a Damien Rice song. The brunch date certainly hadn't been the sort of ride the Cab Driver had taken me on, and Jon was probably even more ill matched with me than the Merchant Marine, who in spite of his ozone-killing toys at least had baby fever. But hey, in the end I still learned a valuable lesson: I may suck at hearing, but I am fucking awesome at talking.

DATE N° 6

The Guy with the Perfect Teeth

LOS FELIZ

The fatigue was setting in. It had been less than a week, but already my new job was starting to take its toll. The scheduling, the meetings, the gussying up, the showmanship. It was feeling more and more eerily similar to auditioning.

I looked at myself in the mirror. I'd been on set all day, and I was worse for the wear. *Do I really need to put on more makeup? Do I have to strap on six-inch torture devices again?* My eyes pleaded with me. *Nope. You don't.* I threw my hair in a sloppy pony, wiped the smeared makeup from under my eyes, leaving the rest, and threw on a pair of Chucks. *That'll do, Amy. That'll do.*

It wasn't really so much fatigue as it was simply missing my friends. I had three separate invites to the movies that night, and another to "find some place to eat with capers." The thrill of a dark theater with zero conversation and the salty goodness of dark green round things were calling, but I had to go fulfill my dating duty: drinks at Spitz with Marvin.

I spotted Marvin from behind and plopped casually down on a stool across the table. This startled him, but he quickly recovered, and offered to buy me a drink. He disappeared to grab a local wheat, and I reached for my phone, finishing my text conversation with Sascha. She was going on her first Tinder date, and needed advice.

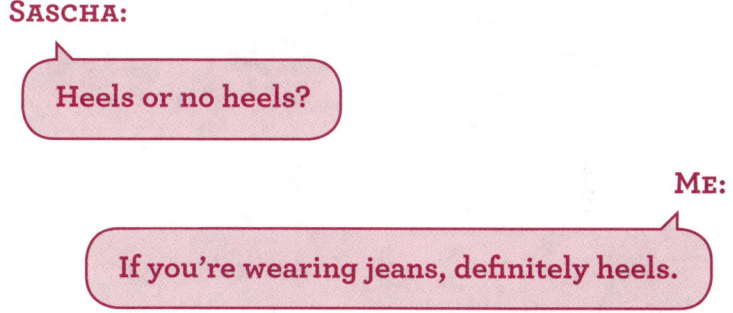

I glanced at my own shabby ensemble. Easier to give advice than take it.

"Here you go." Marvin handed me the beer. I shoved my phone in my purse.

"I promise I won't be using that. My girlfriend was just asking me questions about her first Tinder date."

"Ooh, give me all the details!" He smiled, showing off his perfect teeth.

I filled him in on her nerves, the location, and the wardrobe.

He segued into his buddy's recent anti-Tinder tirade.

"He won't even try it. I don't understand why people are still so weirded out. Sure, it may have begun as a hookup site, but it's not now, and it's not like it was ever Grindr. 'Oh, you're three blocks away? Let's meet in this public restroom.'" (Been there, done that with an ex. Not as sexy as it sounds.)

I laughed. "Yeah, try explaining it to your dad. Now that's a good time."

"So, tell me all about yourself." *Oh god, not this again.* I shuddered, flashing back to Young Jon.

"I'm an actress and a writer," I replied. "Not that I've been paid for my writing yet; more transitioning into that." He nodded.

"So what do you do for the bills?"

I smiled sheepishly. "I stand in for the Wendy's girl."

His eyes went wide. "Are you serious? That's awesome! I feel like there's a documentary in there somewhere." *Yes! Perfect time to deflect! His profile said he was a filmmaker!*

"Do you make documentaries, or ... ?"

"I see what you're doing." He smiled. "Trying to avoid talking about yourself, Wendy 2.0." *Caught red-haired and red-handed.*

I told him about my interest in comedy, my degree in art history, and my plan to spend two months writing in Paris next summer.

"Wait, did you just feel that?" He looked at me intensely.

Shit, am I so self-involved I just missed some sort of seismic activity? "I, uh ... was there an earthquake?"

"No, I just invited myself to Paris." I laughed. "Is that cool? Because seriously, I'm coming."

I happily played along. "Pick up that phone. Book a flight right now!"

At some point in the Exposition of Amy, I made an off-color joke and he chuckled.

"A while back I wanted to start the hashtag *amIracist*, but I was too chicken," I confided.

"Yeah, probably for the best; everyone's so sensitive these days."

I nodded, adding, "Or not sensitive enough, as if Obama has somehow nullified racial prejudice."

And thus began one of the most honest, in-depth conversations I've ever had regarding race politics. The topic took us from his personal experiences ("Why am I always Marvin the black guy? Why can't I ever be Marvin the funny guy? Or Marvin with perfect teeth?") to a USC class we'd both taken with the incomparable Todd Boyd (Race, Class, and Gender in American Film). We debated our covert class system in the United States versus India's and London's ("Wait! Did you feel that? We just booked tickets on the Channel Star!") and discussed the myth of mobility engendered by our current worship of the individual.

The conversation finally wrapped its way back around to the really important issues—dating and having children—and he asked me about my recent Tinder experiences.

"Yeah, with a lot of guys you just know immediately it's not gonna work," I said.

He studied me. "Explain."

I recapped Young Jon and our differing views on babies, then quickly backtracked. "I mean, not like I'm trying to have a baby right now, you know, like tonight or anything, although

I could. But I just can't be wasting time on guys who don't even know if they want kids, you know?" *Ugh, Amy, why do you always do this?* He gave me a funny look. "God, I sound desperate, don't I? I'm just ... Dammit."

He paused, then started impersonating me. "There are *many mens* who want to give me a baby. *Many mens.* I don't have time for all that, cuz I've got *many mens.*"

I laughed so hard I started crying. Tables turned to us, concerned.

"*Many mens.*"

♥

We finished our second beers, and he settled up at the bar.

I thanked him. "This was really awesome. I haven't laughed this hard in a long time."

"Anytime." He smiled with those perfect teeth, leading me out the door. "Let me walk you to your car."

We ambled along Hillhurst, my nerves mounting. I thought about Colin, and end-of-the-night, walk-to-the-vehicle expectations. We approached my car. "This is my Jetta," I said in the lamest voice ever, flailing my arms like a baby T. rex.

He shot me a look. "What the fuck was that?"

I crumpled in mortified fits of laughter. "I don't knoooow, ahhhh. *My Jetta.*"

He moved in close. "Don't make this awkward," he said seriously.

I stared at him, stomach somersaulting. A long pause.

"You're making this awkward!" He backed away.

"I'm sorry!" I said, not sure what to do.

Screw it. I skipped up to him and pulled him in for a kiss. It was sweet, simple.

"We're kissing," he whispered.

"What?" I peeled back. "Now *you're* making it awkward!"

"Come here." He grabbed my waist.

After a few moments, I broke away, not wanting to give away too much on the first date.

"Many mens, in my Jetta," I mocked myself one last time, and climbed into my car, laughing. I couldn't stop smiling the ten minutes it took me to get home. I pulled into the driveway, reached for my phone, and sent Marvin a text.

ME:

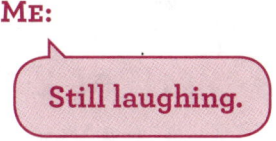

The phone buzzed instantly.

MARVIN:

More smiling. There would be no Facebook stalking tonight.

DATE No 7

The Creative Wordsmith

HANCOCK PARK

Full disclosure: I knew Alejandro and I weren't going to work out before we even met. *I know, I know, I'm sorry, I'm a horrible person!* But it isn't what you're thinking. I really wasn't just trying to fill a mid-afternoon time slot in my forty-day dating schedule with some poor random kid from Barcelona (although it was convenient that he suggested coffee). No, you see, Alejandro and I had been happily Tinder-chatting for almost a week before I realized our almost certainly incompatible fates. And it wasn't until after arranging our coffee meet and greet that he dropped the bomb: he was a broke writer.

Now, you can go ahead and judge me all you want—"Amy, you gold-digging, blog-writing bitch, judging men by their bank accounts"—but I'd been down the broke writer path not once but twice before, resulting in $5,350 in unpaid loans and some serious psychological distress. So nope, there would be no third-time foolery here. I could see the Spanish Wordsmith's potential from a hundred miles away, and I *love* the creative types, but I needed someone who was relationship-ready now. And living on a friend's couch or off Mom and Dad's generosity did not qualify.

So why did I still grab coffee with Alejandro? Well, a) he was beautiful, b) we had a lot in common (writers, filmmakers, UCLA Bruins), and c) this wasn't *40 Lovers & 40 Nights*. Plus, it was coffee, not the altar or Orsa & Winston. So I stuck with our 2:00 p.m. date.

♡

He was running late when I arrived at Graffiti, so I went ahead and ordered a latte. It cost $5.20. For twelve ounces. Without a tip. And no flavors. *Where am I? London? Tokyo? LAX?* I felt guilty for having suggested this ultrahip, not-starving-artist's oasis, but if he couldn't even afford to spot a Lincoln for this date, I was reporting him to Tinder. The barista swiped my card on an iPad and handed me my handcrafted cup of joe.

While I waited for Alejandro, I opted to do some Tindering. *Carl, thirty-five, holding an AK-47?* Left. *George, with the bloodshot eyes?* Left. *Andy, humping a bear statue?* Report. (That really should be an option.) I honestly couldn't figure out what some of these guys' angles were. What were they trying to say? "I practice my Second Amendment rights while blazing up on that Cali weed and occasionally enjoying bestiality?" *Ugh.*

I swiped through at least fifty dudes before stopping on a guy holding a paper mustache on a stick. The backdrop looked like a child's birthday party. Or perhaps a hipster shindig. I clicked on the profile picture to bring up more info.

JAMES, 28
All I'm asking is for a girl to see me the way I see chocolate cake.

His other photos showed him rock climbing and in some sort of mud bath (not a spa; probably a Down & Dirty Obstacle Race). Each of the three photos in some way obscured his physicality, but I could still tell he was good looking. Plus, we had several mutual friends.

My biggest hang-up was his name. Did I really want to get involved with another James? *Jesus, Amy, listen to yourself. You sound like a casting director who doesn't like an actor because they look like a girl from high school who stole everyone's boyfriends.* I swiped right. We matched and I sent off the first message.

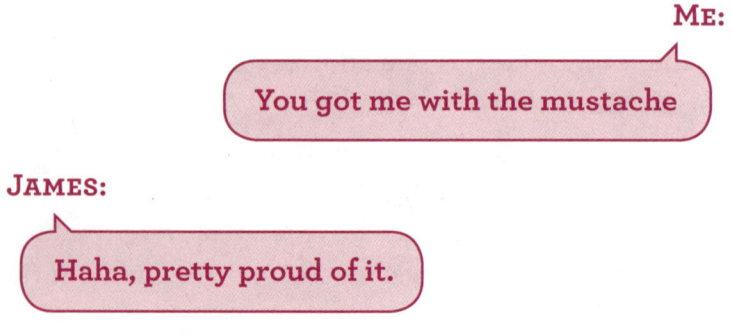

His immediate response indicated he might not have a day job. *Please don't be an actor or a broke writer*, I pleaded with the universe. Then I probed.

ME:

> Are you an actor? I see you're friends with Rory and Brandon

JAMES:

> A rehabilitated one. I made the switch into writing. You?

Ugh, whyyyyy? I was about to go back to swiping when I suddenly had a thought. As a fellow actor-turned-writer, James might actually find this project interesting. And since I clearly wasn't looking to date him anyway, I didn't have much to lose. So …

ME:

> The same actually. I'm doing this blog: Fortydatesfortynights.com

It was the first time I'd outed myself on Tinder. I stared at my phone, nervously waiting for the response.

"Hi! I'm so sorry I'm late!"

I startled, looking up to find Alejandro, even more beautiful in person. I flipped my phone over and stood up to give him a hug.

"Do you need anything?" he asked, his baby blues pleading for forgiveness.

I gently shook my head no, wishing he were less good looking, and he disappeared to grab a beverage. I turned my phone back over and read James's response.

JAMES:

> I'm looking for a girl, a relationship, still not sure what you're looking for—love or just a good blog write-up. I know writers that have done things like this just to try to sell a movie or score a book deal.

Ouch. I winced. Sharing had not been a good idea. *What would Alejandro the novelist think if I told him?* I felt unhinged as I watched him walk back to the table with an iced tea.

"Again, I'm so sorry!" He was apologizing profusely, misinterpreting my guilt for upset. "I thought Second was closer to Fountain, but it took half an hour to walk here."

I gasped. "You *walked* here? From Fountain? In ninety-degree heat?"

He nodded sheepishly. "I know, I should've looked it up on Google Maps. I would've taken a bus."

A bus? I'd taken public transportation exactly once in Los Angeles, a rather harrowing excursion in which I'd been mentally undressed no less than three times and yelled at by a fellow rider.

"I had a car the first couple of weeks," he continued, this

time correctly interpreting my facial expressions, "but I didn't really need one. The bus isn't so bad."

I forced a smile. *He's European, Amy. And you weren't going to marry this one anyway.*

"But hey, it's better than the bus in Barcelona!" he exclaimed.

I laughed, the tables suddenly turned. "I rode the bus in Barcelona," I admitted. He gave me a crooked smile. "Tourist."

If our date was a pendulum, it started on the far left and then swung slowly but surely to the right. I asked him about his published novel, a Catalan sci-fi thriller, and what he was working on in LA. He told me he was here on a student visa studying screenwriting at UCLA.

"It's pretty challenging, but I'm doing all right. I wish my English were better. It's still difficult for me speaking, having to translate, but reading and writing, I'm fine."

I smiled. He actually sounded more proficient than half the guys I met at bars.

"And accents, forget it. Matthew McConaughey should come with subtitles; I can't understand anything he says."

I laughed. Although in our Tinder messages he had said he focused on dark subject matter in his work, I couldn't help feeling he was missing his calling in comedy. His sense of humor was not lost in translation, and I could only imagine what a lady-killer he must be in Spain, euros or no euros.

In response to my thirty or so trips to Sin City: "You're one Vegas away from no brain cells. Next time, comatose."

Regarding Jesus Christ: "Why do people follow him? His magic tricks were shit."

His assessment of his behavior when running after Liev

Schreiber at LAX for a selfie and being blocked by a security guard: "Probably too emotional."

And my personal favorite: "I have a way for you to save money on your trip to Paris next year. Get deported. I'm thinking about doing that here. Free flight home!"

My luxury latte had long been finished when I finally checked the time: 3:45. I could've listened to his accent and stared into those oceanic eyes for several more hours, but there were poles I needed to swing around, and I told him I had to get going.

"How did I end up talking the whole time, when this isn't even my native language?" he asked. I laughed, relieved. Maybe I wasn't a complete narcissist.

"Perhaps someday I'll tell you all about me." I gave him a hug and walked away, no awkward car moment this time.

Will I ever tell him about me? I wondered as I drove to my pole class. *Or about this project?* Maybe yes, maybe no. Probably not, all things considered. I still couldn't shake what the other wordsmith—the other James—had said.

I parked and opened up Tinder. New James stared at me from behind the fake mustache. I wrote one last message, leaving my number in case he wanted to talk about it further. I doubted he would, just as I doubted I'd see Alejandro again, but who could predict the future? If I'd learned anything in the ten years I'd been dating, it was that things never turned out quite how you expected them to. *Ni modo, así es la vida.*

A Word of Caution

In only one week, I'd already met seven lovely guys through Tinder, all totally date-worthy (at least, as long as you had fantastic hearing). But that doesn't mean there weren't some bad Johnny Appleseeds out there. Because there were. Some really bad, genuinely scary, change-your-phone-number, move-out-of-the-country creepsters. Witness Exhibit A.

I first swiped right on Exhibit A because he seemed interesting, a sort of jack-of-all-trades:

EXHIBIT A, 38

Entrepreneur, Photographer, Adventurist, Extreme Sports Enthusiast, Race Car Driver, Horse Enthusiast, Bungee Jumper, Skydiver, Master Chef, Romantic

Quite the mélange of hats! More even than the Tall Prince! But pretty soon it all went south. Like, straight-into-the-heart-of-Juárez south.

Our first few exchanges were nothing too crazy, although I already had a bad feeling.

EXHIBIT A:

> **Are you looking for something special?**

Me:

Yes, aren't we all?

Exhibit A:

Why are you single, and what caught your eye about me?

Me:

Recently out of something. You looked different, fun.

Exhibit A:

I want someone to have fun with and hope that love happens. What city are you in? I live alone in a condo in Simi Valley.

Hmm. Why was he telling me he lived alone in a condo? I didn't reply.

NEXT DAY

Exhibit A:

Amy, would you be interested in meeting for happy hour or lunch next week?

ME:

> I could do lunch Monday.

We exchanged phone numbers, agreeing on a sushi place in the Valley. Then, a couple of hours later, I received word that I had been booked on a commercial gig. I immediately texted him back.

ME:

> Hey. I'm so sorry, but I'm going to need to reschedule. I just found out I'm booked on a job Monday. My apologies!

EXHIBIT A:

> Yeah, I had a meeting on Monday that I called and canceled so I could meet you instead. We all have our priorities.

Whoa. Not what I'd been expecting. I didn't respond.

EXHIBIT A:

> Are you going out of town this weekend?

No reply.

Exhibit A:

> Just text me when you feel comfortable meeting me.

Yeah, let me see—that would be … never. At least I was finally out of the woods. Or so I thought.

NEXT DAY

Exhibit A:

> Help me make a decision. LOL. Pizza or Steak?

Yo, dude, what happened to waiting for me? *Yikes*. But then, radio silence. *Whew*. Until …

THREE DAYS LATER

I received a phone call from an unknown number, and picked it up, figuring it may be work related. Wrong. It was Exhibit A. Cue scary music: *duh duh duh.*

"I, uh…my phone may drop out. I've been losing a lot of phone calls," I said nervously. (This was actually true.)

"What do you have?" he asked.

"An iPhone," I replied.

"Well, that's what you get when you have inferior technology: overpriced bullshit."

Ooookay. You can insult my priorities, but you *do not* insult Apple.

"I love my iPhone. And my iPad, and my MacBook Pro. You know, my agent is calling. I'll call you back." (This one was a lie.)

Moments later I got a text.

Exhibit A:

> Call me back.

Me:

> Sorry, but I'm not really feeling this, I don't think it's a good match.

A minute of silence, and then this (you're welcome):

Exhibit A:

> More lame Tinder excuses why things can't match. Pathetic.

> Oh yeah why because I don't like iPhones?

> How would you know how well we would get along if you know nothing about me and vice versa. Your just scared to take a chance at finding love.

> Bet it would have been different if you met me in the produce isle of vons instead of Tinder

> I'm wondering how much you actually work. I worked on **NCIS: NEW ORLEANS** yesterday. I was in Anaconda 2. I've done tons of tv and movies but it isn't what pays the bills. I'm a very successful entrepreneur. That's what pays the bills in the long run for me. My companies are quite successful and you would have known that if you took a chance. Bye.

Yes, BYE! But was Exhibit A actually done? Of course not.

Exhibit A:

> Thanks for letting me know your true colors because I don't date weak women. Especially ones that are struggling actresses with empty pipe dreams. Classic Tinder girl! Classic!!

I couldn't have said it better myself: *Classic!*

NEXT DAY

Exhibit A:

> Such an amazingly beautiful girl yet so scared at taking a chance at love.
> Please add scaredy cat to your adjectives that describe you.

Noted, Exhibit A. Noted.

TWO DAYS LATER

Exhibit A:

> If your not interested in me then why haven't you unmatched me? Trying to build up courage?

    I was actually grateful he'd reached out this one last time. I hadn't known about unmatching.
    UNMATCHED.

DATE N° 8

An Amiable, Affable, Agreeable Evening
HOLLYWOOD

You would think that after my experience with Exhibit A, I would be as on guard as the Queen's staff in front of Buckingham Palace. But I wasn't. Because only a couple of short hours after pulling the plug on the *Anaconda 2* bit actor, I made Obvious Tinder Dating Mistake #4: Meeting in a Car.

I knew I was jumping directly into the line of fire when I agreed to let Calev, Suitor #8, pick me up on my street. But we had so many mutual friends (fifteen) and the destination was so close (one mile), it just didn't seem like a big deal (it was). I waited for him in front of my neighbor's house.

CALEV:
> What corner do you want me on?

I stared at my phone. *It's a sign*, I thought. *Pimps and hos lingo!*

Me:

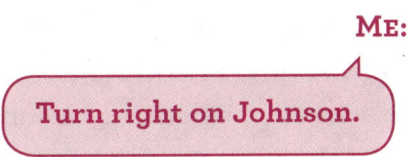

Turn right on Johnson.

Within thirty seconds a 1990s Dodge Intrepid came around the corner, slowly creeping down my street. *Oh god, RUN!* my mind ordered me as I stood stick still, glued to the ground. (No fight-or-flight response for me in a near-death situation, apparently; I just *freeze*.)

The Intrepid passed and a brand-new Range Rover took its place. *That's more like it*, I thought, climbing into the passenger seat, as if expensive SUV drivers couldn't be serial killers.

"Hey." Calev smiled warmly and gave me a hug across the divider.

"If you try anything funny, I've already told Jerry Roth about our date," I half-joked.

"Jerry? Of all the friends we have in common, you trust Jerry?" He laughed.

"Good point," I said, my Intrepid adrenaline dissipating. "Hold on, I'm calling Steve."

I had suggested our date spot, a new restaurant/lounge called The 9 on Vine that I'd never been to. For a reason, apparently: it was dead empty. Two girls with multicolored hair sat at a booth, three hipsters loomed at the bar, and one sad piano man sang Cat Stevens songs.

"This guy's not too bad," Calev said optimistically.

"We can just grab a drink here and go somewhere else," I told him, embarrassed at my choice of venue.

We ordered cocktails and started talking about Jerry. He was a very successful screenwriter and represented a certain type of LA guy: the over-forty playboy with a penchant for models and a deep-seated loneliness that drives his work. (I had gratefully managed to avoid dating this type, probably because I wasn't a model.) Calev knew Jerry through his agent, Peter, who'd also been one of these guys until he recently succumbed to baby fever and simultaneously impregnated and married a Guess girl.

"I mean, I understand why they do it: they're having a blast, throwing parties at their mansions, different girls every weekend. But it's sad. One day they wake up at forty-five like Peter and realize their lives are missing something," Calev said. I nodded in agreement.

"But hey, at least they wake up at all!" I pictured Jerry in a coma for the rest of his life, then felt my own baby fever rising.

I could have gone on for hours with Calev about my desire for a family, how it stemmed from my upbringing and the immense love my parents gave my brother and me. How I'd always wanted to be able to share that with my own children, to replicate the strength of those bonds. How nothing was ultimately more important to me than one day, preferably in the next six years, having two little ones, hopefully a boy and a girl.

But I'd learned the hard way the previous spring that this sort of misty-eyed sharing of one's deepest longings does not settle well on a first date. After a beautiful afternoon spent with an exquisite bachelor of Greek god stature, I'd literally started crying while talking about having my own family. Endearing? Yes, in a long-term relationship or with your therapist. But two margaritas deep, three hours after meeting an Adonis? He'd stared at me like I was a fertility time bomb. (Needless to say, I never saw him again.)

"So, you were running late because of a haircut?" I asked, shifting 180 degrees away from baby-making.

"Yeah, sorry about that," he replied. "It's actually a super Hollywood story. I've been going to this stylist for three years, and she cuts it perfectly, but then she met a guy from Hawaii on Tinder, and now she's moved there for him and only comes to LA on occasion. So I drop everything when she's here."

True Tinder love did exist!

♥

We left The 9 on Vine in search of signs of intelligent life, and ended up at Katsuya. Calev hadn't eaten since breakfast, and it was the only place still serving at ten thirty at night. The hostess sandwiched us between two tables of old men and young girls, the universe laughing along with our earlier discussion, and we continued our agreeable banter: travel, his upcoming birthday trip to Cuba, mine to Europe, his shellfish allergy, Burning Man.

"Wait, *you* go to Burning Man?" I laughed, imagining the Range Rover–driving real estate broker with perfect hair not showering for seven days.

"Twice." His eyes twinkled. "I didn't get to go this year, but I'm already planning everything for next. It's the most incredible experience you'll ever have."

I smiled. "I'm afraid I would die. I can't do drugs like that."

"Neither can I," he responded. "Just alcohol and Pedialyte."

I grinned and shook my head. "Yeah, that's a nice idea, but I know myself too well. It'd be like Vegas: I always say I'm not gonna go hard, and then ... I'm easily swayed by others. It's something I need to work on. So yeah, naked communal baths! So Roman!"

♥

He paid the check, and we walked back to his car.

"You sure you don't want to go dancing? I can find you a pole," he offered.

If there had been one consistency between all of my dates, it had been my absolute inability not to mention my favorite hobby. I didn't want to send the wrong message, but now that I was getting back into it, I just couldn't help it.

"No, it's okay—although if you spot a good-looking stop sign, you should probably pull over." *Maybe with the next suitor I'll try and save pole dancing until date two*, I thought. *Or even three.*

"It's this one, right here." He pulled into my driveway and parked. "Now you know where I live, ahhhh," I joked. "But it's okay. Facebook has vetted you, and it never lies."

We spent a few more minutes laughing about some of the old-school Hollywood peeps: the club kids who'd grown into club adults, the scenesters who'd been around so long they were now part of the scenery. There was something comforting in this sort of silly gossip, a connection that was being built, like "I did that, too. We both experienced the same fun dumb things in our early twenties."

"I had a nice time tonight," I said.

"Me too." He smiled, and leaned in for a kiss. It was enjoyable, if not, well ... pleasantly generic. "Next time I want to see those moves," he teased as I got out.

"Oh, I'll show you!"

I playfully strutted across my driveway, hips out, the occasional hair flip. He flashed his brights and drove off. I stepped into my place and threw my purse to the side. *What am I feeling right now?* Not crazy excitement, or crippling depression; nothing at all extreme like other dates had produced. No, I just felt ... like me. Happy.

THE WAR OF DATING: A MINI-ESSAY

Dating is a battlefield. Night after night, dinner after dinner, singles all over the world lay themselves down on the line, fighting over perhaps the single most important ideal of all time: love (at least according to pop songs, and Keats poems). They go in, arming themselves with as much ammunition as they can muster—perfect hair, college degrees, conversational French, fresh breath—and then let the verbal and nonverbal forms of communication fly. If they are lucky, these forms collide with the other side's forms and create sparks, sometimes even fireworks. Victory! If not, well...things can get ugly.

With Tinder (and any other form of online dating), the battle begins with a profile picture. This single photo is worth a thousand arrows, as they say, and you need at least a halfway decent one to advance to the next stage: text message sparring. Here, you can truly make it or break it. You might look like Henry Cavill in your photos, but if you lead off with "Girl, u so fine. U like pizza?" the answer is no.

Conversely, if you only have a halfway decent photo, now is the time to make up some major ground. For instance, "Dang, I was going to suggest taking a limo to the Fred Segal in Vegas for our first date, but it looks like you've already done that" is a perfect lead-in and indicates you've taken the time to study every one of your opponent's carefully selected photos. Then, after securing an actual physical meet and greet through pics and texts, it's time to hit the field, guns waving, grenades tossing, axes wielding. Nothing is off limits. Go for broke.

DATE No. 9

The Strategist

BEVERLY HILLS

I had a commercial audition Wednesday morning. I was supposed to be a sexy mechanic working on her motorcycle, so I toughened myself up as much as I could: badass leather jacket, black ripped jeans, black leather boots. I was in it to win it, as Randy Jackson would say.

When I got to the casting office, fifteen or so other girls with red hair and biker attire had already signed in. The same old thought patterns emerged: *You're never going to book this. That girl looks so much more like a mechanic. Your arms are too big. Turn around and go home.* I wrote my name on the clipboard, then found a spot against the wall. I pulled out my earbuds and put on some Nirvana. *Not this time, actor brain.* I focused on my breathing. *I am a badass.*

My phone buzzed: Marvin, the Guy with the Perfect Teeth.

MARVIN:

> want to come to a screening with me tonight at USC?

I did, of course, but I'd already scheduled a date with another guy: Steve. Who I'd already considered canceling on, thanks to the semi-creepy texts he'd been sending the last couple of days. *Maybe I'll—*

"Amy?" The casting assistant called my name loudly. I ripped out my earbuds and shoved my phone in my purse.

"Here!"

I entered the room and instantly felt a cold chill. *Did they turn the AC down to fifty-five?* The casting director rattled off a ton of directions, stone-faced. I struggled to remember all of them while simultaneously trying to make some interesting choices.

"What's your martial arts experience?"

"I, uh..." I'd taken some Les Mills combat classes at 24 Hour Fitness a couple of years earlier. "I've taken tae kwon do," I lied. I could always learn some if I booked the job.

"Great. At the end, give me a series of moves for a couple of minutes." *Fuck.* My head started to spin. "Ready?" I nodded, not ready at all.

I screwed up the first part, working on the fake bike, and could not have felt less sexy or empowered. I was too worried about my lie. When I got to the kicking and karate-chopping part, I just did whatever I could remember. A roundhouse kick, a closed-hand strike.

"Thank you very much," the casting director said after twenty seconds. He could clearly tell I had zero experience.

"Have a great day." I forced a smile and walked out. *Why did I lie? Why couldn't I just be myself?*

Back at my house, I nursed my acting wounds with several squares of dark chocolate and figured out what to do about my evening. *Do I cancel on Steve to go out on a second date with Marvin?* I hated leaving people high and dry, especially when plans had been in place for a week, but Steve's recent texts had been so off-putting. Drilling me with questions about my daily plans? Weird. Asking for a selfie before we met? No thanks. Couple that with Ashley's comment that he looked "rapey" and I was having major doubts.

But our date wasn't the only thing I was doubting. I was also reconsidering my initial decision to write about second and third dates, and I was leaning toward no. It felt too invasive, and it would probably not be as interesting to readers. First Tinder dates felt totally like fair game, but after that, you started revealing more of yourself in confidence. The more I thought about it, the more I definitely did not feel comfortable with the idea of blogging my second date with Marvin. Of course, this meant I would be breaking Rule #2. Unless...

I decided to ask Steve if we could move our drinks to happy hour. I would uphold Rule #2 and sacrifice Rule #1. I still wanted to post one blog entry each day, so now I would just have to do forty first dates in forty days. And second and third dates? Well, this was going to get even crazier than I'd intended.

I texted Marvin that I was in for the screening, then asked Steve to meet at four thirty. Steve responded that it would be fine (although later would be "more fun"), but under one condition: that I send him a selfie. *This guy's not going down without a fight*, I thought, annoyed. I surrendered and sent him a hideous car shot that would never end up in a spank bank. If only I hadn't …

♥

There was no way I could have known the battle I was entering into at Gyu-Kaku, or the strength of my opponent. It began on La Cienega Boulevard. He came from the south, I the north, and we spotted each other from several hundred feet away. He waved, and as we drew closer and closer, the tension mounted. *Soldiers, draw your weapons!* We finally made it to each other, hugged, and then stepped into the restaurant, ready for Sapporo and round one.

Steve had never been to the Japanese BBQ joint, which I found pretty surprising (it's an LA classic). So I did the ordering: pitcher of beer, New York steak, ahi tuna poke, and shishito peppers. This proved to be the first and last time I had any real control over the afternoon, because shortly after our waiter left, Steve dropped the bomb. Now, I'm not talking about some amateur bomb, some Molotov cocktail or eighth-grade science experiment. Oh no, I'm talking about a *big one*. Maybe not Hiroshima big ("I have six baby mamas" or "I just got out of jail for manslaughter") but nevertheless big for a first-date Tinder confession.

"So, I didn't mention this to you before, but it's actually my birthday." I paused, studying him to see if he was serious, then burst out laughing.

"Today's your birthday? Oh my god, cheers! That's crazy!" I picked up my glass, masking my horror. "How old are you?"

He took a sip, then answered, "Thirty."

I took a gulp. "Wow, your thirtieth birthday…and you're spending it with me. That's"—*insane*—"so cool!"

I had to excuse myself to the bathroom, for fear of laughing or crying or both. In the stall, I had my rom-com movie moment, literally bursting at the seams and mouthing "what the fuck" over and over again. I couldn't have asked for a better story for my blog, but at the same time, this was going to be brutal. Thank God I had the screening as a hard out.

I returned to the table and tried to recover from the shock of the blow, but never really got back on my feet. I knew I needed to make the most of it for his sake—I mean, it was his *thirtieth goddamn birthday*—but it was tough going. He couldn't stop talking about himself, and any time I tried to add to the conversation or tell a story, he cut me off. I decided to just let him run with it (again, thirtieth birthday), and I learned a lot about his life: his actor origins, his switch to sales and then law, his excellent LSAT score. At a certain point, I wondered if he didn't maybe have bad hearing, and I started talking louder and sort of angrily. But this had no effect; I still got cut off.

The check came, and I reached for it. He got it first. I

pulled out my wallet. "Let me take care of it; it's your thirtieth birthday."

He smiled and gave his card to the waiter. "I know, but I just sprung this on you." *Yes, yes, you did.* I looked at my watch. Twenty minutes before I had to leave to meet Marvin.

"How about we jump next door to the Phoenix so I can at least buy you a drink?" I offered.

He smiled. "That sounds great."

As we walked to the bar, Steve put his arm around me, and it took everything in me not to throw it off. *Oh c'mon, Amy, run in the other direction! Channel that inner badass motorcycle chick! Why are you doing this?* my mind screamed at me. *Oh, right, it's his birthday.* I bought a round of three-dollar happy hour beers, and we cheers-ed. I took two sips, and felt his eyes on me.

"Why are you looking at me like that?" I asked, knowing perfectly well why he was looking at me like that.

"I just...want to kiss you," he said, and leaned in. *Oh god, birthday present birthday present birthday present.* His lips met mine for a brief second, and then it was over. I pulled out my phone.

"Oh no, I have to go. Happy birthday!" I gave him a quick hug and scrambled toward the exit. Out in the open, free at last, I took a deep breath and then headed to my car. Within one minute my phone buzzed.

STEVE:

> Thanks for spending my birthday with me 🙂 I had fun.

"You may have won this round, Steve, but you've lost the fight," I almost replied. But instead, I typed the only thing I could.

ME:

> Happy birthday!

DATE N.º 9.5

Miles of Perfect Smiles

DOWNTOWN LOS ANGELES

After circling around the streets of my old stomping ground looking for parking, I finally found a spot and called Marvin. He came and met me on the closest corner, and what a relief it was to see him. *Yes! Someone who knows how to talk and listen!*

After our first date, I expected nothing less than great conversation and a six-pack of abs from laughing. And that's pretty much exactly what I got, minus the abs: another fun evening with one of my *many mens*. We got frozen yogurt after the screening (why does mine always end up looking like a four-year-old's art project?) and walked around the quiet campus. It was lovely.

But I couldn't help feeling that something wasn't quite

firing on the romantic level for me. Yes, he made me laugh, and yes, I thoroughly enjoyed his company, but I didn't feel the physical chemistry. When he kissed me in my car at the end of the evening, I was thinking about my yoga class the next morning and how good sleep sounded. Not exactly the mind-set of someone in the throes of passion.

And he picked up on it. He actually called me out, saying I seemed a little disconnected, "not quite there." As weird as it felt to have my behavior named, it made me appreciate Marvin even more. His awareness, his willingness to say things how he saw them—it made dating feel less like the war I'd just fought with the Strategist. There was no winner or loser in this scenario, just two people coming together looking for a connection. And we'd found one, just not of the "till death do us part" sort.

When I finally got home after midnight, I collapsed onto my bed, spent from my back-to-back dates. But I felt absolutely certain I'd made the right decision to not write about second dates. The world didn't need to know in depth about our frozen yogurt or his family struggles or that I just wasn't really feeling it. Oh well, if this meant a few more dating duties than I'd signed up for, I would just have to suck it up.

DATE N⁰ 10

Blast from the Past

BEVERLY GROVE

FADE IN:

INT. GORDON RAMSAY RESTAURANT KITCHEN — SIX YEARS AGO

AMY POLISHES GLASSES NEXT TO ANDY (32), CUTE, GOOFY.

>   AMY
> So I got this random call today from this
> company Extra Extra—

>   ANDY
> Oh my god, register!

AMY
But I'm shooting this—

ANDY
Doesn't matter, you HAVE to register!

END FLASHBACK

    For all of the millions of people in LA, it never ceased to amaze me how small the circles I ran in were. No, I didn't see a familiar face every time I was at Pavilions, like I probably would in Boring, Oregon, but it was a rare day when I was out buying lightbulbs at Target or hiking Runyon Canyon or laughing at the Comedy Store and didn't bump into at least one person I knew, or at least recognized (for example, the guy from *The Drew Carey Show* who was in my yoga class that morning). So it was only a matter of time before I had a first Tinder date with someone I already knew: Andy.

    I was honestly a little surprised (disappointed?) that it hadn't been my friend Scottie, the only guy I'd ever talked at length with about Tinder. (He'd even invited a Tinder date to join us at a bar one night when we were having drinks!) He was the first friend that had popped up on my Tinder screen, and I'd excitedly swiped right on him, thinking it might even be fun to go on a real date after all of these years. But to my chagrin, nothing happened. No happy matching, no congratulatory message, no winning. Nothing. Apparently not everyone shared my level of enthusiasm for this form of cyber peekaboo.

    But Andy did. It had taken me a few seconds to recognize

him when his picture graced my phone, but once I did, my finger happily slid right. *For the win!*

ME:

Andy!! How the hell are you?

I'd run into him maybe twice since our days in Gordon Ramsay's hellhole.

ANDY:

Haha! Amy! I'm amazing as always, how bout yourself? Oh, the internets are always a funny place, eh?

ME:

They are indeed!

I told him about my experiment, and he asked if he could take me out in fifty-two days, to give me some time to recover before blowing my mind. I responded that it might be too late, I may have found my husband by then, so he agreed to take me out as one of the forty.

I suggested lunch, and he chose a new place on West Third Street I'd never been to, Blue Plate Oysterette. He got there early and I got there late.

"This is so going in my blog," he joked. "Amy was late. Minus three points."

I laughed. It felt nice being on a first date with somebody I already knew, whom I had a shared history with. As much as I enjoyed meeting all these new guys, it really was exhausting trying to make so many good first impressions.

We got seated, and I jumped right in. "So, I need to thank you for something, because you've pretty much been the reason for my life the past six years."

He looked at me, curious. "Oh?"

I smiled, realizing that sounded a bit intense. But it was the truth. "Do you remember that night I came into work and I asked you about Extra Extra and you told me to register no matter what?" He nodded. "Well, that one decision to race up the 405 during a lunch break from shooting—a decision entirely influenced by you—changed my life. And I never got to properly thank you. So thank you."

He laughed. "Wow. Well. You're welcome."

We started talking about dating, and I told him all about the Strategist, still trying to wrap my mind around the previous day's events. Our waiter overheard my story and interrupted: "That sounds awesome! I want to read!" *This is one way to get fans*, I thought, writing down my website for him.

Our conversation jumped around from the birthday fiasco to his recent car fiasco (his apartment complex's garage door had crushed his hood) to a commercial fiasco (a DirecTV spot he'd been in last year had been pulled because it offended "mountain people").

Perhaps my favorite moment of discussion was his recollection of a run-in he'd had with Jeremy Renner. They'd been at the same bar for a football game, and had both gone out back to smoke a cigarette. Not one to be starstruck, Andy had nevertheless always been curious about the costuming process for superhero movies, and so he asked the actor, out of nowhere, "What was the fitting like for *The Avengers*?" Jeremy looked at him, steely eyed, took a deep inhale, and replied, "It was a long haul." Perfection.

Andy was an East Coast boy with roots in Philadelphia and Maine, so I trusted him to do the ordering, and he did not lead us astray. We got the lobster tacos (not on the menu, but delicious), bouillabaisse (which I had somehow never had—also delicious), and, of course, a dozen oysters. The food, like the company, was, well ... *stimulating*.

After we finished eating, we shot the shit for a little while longer, and then he walked me back to my car. "There were, like, a bunch of other ideas I had for our first date, more original than lunch."

I smiled. "Oh yeah?"

"I was going to see if you wanted to go to the Tom Petty concert tomorrow night, but my friend was like, 'Dude, what is she, sixty-five?' So that didn't happen. Or, you know, batting cages, or miniature golf."

I laughed. "Well, I happen to love Tom Petty, batting cages, and miniature golf, so you couldn't have gone wrong."

He gave me a kiss, the kind that neither makes a relationship nor breaks a friendship, and I got in my car. *Who would've thought six years ago, schlepping tables together in a fine-dining nightmare, that Andy and I would one day reconnect through Tinder?* I was glad we'd both swiped right.

DATE N°. 10.5

The Tall Prince Returns

HOLLYWOOD

The thing about rules is, once you break them, it's hard to stop. My decision to not blog second dates had unleashed a monster: I ended up going on four dates in two days. I was turning into a female Casanova. *Bring on the boys!*

In spite of my firm declaration after our first date that Jordan was not my Prince Charming, I ended up going out with him again anyway. His follow-up had been really sweet, and there was so much to recommend him: good-looking, funny, successful, multitalented, apparently cooked an insane rib eye. I couldn't help thinking I should give it a second chance—especially after Sascha's phone call telling me I needed to. So what if the kiss had been a little awkward? Maybe I'd intimidated him.

Indeed I had. Shortly after sitting down at littlefork, a quaint French-Canadian restaurant, Jordan confessed I'd made him incredibly nervous with my beauty. And personality. But mostly my eyes.

"They're just ... captivating," he said shakily.

My tendency with compliments like these had always been to deflect them. I never felt that I merited them. But now I wanted to accept. After all, I had been feeling beautiful and sexy again. Why not own it in the world the way I was owning it on the pole?

"Thank you, I really appreciate that," I replied, then added, "But you don't need to feel nervous. I'm a huge dork. I cry to Celine Dion and read books by evolutionary biologists. And I'm *super* clumsy."

I told him about running into a parking meter in high school so hard I drew blood. And falling flat on my back in the middle of the hottest restaurant in Hollywood on a Friday night (I took a bow after that one). And how I'd somehow never learned how to properly eat, and rarely made it through a meal without something ending up in my lap. Case in point, I accidentally spilled my wine. His jitters dissipated.

The evening continued pleasantly, as we revealed more about ourselves over baby kale salad, charred octopus, and chicken confit. He was still charming as a Disney character, and the kiss at the end was gratefully less awkward. But as with Marvin, even though we connected on multiple levels, there was something missing. *What is it?* I still couldn't say. But maybe by Date #40 I would find out.

DATE No. 11

The Thespian

LARCHMONT VILLAGE

Back in my late teens, when I worked as a hostess at a restaurant on Sunset Boulevard, a wise old waitress once told me that the problem at the beginning of any relationship would be the cause of the end of it. I remember thinking how profound this sounded, then proceeded to completely disregard it for the next ten years. I jumped into relationship after relationship where I willfully ignored large inherent problems up front, believing that either I could change or they could change or love would ultimately win out. *Major age difference and a degenerative eye disease? No worries! I'm in love with you! Differing goals concerning family and children? Don't sweat it! I'm in love with you! Crippling emotional baggage from childhood? Woo-hoo! Let's ride this train!*

In retrospect, I could have predicted the demise of every one of my longer-term relationships using the Wise Waitress's wisdom. It essentially went hand in hand with that other practical piece of dating advice: "Don't try and change someone." It was so very simple, and yet over and over again I found myself bending this rule, talking myself out of it.

"If you're not comfortable with me being an actress, I'll quit my dreams and marry you." *Wrong.* Thank god one of us was smart enough to see the danger in that (hint: it wasn't me).

"Well, it's not fair to expect him to have a consistent salary when I myself am an artist." *Wrong.* I hadn't lived paycheck to paycheck since the age of twenty; it was okay to want at least the same from a future father.

"With the right amount of love and tenderness, I can treat his borderline personality disorder." *Seriously wrong.* I was neither a licensed therapist nor an emotional punching bag.

Now, it wasn't that there was anything inherently wrong with dating actors (I'd be totally screwed if there was!); it was just that through my years of experience I'd decided it didn't work for me. I'd hopped aboard that carousel enough times to know what happened: it went around and around and never got anywhere. That being said, I still found myself drawn to actors, especially the really talented ones, attracted by their charisma, their quick wit, their empathic nature, their listening skills. But I knew better.

So why did I decide to go out with George, a thirty-nine-year-old actor from Koreatown? Well, I didn't realize he was an actor until after I had swiped right, and then it was too late, because it was impossible to say no to this intro:

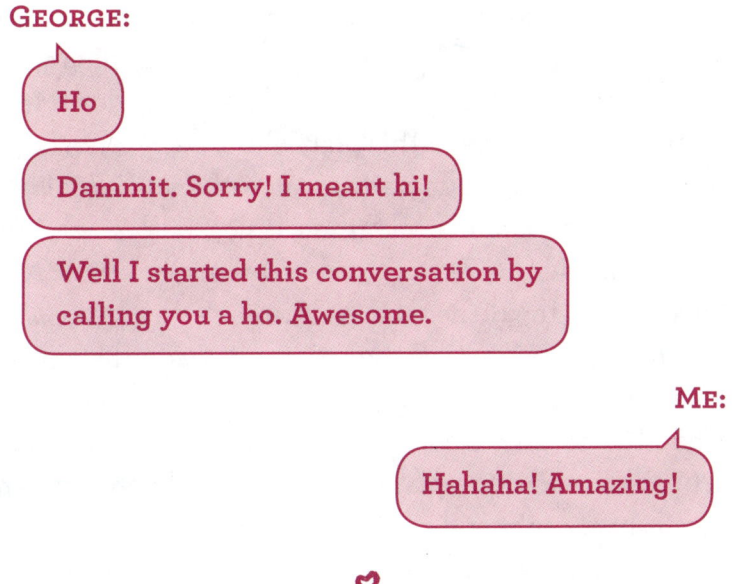

We met for lunch at Café Gratitude, my favorite vegan restaurant in Los Angeles. It's a space all about positive affirmations and energy, and I liked his from our first sip of water. "This is a great vintage, been aged perfectly," he said, swirling the small taste the waitress had poured. "You can smell the balanced minerality, and what a smooth finish!" I laughed, picking up the carafe and pouring us proper glasses. He definitely had an actor's charm.

Within minutes, we figured out that we had studied at the same acting studio based on our mutual friends. This ingratiated me to him immediately, and gave us a shared language. He had studied with my current teacher for seven years, and I knew right away what kind of actor he was: a really talented one.

"I spent several years traveling around the country doing

regional theater, honing my craft. I did a full year acting in *Hamlet* at the Oregon Shakespeare Festival, then finally came back to LA to work more in TV and film." I nodded. He was a serious working actor, a thespian who'd been following his calling since a third-grade performance of *Snow White*.

Our waitress came back three times before we finally looked at the menu. We both ordered the same thing: I Am Fortified. (All of the dishes were named like this: I Am Whole, I Am Gracious, I Am New Age. Okay, I made that last one up.) Our conversation about dogs and writing and traveling continued over quinoa and rice bowls laden with kale, squash, corn, broccoli, and other plants. I sipped kombucha as he told me about his family and his nephew and a crazy solo Rome trip where a couple he had met at a restaurant gave him their car to borrow for two days. (*What? Only in Rome...*) I told him about my love of Paris and my shift toward writing and how grateful I was that I hadn't made it when I was eighteen. "I would have been Lindsay Lohan. Fame would have destroyed me."

Talking with George was easy, never dull, never forced. But still, I knew from the beginning that this was not my guy. Or rather, *man*, because George was fully, 100 percent a man. More than any of my other dates, he was a capital-*A* Adult. *Which is what I want, right?* Well, yes and no. Because while I was looking for someone serious about marriage and kids and family, I was also looking for someone I felt on the same page with. And as I looked at George, the lines on his face, the twinkling knowledge of thirty-nine years in his eyes, and we spoke about our passions and our paths, I couldn't help feeling we were in different places, from different generations.

And we were. Because even though age is just a number, that decade between us was real, and filled with a world of varied experiences. I mean, I'd always considered myself a pretty old soul, but let's face it: I was writing a blog about Tinder dating, and he was playing Hamlet. And if I was already worried about the age difference and our maturity levels on date one, well, you could bet that wasn't going away anytime soon.

And besides, even without looking at him and seeing a second father, he was still, no matter how awesome, an actor.

Date Nº 12

The Jock

MARINA DEL REY

It was Sunday, and my week ahead looked crazy. I was working on three background jobs and had two commercial auditions, my acting and improv classes, plus a "Why I Dance" meeting. We'd officially locked in the date for our shoot, less than a month away, and there was a lot to take care of. I shuddered at the thought of trying to squeeze in 11:00 p.m. drink dates only to wake up at 6:00 a.m. for work. I knew what I needed to do. Break Rule #1 again, and stockpile a couple of dates while I had the chance. Better to be ahead of schedule than try and cram it all in at the last minute.

I already had a coffee date slated in Marina del Ray, so I figured I'd try and stay down by the beach. Up until now, my dates had all been relegated to the Eastside. This would be a good opportunity to experience the Tinder offerings in another part of town. I widened my radius back to ten miles (I'd shrunk it to five from twenty-five after Exhibit A in Simi Valley) and started swiping on beach boys. I found one relatively quickly who happened to be free in the late afternoon. He suggested wine by the water's edge while watching the sunset. Cliché, but problem solved! I finished my home-brewed latte, then got ready to go have another.

My first date of the day started off normally enough, if not a little awkwardly. I walked into the Starbucks and did a quick scan for my suitor. My eyes landed on a tall guy in a yellow shirt in line, sporting Ray-Bans and bedhead. I smiled. *Is that him?* He smiled back but said nothing, stepping up to order his orange juice. *Guess not.* I pulled out my phone and looked at the Tinder profile. *Hmm, this aviator shot has the same scruffy hair.* I studied the back of his head. *And he's built sort of like this guy.* He turned and caught me staring.

"Amy?" It was him.

"Matt." I stepped in and gave him a hug, feeling his solid form. *Not bad.*

I ordered a drink, and we got a table outside. He started to take his sunglasses off, then changed his mind. "Nope, not ready."

I laughed. "Long night?"

He nodded. "Lots of Scotch. Trying to flush it out, but so far it's not working."

I smiled. "Yeah, when you get to our age, those hangovers, yikes!" *Total jock*, I thought, already stereotyping.

I reached into my grab bag of small talk questions and pulled one out. "So, how long you been in LA?"

"Two weeks," he replied.

My jaw dropped. "Seriously?" *Oh god, a newb.*

"Yup, from Houston, but don't worry, I'm a liberal. Born and raised all over. Engineer brat." I smiled, reaching for the next question.

"Why'd you move out here?"

"The industry. Acting and producing." *Shiiiiit.*

Romantic possibilities dead, the pressure was off, and we eased into an open conversation about acting. He told me about his experiences in Houston on various film sets, the reason he began acting (Daniel Craig in *Casino Royale*), and his previous passion and lifelong love (hockey—I knew he was a jock!).

"I was set to get drafted, then tore my shoulder. But everything happens for a reason." He spoke with such heart and confidence and enthusiasm, it was hard not to root for him. A refreshing breeze in a land of stale, jaded air.

He was in the middle of talking about a TV pilot he was producing when I committed Obvious Tinder Dating Mistake #5: Checking Cell Phone. My home screen showed a missed call from Andy and a text from Steve. I couldn't help myself; I opened the latter up.

STEVE:

> Wow, just read your blog. I guess the date didn't go so well. I'm sorry.

HOLY @&%#!!!

You know that feeling you get when you've been caught doing something really bad, like cheating on a test or on a boyfriend/girlfriend? When a wave of panic and nausea and guilt just knocks you off that surfboard you've been gliding on, pulls you under, chokes and suffocates and drowns you? Yeah, that's what I was feeling. Matt kept talking, but I didn't hear a word he said, like in a movie when a realization hits the character and everything around just blurs and the soundtrack gets fuzzy.

"I'm so sorry. I have to tell you what's going on," I blurted out, and word-vomited the entire thing on him.

"Wait, so this is a blog? You're going to write about this?" I nodded. "That's so cool!"

Well, at least he's not upset, I thought, racked with guilt.

This had been my worst nightmare when I started *40 Dates & 40 Nights*: getting caught and hurting someone. And yet I hadn't adequately prepared it. I'd set up rules for myself, to protect my own heart in the project, but neglected to fully consider the other side of the equation. Now I was reaping what I'd sown.

Not that I hadn't known when I'd written "The Strategist" that there was a chance Steve would read it and be utterly humiliated. But I'd taken it anyway, figuring the odds were about the same as the Dodgers winning the World Series. *Wrong*. I'd failed to judge the strength of my opponent once again, and failed to recognize my own.

My uneasiness finally abated enough for me to reengage with Matt for the remainder of the date, and he told me more about his pilot idea. It was actually pretty great, and he'd already gotten some high-level people on board. I'd misjudged him at the beginning as well, pegging him as just another jock, but he was more than that: a genuine, intelligent guy with a helluva lotta drive and a super-positive outlook. *Guilty again.*

He hugged me good-bye, and left me alone to my inner turmoil. *How did Steve find my blog?* I'd used fake names (including mine) for a reason. And we had mutual friends, but none of them knew about it. Oh well, that was beside the point. The point was, I had seriously hurt someone's feelings, and forever ruined his thirtieth birthday. It had been a really weird bad date, but he didn't deserve this. I shuddered at what my parents would think. *Ugghhh.*

I had an hour before my beach date, and I spent most of it struggling to craft a response to Steve. I wanted to—needed to—apologize, but didn't quite know how. Finally I just sent him something simple and to the point.

ME:

> I am not sure what to say, except I'm very sorry I hurt your feelings. I didn't mean for you to read that, obviously. But that's not an excuse. I'm sorry.

STEVE:

> Thanks for apologizing.

And that was that. *What should I do now?* I thought, as

I sat in my car down by the ocean. *Should I stop the blog? Should I fold my cards?* I felt conflicted. *I'll decide after the next date.* I closed my eyes, trying to shake my well-deserved uneasiness. I knew one thing for sure: after this blog, I was only writing pure fiction.

My phone buzzed. I picked it up, expecting another text from Steve. Instead, it was a day one Tinder match who had fallen off the deep end.

DAN:

> **Hey stranger! Sorry I totally dropped the ball, but I was hoping we could reconnect. I'm actually free tonight if you wanted to grab dinner?**

Hmm. I looked back through our past messages. Things had started out great, with fun, witty banter, but any Tinderthusiasm had quickly cooled after he sent me a picture of his wine rack as a suggestion for our first date. This bold, obvious move had dispatched Dan to the Tindether of Forgotten Matches.

But now he was suggesting dinner. And he did live in Hermosa Beach. And I could kill a third bird in one day after sunset, which would help with my schedule, should I choose to continue.

ME:

> **Sure. I'm already down by the beach so why not? 7:30?**

DAN:

> Great, let's do the Rockefeller.

ME:

> See you then.

Just like that, I had three dates in one day. A true Tinderella, if ever there was one.

DATE N° 13

The Free Love Activist
SANTA MONICA

*Q**uestion: How many times can you remove a guy's hand from your leg before he gets the picture?*

Up until now, I'd never felt like Tinder was anything more than a conversation starter, a way to potentially initiate a first date based on very brief first impressions (and maybe find love!). Plenty of friends had asked me if I'd run into creepy guys sending dick pics or requesting orgies, but of the one hundred or so I'd matched with, only one had been blunt in terms of sex:

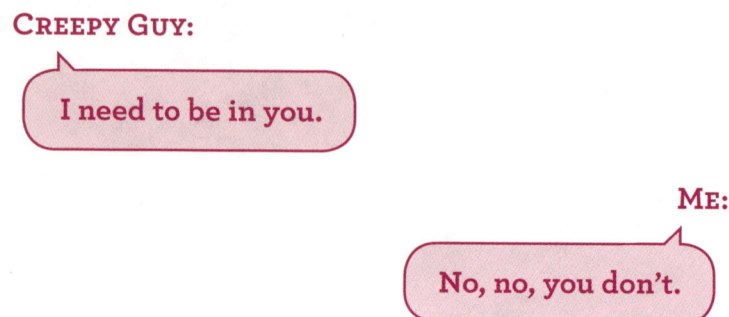

Other than that, Exhibit A, and Dan's wine rack, most of the guys I had Tindered with were respectful, if not stand-up Colin Firths. And all of my first dates had been, well, first dates: that sometimes fun, sometimes awkward period of getting to know someone.

But from the moment I met Ainsley in the park overlooking the coast, I knew this was going to be different. He went in for a kiss on our very first hug. This both caught me off and put me on guard. *Really?* I quickly turned my cheek, allowing his whiskers to exfoliate it.

Ainsley could have been Glen Hansard's brother, or at least a cousin, and he had the wandering Irish musician attire to match. I knew he'd lived in Portland from his 503 area code, so I started the conversation there. From the looks of it, that might be the only thing we had in common.

"Yeah, I'm from San Diego originally; was living up north for work and a girl," he said coolly. *So, not a native. Coulda fooled me, with the unwashed hair and hobo knapsack.*

We trekked down to the water, removing our shoes and rolling our cuffs. The cool sand felt like silk underfoot, and I regretted how little I came down to the ocean. The year I'd lived in Santa Monica, I had run on the beach every day, but now I only visited maybe four times a year. I was happy to be here.

"So, what do you do?" I asked, breaking the silence.

"Oh, that question again. Everybody just wants to know how they can benefit from people."

I bristled.

"I'm not trying to get anything from you; I just think it's a fairly important question. Presumably you spend a lot of time doing your job, so it makes up a part of who you are. I'm not saying it fully defines you, but it's certainly a pretty key circumstance in your life."

He submitted, and told me the various things he did: documentaries, graphic design, visual effects for concerts, web development.

"So eighty-five hats," I teased. He didn't laugh.

We spread the blanket out and sat down. He pulled out a bottle of wine ("Merlot, seven dollars") and poured it into a silver mug for us to share. I sat on the edge, looking out at the sailboats traversing the water, my polarized lenses coloring the scene with Turner's palette.

"C'mere, get in between my legs. I want to get close to you," he said, moving my purse and grabbing for me.

"I'm okay right here for the moment," I replied.

He placed his hand on my thigh. I politely picked it up and handed it back to him.

"I'm trying to get to know you," I said calmly. Part of me wanted to run for the waves right then, but I also wanted to hear his story. Everyone had one, right? Plus, it was an opportunity for me to stand my ground, something I still needed to work on.

"So you're a writer. What are you currently reading?" he asked. *Well, this is a start.*

"Oh, this awesome book, Jonathan Franzen's *The Corrections*! I know I'm a little late on the bandwagon, but—"

"Yeah, never heard of it," he interrupted, reaching to touch my neck. Once again, I retracted.

I asked him more questions about himself, slowly prying out his story. He had lived in India for six months and Amsterdam for four years. His father was also a documentarian, and they'd traveled and worked together. He didn't elaborate much on anything, and spoke about everything in a sort of neo-hipster, sardonic tone. And every five minutes or so, he tried again to touch me—grabbing my leg, rubbing my back—to which I promptly deflected his advances.

If there'd been any attraction at the beginning (there hadn't been), there was absolutely none by the time the sun actually set. I'd given up on "getting to know each other." The only part of me he seemed interested in were my upper thighs. Worse, I found myself matching his over-it attitude. I thought of something the Jock had said: "You become like the people you surround yourself with." I pictured myself in that *Wanderlust* commune, sporting dreadlocks, smoking a joint, engaging in the free love Ainsley so clearly practiced. I shivered. (I actually was shivering. It was cold.)

But at least in *Wanderlust* there was laughter. Here, there was none, except when I uncomfortably squirmed away from his grip: "Ha-ha, that move again!" A previous version of Amy may have eventually succumbed to these advances, too afraid to defend myself, too eager to please, but seasoned-dater Amy knew better. "Yup! Still don't really know you!"

The sun vanished, taking with it any last bit of warmth. "So, we should probably grab some dinner," he stated matter-of-factly. *Let me guess: Chinese takeout? Pizza delivery?*

"Actually, it's my friend Marcia's birthday. We're having dinner for her," I half-lied (it was Marcia's birthday, but she lived in Florida, and I was having dinner with Dan). He nodded and we walked back up the beach.

Ainsley made a pit stop at the restrooms, and I considered making a run for it. *Free yourself, Amy! This guy sucks!* But I had already come this far. What was an extra five minutes, even if it meant dodging one more kiss?

Which it did. Up at the park, he went in for the kill and came up with a mouthful of cheek. Even after this failed attempt, he held on to me a few seconds longer, as if there'd been some sort of mistake. And of course there had been—I should've left an hour earlier. *Why did I give him this much of a chance when I knew so quickly I wasn't interested?* Guess I still needed more seasoning.

"Let's hang again sometime soon," he said.

"Have fun!" I yelled back non sequiturally, and disappeared along the boardwalk. When I'd finally walked far enough to feel safe from his wandering hands, I let out a deep sigh. *What was that guy's problem?*

But more importantly, what was *my* problem?

Answer: As many times as it takes until you leave.

PART 2

Too many boys, not enough time.

What happens on date two stays on date two; not everything should be on the Internet.

●●●●○ AT&T　LTE　　12:31 PM　　79% ▮

‹ Back

June 19, 2015, 12:31 PM

1. A date a day for 40 days.
2. A blog a day for each date.
3. All dates from Tinder.
4. Maximum of 3 dates with any one guy.
5. No sex till monogamy - courtesy Patty Stanger

WHAT THE F~~UCK~~ AM I DOING?

I sat in my car and cried. I had an hour before my date with Dan, and I thought about canceling. In fact, I thought about quitting altogether. *What am I doing? Three first dates in one day? Nine dates in five?* This was quickly spinning out of control. After just thirteen first dates, a mere third of the way through, I was already exhausted, still stuck on James, breaking rules, and worthy of membership in the Plastics for what I'd done to Steve. How could I possibly keep this up for another month? And why?

Not that it had all been bad. Not even close. Some moments had been downright Kodak-worthy: *many mens* with Perfect Teeth, the non-kiss with the Cab Driver, the Spanish Wordsmith's beautiful baby blues. I had met some really great guys I never would have come into contact with. And the dates themselves had mostly been fun and easy, with lots of enjoyable conversation and delicious food (if not a few too many cocktails). As a storyteller, foodie, and general lover of humans, I'd struck gold. If my dating experiment had proven anything thus far, it was Tinder's value as a tool for connecting people outside their usual circles and for supporting local restaurants and bars.

But I still couldn't shake thoughts of James, or the idea that I was a horrible person. At night, alone in my bedroom, the questions would echo off the four walls: *Who am I? Why am I still single? Why can't I find another James?*

I knew I needed to stop comparing every date to James. It was a futile exercise, and I'd vowed not to after Gordon and my Great Expectations. But I'd still been doing it, and it was preventing me from having pure encounters, from being fully open to any new possibilities, like Sascha had warned.

That was one of the reasons I felt horrible. Another was not telling my dates what I was doing. The ethics of this haunted me. I'd certainly considered it in preproduction (*to tell or not to tell, that is the question*), but ultimately I'd decided that for the sake of the project, it was better to hold off. I didn't want the guys thinking it was a stunt to "score a book deal," as New James had so eloquently put it. Or worse, for my blog to cause someone to behave super weirdly or even vindictively. I wanted to avoid that sketchy Dumpster. Thankfully I had. Too bad I couldn't also avoid the guilt over my literary trespasses.

Speaking of guilt: I felt guilty for kissing guys I knew I wouldn't continue dating. I felt guilty for *not* kissing guys I wouldn't continue dating. I just felt guilty in general about all the guys I wouldn't continue dating. Since eleven out of thirteen of them were decent, interesting people, I couldn't help questioning my own judgment. For instance, Calev and Andy had already asked me out again, but I'd decided I wasn't going to give them a second chance. I just wasn't totally feeling it. But *why*? Was it because I was shallow, or only liked douche bags? I was beginning to think there was something seriously wrong with me. That I had impossible standards or only wanted what I couldn't have (*cough, cough*—James). And my second dates with the Tall Prince and Perfect Teeth had only compounded the guilt, because while their attraction appeared to grow (both had asked me on a third date), mine had shrunk. *Ugh, misery.*

And then, of course, there was Date #9, the date that had launched a thousand regrets. From the moment "thirtieth birthday" passed through Steve's lips, I'd known how badly things would go. How cruel and funny a post it would make. How much people would enjoy laughing with me at this poor guy. How terrible I would feel if he ever read it... Well, we all know how that turned out.

Maybe it was time to throw in the towel. To cut my losses, jump on the 10 East, and get back to my regular life in Hollywood. To screw my dating project, and focus on my dance film and acting.

I missed my friends. I missed watching movies, and reading the *New York Times*, and imagining the lives of characters in plays and TV scripts. I missed the days when going to yoga actually cleared my mind, instead of producing visions of Tinder profiles. *How quickly I've become a Tinder addict!* I could think of nothing but men and my relationship to them. I was officially boy crazy. This was unhealthy.

But how unhealthy was it really, when compared to my state of being just a month before, sobbing in bed day after day? That had been a true clinical condition: depression. At least now I was getting out in the world and having a good time, spending my days writing and sharing stories with others. And whether I liked the results or not, my project *was* teaching me about myself.

Maybe I just needed to re-center. To take a deep breath, go to a pole class, and dance out my frustrations. Put on a little Eminem, or maybe Metallica, something dark and stormy, and let it all go ...

Then come home and remember the essential reason why I was doing this: to find my perfect match. That man I wanted to spend the rest of my life with. To raise a family with. To share travels, and holidays, and illnesses, and successes, and failures with. To wake up to every morning, and fall asleep with every night. To talk with about politics and TV shows and religion and life and death and what I ate for lunch. To grow old with. To love and be loved by. This was no small order. No one said it would be easy.

But was this the right way to go about it? An onslaught of Tinder dates? Maybe I had it all backward. I mean, people were always saying things like "you shouldn't go looking for love" or "you have to let it just come to you." I considered this.

And the more I considered it, the more I wanted to scream "bullshit!" Would I have just left my education to chance, let my career just come to me? No, of course not. I studied my ass off, researched colleges, explored different fields, spent thousands of hours in acting classes. I discovered what I wanted, made informed decisions accordingly, and prepared myself for when the opportunities came. Why would I treat one of the single most important relationships in my life any differently?

I needed to keep going. Yes, I was tired and consumed by dating, but I could just think of this as finals week (or month). And so what if I'd hurt Steve's feelings, or felt bad about mishandling Ainsley's advances, or harbored guilt over not continuing to date every guy? It was all part of the learning process. Even Steve might have learned something through our date and the mirror my writing presented him with. Like not to have a first Tinder date on your thirtieth birthday. Or to let your date finish her sentences and stories. Which was what I would do now. Because this one wasn't over. I turned on my car and headed south, toward Hermosa Beach.

DATE NO. 14

The Full Stein

HERMOSA BEACH

I arrived before Dan and went straight to the restroom. I looked salty and war-torn. *Well, at least he won't want to go home with me,* I thought, trying to poof my limp ponytail. I didn't even bother putting on lip gloss, resigning myself to my fate. *You chose this, Amy. You got this.*

I walked back into the restaurant, and he showed up a minute later. He was cuter than his pictures, but definitely had a fratty, "show you my wine rack" vibe. They don't call it Bromosa for nothing. We sat down at a table in the back, and our server, Mike, brought us menus.

"Can I get you guys something to drink?" he asked.

I looked at the beer list and noticed they had special refillable steins for Oktoberfest. "You should totally get a stein!" I teased Dan.

"It's a great deal if you'll be in here again!" Mike interjected. Dan looked at me, then at Mike. "All right, I'll do it."

I laughed approvingly and ordered myself a pint of hefe.

Mike disappeared and we quickly covered the basics. Dan worked for AEG, specifically with the Galaxy.

"David Beckham?" he offered, as if I thought he were referring to the Milky Way.

"I know my soccer! I even watched a few of the World Cup games," I mock-protested, then added quickly, "But I don't really follow sports." I didn't want to give the wrong impression, like I enjoyed Monday Night Football at bars.

"Great!" he said. "I spend so much of my day focused on sports, I don't want to date a girl that's all about that, too." *All right—so far, so good.*

Mike returned with our beers. Dan's stein was ridiculous. "This was definitely a mistake," he lamented as soon as Mike left. I took a picture of it. "Christ, I'm gonna end up in some story to your girlfriends about your awful Tinder dates."

I smiled. *Oh, you have no idea.*

The sparks started flying from here and didn't stop. You know when you're having such a good time with someone, you just sort of forget where you are and what you have to do tomorrow and next week and for the rest of your life, because all that matters is this moment and what the other person is saying and "holy shit, you feel that too?" Well, that's what this was like.

Everything seemed to be spiraling and buzzing back and forth, bubbling up like a chemistry experiment. We talked about Wes Anderson, and Woody Allen, and M. Night Shyamalan (but only *The Sixth Sense* and *Unbreakable*). Sleep paralysis and death and Einstein's relativity. Chaos theory and information theory and equity theory and Tinder theory. Yup, Tinder theory. It's a thing; we invented it.

"I want to apologize for coming off so aggressively at the beginning. I'm not really sure anymore how to treat Tinder," Dan said, mid-theory development. "But obviously that's not actually who I am. I'm more of a nerd, and I really don't go for casual sex. A lot of my buddies can date girls just because they're hot, but I can't do it anymore. There's nothing in it for me, except some awkward sex." He told me about one awful experience in which the girl burst out sobbing midway through. When he stopped, she wiped her eyes and said they could keep going. Tinder fail.

"Yeah, you almost ruined your chances with me," I said, grateful I'd chosen the 405 over the 10.

"Well, I'm glad I didn't." He smiled. "Because you're beautiful and smart and interesting. Don't laugh, but I was starting to think that there was really some truth to that 'men are from Mars, women are from Venus' thing. I really didn't think I could find a girl I could connect with on this sort of level." I nodded, leaning so far over the table I was practically out of my seat.

"I need to tell you something," I blurted out impulsively.

"Shoot."

"I'm actually writing this as a blog. On Tinder and dating. And you're a part of it." I shrunk back, nervously anticipating his reaction. *Is he mad? Is he going to freak out and smash his stein?*

"No way. That's awesome!" His eyes lit up. "I actually thought about doing one at one point, but I'm not a writer. So good for you! How do I stack up?"

I smiled. "Oh, you're winning." He laughed, and all the

tension released from my body. Maybe I wasn't as horrible as I'd thought. Maybe this could actually work. Maybe it was just a numbers game after all.

The whole restaurant had cleared out except for us. Mike stacked chairs on tables, and the lights came up. "We should probably get out of here and get you home," he said, and we walked to my car.

"Oh no! I have a ticket," I exclaimed, although it surprisingly didn't bother me. Usually a parking infraction raised my blood temperature a few degrees, but right then I could have cared less.

"I'll tell you what," Dan said. "It's partly my fault, since I kept you here over two hours, so I'll split it with you. And I'll give it to you the next time we hang out." I leaned in and kissed him. I didn't need him to pay my ticket, but I loved the not-so-subtle sales move, selling me on date two.

"Deal."

Driving the forty-five minutes home, I felt excited. My body ached, my throat burned, my head pulsed, but I felt excited. *What if this is the one? Number fourteen?* My mind raced. Old thought patterns emerged. *He lives in Hermosa Beach—is that going to be a problem? What if he has cats and I develop an allergy to them? Will I like his parents? Will they like me?*

SLOW. DOWN. AMY. I took a deep breath. This was one of the habits I was trying to break, and Obvious Tinder Dating Mistake #6: Planning Our Entire Future after Date One. I smiled, reminding myself of all that I was learning. My heart rate slowed. *That's better, Amy...*

But I was still excited!

DATE Nº 15

The Softer Side of Tinder

LOS FELIZ

If Dan and his stein hadn't been enough to convince me I'd made the right choice about continuing my project, then the text I got from James the next morning did. Not James my ex, the *40 Dates* catalyst, but New James, the writer who'd accused me of doing this to score a book deal.

JAMES:

> So I checked out your blog today for the first time since we talked... I have found every one of your posts to be full of heart and compassion. With a blog like this, it is actually easier to

JAMES:

> write something that would make fun of or cut your dates down. This town can turn a person bitter and cynical. I haven't found that in your writing at all

I wanted to jump for joy. *I'm not a bad person! I have heart and compassion!* I knew I shouldn't care this much about one guy's opinion, but his words affected me.

ME:

> So are you ready to go out then?

JAMES:

> Already planning it.

I grinned. But our date would have to wait until the weekend. For now, we would just have to text. Which, as a writer, he happened to be quite good at. I let myself enjoy our banter, but not too much. I was adamant about having no expectations, like with Diego, Suitor #15, my lunch playdate.

It almost felt like cheating to include Diego as one of my forty dates, but I decided to anyway. You see, when I matched with the thirty-six-year-old actor a couple of weeks prior, his profile said he was on Tinder for social purposes: meeting new friends, promoting his work, building his Instagram following. Obviously this didn't exactly fit what I was looking for, but from his pictures he looked like the kind of guy I wanted to karaoke with, and Journey knows we can all use more people like that in our lives.

Our Tinder messages were friendly and casual. He told me about the show he was currently shooting in Atlanta ("I have a huge fight scene tomorrow!"), and I shared with him some of my writing (*not* my blog, although now I was considering it). At no point did I get the impression that he had any romantic interest in me, and I was just fine with that. I love meeting new people, clearly, or I never would have agreed with myself to do this project.

After our initial daily text convos, there was a week of radio silence, and I figured our new cyber friendship had ended as quickly as it'd begun. But then, Diego shot me a message on Saturday.

DIEGO:

> **Back in town Monday to Thursday, let's fucking grab some drinks!!**

How could I turn down such an enthusiastic invitation? I really wanted to meet him, but the only way I could justify it with my schedule would be to include him as one of my dates. So be it. Tinder has more uses than just one-night stands and finding the love of your life, and I found it important to show this.

ME:

> **Fucking fantastic! Let's do lunch Monday 1:30pm at Home in Los Feliz.**

Diego was already having a beer at the bar when I arrived. Two Original Hipsters (sixty-year-old bearded men in plaid) joined him at either end. I snagged the stool to his right. It could not have felt less like a date.

"How the hell are ya?" Diego gave me a great big bear hug. His presence had a warming effect, like a cup of hot cocoa on a snow day. With extra marshmallows. "It's awesome to finally meet!" he exclaimed.

"I know!" I grinned. "Welcome home!"

He hadn't eaten since lunch the day before, a feat that would have turned me into Exhibit A, so we ordered right away. He went for the steak sandwich with mash, while I opted for a salmon salad, trying to be healthy. (A friend of mine told me when I started this project that I should call it *40 Dates, 40 Nights, & 40 Pounds*. He was joking, but he may have been right.)

The conversation naturally began with acting, and pretty much stayed there the whole time. Under normal first-date circumstances, this would have driven me nuts, but not with Diego. Like George, he'd been a working actor for more than a decade, and his passion for story was infectious. He possessed no arrogance, no self-involvement, no concern over fortune and fame—just a love of playing pretend.

And craft services. "I remember being an extra on my first set, playing this homeless Mexican kid running around dirty and barefoot, and stumbling across this mountain of food: chips, cookies, candy, Coca-Cola Classics up to my ears. I knew right then what I wanted to do with my life."

He talked excitedly about his part in the TV show—"I get to play a cop, with the gun, the uniform, the whole thing!"—and the stunt sequence they were shooting next week.

"Have you never played a cop?" I asked, even though I'd already deduced the answer.

"Oh no, I'm always the bad guy. The drug dealer, the serial killer, the rapist."

I laughed. "Oh yeah? How many rapists have you played?"

He thought about it. "Two ... no, three. Yup, three rapists." More (inappropriate) laughter.

"It's funny, because it's so hard to picture you as a bad guy," I said. "Actually, that's not true; you totally look like a criminal, but your energy is just so positive and happy!"

"Yeah." He laughed. "But that's what's great about acting! Getting to be all of the things that you're not. But it's nice to finally be liked. After my part on *Breaking Bad*, I had people coming up to me and telling me they hated me." *Burn.*

We finished eating and closed out with the bartender. Diego had lent his car to a friend and was planning to take an Uber, so I offered him a ride home.

"You sure?" he asked. "I know you're really busy."

"Yes, definitely. I'm not that busy. I mean, you're not actually a rapist, are you?"

He shook his head.

"Hop in."

On the drive to his place, we discussed the bane of every actor's existence: waiting tables. He'd worked at restaurants in Los Angeles, New York, and Louisiana, but by far his worst experience had been the night shift at Jerry's Famous Deli on Beverly Boulevard. "I worked from ten p.m. to five a.m. almost every night. All the drunk, delinquent customers loved me and would always request me. I think the lowest night of my entire life was the Christmas shift I worked there. It was three thirty on Christmas morning, and some guy had spilled ranch dressing all over the floor. And I was on my hands and knees, soaking it up with napkins. Yeah, that was pretty bad."

My worst experience hadn't been quite that demoralizing, but it had been life-threatening. It happened at Ketchup, one of the trendiest, most ridiculous restaurants in LA for a brief period, thanks to its celebrity associations. On this particular night, a gang of Armenian twentysomething males had come into the hot spot wanting to host a party for a sixteen-year-old girl and her friends. When the manager told them they were too drunk to accompany the girls, the men pulled out guns. The cops showed up seconds later and arrested them in the middle of Sunset Boulevard.

"Geez, that's intense," Diego said, eyes wide. "You may have me beat."

"Well, if it ever gets turned into a movie or TV show, you can play the cop." We shared a laugh.

He showed me where to pull over, and I stopped.

"Hey, you're awesome," I said, giving him a hug.

"You are, too." He smiled and got out of the car. "Let's hang again when I'm back."

I nodded. "For sure! Have fun catching bad guys!" He shut the door and I took off.

My lunch with Diego certainly hadn't been like my date

with the Cab Driver, or Perfect Teeth, or the Full Stein. Heck, it hadn't even really been a date at all. But I was happy I swiped right. Not only had I made a new buddy, one I could play cops and robbers with and who would one day hopefully join me at Brass Monkey in a horrible rendition of "Don't Stop Believin'," but he had helped me to solidify one of my key arguments about Tinder theory: that it's not all about sex.

Maybe it was time I started Tindering with girls, too. *Just kidding.*

DATE No. 16

All Things Reconsidered

HOLLYWOOD

Human beings change. They grow up, they grow out, they grow older, they grow wiser. They change their hairstyles, their clothes, their music tastes, their sheets (hopefully). New information comes along and people adapt. Last election they were against gay marriage; this election their brother is out of the closet and they support it. Last spring they ate gluten-free; this fall it's Paleo. Things happen, people change.

My dating project was changing me. I could feel the shift. With Diego, with Dan. I was dropping into myself, letting go of pretenses, owning my experiences, my thoughts, my behaviors. Good and bad. And nowhere was this more clear than in my pole dancing.

I went into class that morning thinking I might dance to

something raunchy or sassy: Nicki Minaj, Ace Hood, Rihanna. But when it came time for me to get up in front of the class, I couldn't choose a song.

"What have you been holding on to?" my teacher asked. "What song have you wanted to dance to but been too afraid?"

"Volcano," I said without hesitation.

If Damien Rice's ballad seems like the antithesis of pole dancing music to you, you're not alone. My response surprised even me. Sure, women danced to slow, emotional music all the time in the studio, but I always went for more provocative, sexier songs. Ones that screamed Coyote Ugly. Not right now.

I lay down on the ground, and let the opening chords work their way into my bones. An intense rush of emotion pulsated through me. Through the lyrics, through the music, through my body, I was speaking to James. But not just James. To every lost lover, to all the guys who had broken my heart. I felt like I was exploding, hot lava pouring out into the room.

By the last note I was sobbing. My teacher came and held me on the floor.

"That was it. That was so beautiful. That was so powerful," she whispered in my ear. She was also crying.

"Thank you," I choked. "Thank you so much. I needed that."

My dance had been a sort of forgiveness, a reconciliation. Yes, my heart had been broken, but I was coming out stronger for it. James didn't need me, but I also didn't need him. It was time to move on.

And perhaps date actors again. As I swiped through Tinder later that afternoon, checking out profile after profile belonging to creative Hollywood types, I considered my reasoning behind my No Actor clause. It was rooted in some pretty heavy shit. Shit dating back to my late teens and early twenties.

Back then, all a guy needed to say was "I'm on a CW show" and I instantly fell in love. I was enamored with working actors. The sheer fact that their talent was being recognized on the screen validated them in my mind. I desperately wanted that same validation, and if I couldn't get it from booking my auditions, at least I could get it from dating someone who was.

For instance, Cameron Daughters, my first LA boyfriend. I met him in an acting class, and he blew me away with his talent, his sensitivity, his intelligence, his thoughtfulness. And yes, his mid-level success. I fell desperately in love with him, even lost my virginity to him, and we dated for almost a year. But here was the thing: even though we spent tons of time together, immersing ourselves in each other's worlds, he never once called me his girlfriend. It was like he was always waiting for something better to come along, someone prettier, more talented, more ... Natalie Portman. It devastated me.

More painful experiences followed. Like waking up after a day at Disneyland and a passionate night to be told by an ABC Family star, "I'm getting back with my girlfriend." Or my romance with the superhot, about-to-be-famous Aussie who simply ghosted me after three weeks. Or the kicker: spending Valentine's Day with my longtime friend and on-again, off-again lover only to find out he had a girlfriend. (They are now married. Mazel tov.)

Finally, I quit dating actors. I stopped seeking out guys with impressive IMDB pages, and started searching for qualities like compassionate, intellectual, funny, selfless, monogamous, and financially stable. And I found this to be a wise move, saving me from lots of heartache and potential STDs.

But now, as I studied the profile of Matt Two—his huge, friendly smile, his goofy headshot, the picture of him and his droopy-eyed puppy in matching sweaters—I couldn't help thinking maybe it was time for an amendment. How bad could a guy with this About Me section really be?

MATT, 38

I am kind, funny, smart, and fun to be around. I work hard and continue to learn new things. Stop by and say hello when you get a chance. Also, my dog's name is Doug.

Awww. Not only did his dog dig up nostalgia for Saturday-morning cartoons, but he was friends with Sascha. And anyone who was good in that pole goddess's book was also good in mine. I swiped right. I wanted to say hello to Matt and Doug.

As fate would have it, I got my opportunity that night. While I originally had plans to go out with Daniel, the guy I was supposed to go out with all the way back on Date #1, he once again bailed on me. But this time, instead of having ten hours to fill his slot, I had sixty minutes. I got out of my improv class at ten o'clock to a text that he was sick. I assumed this was true, because he apologized profusely, but I was still annoyed. I had two tickets to a UCB show at eleven, and finding a date at this hour on a school night might prove difficult.

But it wasn't.

MATT TWO:

> Yeah, fuck it! I'll try and get there in a half hour

Score! This was one thing I'd always loved about dating actors: spontaneity and insanely flexible schedules.

We met twenty minutes before the show at the Oaks, a gourmet food and beverage store next to the UCB theater. I stood staring at a refrigerator full of beer for a solid ten minutes before Matt Two showed up, and the clerks kept eyeing me suspiciously. *Just waiting for a Tinder date! Not trying to steal a Stone IPA!* I smiled weakly. The door finally swung open and Matt Two strode in.

"Yay! You came!"

We bought a couple of beers, concealed them in my purse, and queued up for the show.

"Thanks for getting me out of the house! I was just watching a documentary, about to go to sleep. But I never regret last-minute decisions to hit the town!" he said eagerly.

"I'm thrilled you could make it!" I exclaimed. "It's bangarang, they're awesome, I promise you'll laugh."

"Do you do improv?" he asked.

"Badly," I replied. "But it definitely helps with my writing."

"Absolutely. It's helped with mine, too."

So he's also a writer. I smiled.

We found seats in the theater and covertly cracked open our beers. I managed to cheers, drink, and look him in the eye at the same time from our crouched position among the battered seats. Quite the accomplishment. The lights dimmed and the show began.

It was Halloween themed and split into two parts. The

first involved playing a clip from an eighties horror flick and then doing the next scene. The second featured a half-hour set all improvised from a suggestion of place, in this case a cellar. It included, but was not limited to: bodacious boobies, a humanitarian obsessed with orgasms, and a killer Santa attacking Fran Drescher, Corky Romano, and James Caan. (I should also note my gratitude for the riotous laughter. It really helped mask some rather embarrassing beer belches.)

After the show we skipped over to neighboring Birds to finish off the evening with a nightcap. My cheeks hurt from laughing, and Matt Two would not let them rest. Like me, he made his living in the commercial world, and had been a working actor for a decade. He thrived in comedy.

"I've been in a sketch group for over ten years, and I can honestly say, if I were to never work again, it would all have been worth it. Being able to make people laugh is one of the best feelings in the world." *Agreed.*

We said good night shortly after one. Ultimately, I didn't feel Matt Two, or that special chemistry I'd experienced with the Full Stein, but he was smart, funny, successful, empathetic, and others-centered. And when I thought about it, the other actors I'd been out with—Matt One, Diego, and George—had also been these things. *Imagine that!*

When I got home, I discovered Matt Two was a one-hundred-dollar donor to our Kickstarter campaign. *Wow, what a guy, supporting female sexual empowerment.* And to think I'd almost swiped left because he was an actor. In that moment, I made peace with the past and decided to no longer cross actors off my list. After all, actors were people, and people changed, and I was an actor, and I changed.

DATE N° 17

The Duck

WEST HOLLYWOOD

I went from my dating job into my day job, managing to catch a few hours of sleep post-#16 before heading to set at six in the morning. For once I felt grateful to simply be standing there instead of being the one filmed for national TV. I thought about my friend Olivia, working two restaurant jobs while getting her master's and raising an eight-year-old by herself. If she could do that, I could certainly hold this position with my eyes open for a few hours.

We wrapped at two o'clock, and I drove straight to my next Tinder date at Urth Caffé, looking like a hot, cakey makeup mess. As I examined myself in the rearview mirror, finger-combing my ratted hair, I thought of that overused but completely applicable Marilyn Monroe quote: "If you can't handle me at my worst, then you sure as hell don't deserve me at my best." *Well said, MM.*

I strode up to the café, slightly out of breath, and checked the time: two minutes early. Sweet! I glanced around, and then realized something horrifying: I didn't know who I was looking for. I mean, I knew his name, and at one point I'd seen his pictures, but I'd totally forgotten which guy it was. *ALERT ALERT–TINDER OVERLOAD–EMERGENCY EMERGENCY!* I quickly pulled up my account and scrolled through: *Matthew ... Daniel ... Braxten ... Diego ... Justin!* Whew, I had a visual.

I waited for him inside, enjoying the people-watching. Urth is one of those super-trendy places you go to forty times the first year you live in LA, in hopes of spotting a celebrity. Usually you don't, but every once in a while you'll see a Real Housewife, or Pauly Shore. It's a treat. And they have really incredible Spanish lattes.

As I observed a woman of indeterminable age (thirty? Seventy-five? Impossible to tell) trying to return her iced chai blended, Justin walked up.

"Hi!" He gave me a big hug, and we stepped up to order. "How was your job today?" He was definitely cute, ethnically ambiguous, but *very* metrosexual.

"Great! Just tired, but always thrilled to be working," I replied enthusiastically, channeling Olivia.

We placed our order—decaf coffee for him, green tea boba for me, and tiramisu for both—then found a table outside.

"So we have a lot of comedian friends in common. Are you a stand-up?" he inquired. I laughed. Hard.

"Oh no, not even close. I would faint. Are you?"

He nodded. "Five nights a week, all around the city."

I squinted at him with admiration. Ever since I'd read Steve Martin's memoir, *Born Standing Up*, I'd been completely in awe of stand-up comedians.

"That's amazing. I need to come to one of your shows. Can we move seats?"

I slid over to the next table, dodging the afternoon sunlight. He followed suit, nearly spilling his entire cup of coffee when he kicked the table.

"It's my feet; they're enormous," he remarked.

"What size?" I asked, as if I knew anything about men's feet, other than that my six-foot-two father wears a size 11 or 12.

"Thirteen. And I'm five-foot-nine," he replied.

"Holy cow! You should have been a swimmer with those flippers!" I exclaimed.

"I know, and they're webbed. My nickname growing up was Duck," he confessed.

"You should totally use that for your stand-up name! The Duck!" I laughed. *"Ugh, no, I hated being called that."*

"Well, too bad, Duck," I smiled.

Our drinks and tiramisu landed.

"I'm having you be a guinea pig; I wanna see what their tiramisu is like compared to my coffee shops," he said.

I took a bite and nodded my approval.

"What coffee shops?" I hoped he meant the ones he was frequenting, not ones where he was a barista.

"Grind House and Rockpaper Coffee," Justin replied.

"Awesome. Do you go there to write or something?"

He laughed. "No, I own them." *Wow, had I been off! Happy surprises.*

I continued to ask him questions about his work, his life, his passions. In addition to running cafés and making people laugh, Justin also consulted on the side for GM and studied art history at SUNY.

"I studied art history, too—that's crazy!" I exclaimed.

He smiled. "Yeah, I could tell you were creative. I always try and surround myself with creative people. If you don't, it's game over. What do you do, work all week for the weekend and then what? Kill yourself?"

I laughed. I would definitely hit one of his shows.

Halfway through my boba the conversation drifted into traveling. He envied my European escapades the previous summer, particularly my time spent in the south of France. His dream was to ride a Jet Ski in a full white linen suit. He also admitted he'd never been to the Philippines, even though it's half his heritage (the other half is Puerto Rican).

"But I'm going next year with a comedy tour," he said eagerly.

"Fantastic! I love Southeast Asia! I lived in Thailand when I was younger; my parents did humanitarian work there." More fawning.

Things momentarily took a dark turn—Ebola, depleted fishing populations, the effects of global warming on the Galápagos Islands ("You haven't been there? Perfect. I'm taking you to see a beached turtle")—and then somehow found their way to game shows. He was pitching one the next morning.

"It's a little like *Fifth Grader*," he said.

"I was on that show!" I interjected.

"No way, me too!"

"Wait, hold on, did you drop out as well?" I couldn't believe we'd both been on the same game show.

"You know it!" He grinned.

I laughed. "I love that we are both fifth-grade dropouts! So how'd you do?"

He frowned and told me he had missed a question toward the end about oxygen in the atmosphere.

"Don't worry, I also missed an easy one in the middle. 'What's another name for the windpipe?'" I questioned him.

"Esophagus," he replied assuredly.

"No! That's what I said! It's the trachea! But I still won ten g's." I grinned. *Not bad for a day's work.*

The sun dipped closer to the horizon, and I needed to leave for my pole class.

"I'll walk you to your car," Justin said.

Of course you will, I thought, concealing my own inside joke.

"So what are you doing Sunday?" he asked as we approached my Jetta.

"I, uh ..." I tried to think of what date I had planned. "I have a lunch in Malibu, but—"

"Great. I'm taking you to Pace for dinner."

This took me aback. Justin was the first guy to try and nail down a second date before the first had even ended. I thought about it for a second. He wasn't exactly my type—I really didn't feel any sexual attraction toward his metro-ness—but he was certainly funny and charming and a bunch of other great things, and we'd both been on *5th Grader* (I mean, what are the odds, right?), sooo ...

"Okay, cool!" I gave him a hug and got in my car. "Good luck with the pitch, Duck!"

He scowled, then laughed.

As I drove off, I wondered if I had confirmed too quickly, if I should have told him I'd get back to him so I could really decide if we should go on a second date. I waffled back and forth. On the one hand, it was just dinner; I knew we would have a fun time and have a gazillion things to talk about. But on the other, I didn't want to waste either of our time when I had a pretty strong inclination that he was not the one. *Is it being honest if I cancel? Dumb? Shallow?*

I'd have to figure it out later, because my day still wasn't over ...

DATE No. 17.5

The Time Traveler

Downtown Los Angeles

My third double-dip. I'd gone ahead and officially erased Rule #1 from my playbook, so I was no longer breaking rules, just owning my new identity as Dating Machine. And this second outing with Colin the Cab Driver was frickin' *awesome*.

He was easily one of the most interesting human beings I'd ever met. I mean, I'd kind of gotten that impression after our titillating conversation over our stupidly expensive dinner in which he told me about the twenty-five different lives he had lived. But this solidified it.

We originally planned to do the Norton Simon, then dinner downtown and a play at the Mark Taper. But Colin didn't make it in time for the museum, due to traffic on his drive from San Francisco. Instead he picked me up on his way down the 5, and we headed straight to Faith & Flower.

"This is such a drug dealer's car!" I teased, raising the passenger seat of the 2007 Mercedes-Benz S55.

"I have not been Walter White, if that's what you're wondering," Colin replied. "But there is a funny story behind this car. I was in Vegas a year or two ago, and I went into this casino on a whim and won eighteen grand. I needed a car to drive between SF and San Diego at the time, so I went to the lot and this one was eighteen thousand dollars. When the universe speaks to me, I listen."

I laughed, in awe. "Well, I can't beat that. But I did fly to Vegas once on a first date! We were having dinner at Asia de Cuba, and we were talking about how much we loved Sin City, and I said we should go, so he called his assistant and we got our food to go and went straight to the airport."

Colin raised an eyebrow.

"Don't worry! He was British and a gentleman and sober; all we did was kiss!" I defended my chastity. "But he did buy me an Ed Hardy hoodie."

"Gross." Colin smiled.

"It's never been worn since. And Alexander and I are still friends."

We got to the restaurant, and Colin relayed a crazy first date of his own: his Tinder experience the night before. It had started with dinner in San Francisco, and ended up in Reno. But here's the best part: he wasn't even interested in her! At least, not sexually. He simply found her intriguing, and had been bored by five days in SF, and thus pulled a Fear and Loathing in the poor man's Las Vegas (not coincidentally a movie he credited with many of his life decisions). That was why he'd missed the Norton Simon.

Emboldened by this Tinder admission and the establishment we were dining at, I took a leap of faith and told him about my project. Like with Dan, if this were to ever get more serious, he would need to know anyway.

"Incredible," he replied. "I could have sworn I was being filmed or something on our first date. Now I know what I was picking up on. Tell me everything."

So I did. And he loved it. I showed him the post I'd written about him, and he approved—minus his nickname.

"I wish you'd called me the Time Traveler, but I'll take it."

We launched into wormholes and parallel universes and past lives while downing English milk punch cocktails and California rustic cuisine. I didn't even mind sharing all vegetarian options; our discussion was that good.

We rounded out the evening with a trip to the Mark Taper Forum, further immersing ourselves in the realms of science fiction with the thought-provoking *Marjorie Prime*. I couldn't decide which performer was more captivating, Lois Smith as an elderly robot mother or the Cab Driver holding yoga positions in his seat.

"Not sure how this date'll get topped," I said with a smile as he dropped me off at the end of the night.

"Oh, trust me, I've got something in mind to create some real chaos."

"Chaos?" I asked nervously.

"The good kind."

He gave me a hug. Still no kiss. I had no idea what this meant, but I was willing to embrace the chaos and find out.

DATE N° 18

The Casting Couch

HOLLYWOOD

At our "Why I Dance" meeting that morning, we discussed casting. Initially we'd been concerned with whether we could find twelve women to share their experience in this way. After all, we were asking them to dance in next to nothing on camera for everyone to see—friends, coworkers, grandparents. But our production email had filled up with applications. Now the question was, how would we choose?

We wanted a diverse group to illustrate our message: that every woman is beautiful and sexy. This meant casting a variety of ethnicities, body types, ages, and backgrounds. As we poured over each of the magnificent women, all unique and gorgeous in their own way, we had to make difficult cuts.

"I love Angela, Jenny, Cassie, and Marianne, but we don't

need that many Caucasian girls in their twenties with athletic bodies," the director commented. We agreed. We chose just one.

We ended up casting sixteen dancers. While not the most enjoyable process, it was a profound moment for me as an actress. Because even though we'd rejected a dozen or so women, it didn't mean we didn't find them wonderful, or worthy of this project. It just wasn't the right fit this time around. I'd been hearing this for years—"you're not quite what we're looking for"—but I'd somehow always managed to interpret that as "you suck at acting and life." Now I finally understood it in a different light. No matter how many awesome, talented people are up for the role, still only one gets cast.

And yet that night I still tried to cast two. My Tinder match, Rich, and I had made plans earlier in the week to grab drinks, but when my mysterious, Bruce Wayne-esque friend Clancy magically reappeared from his Batcave and invited me to join him at his buddy's new Hollywood haunt, I couldn't resist. I wanted both.

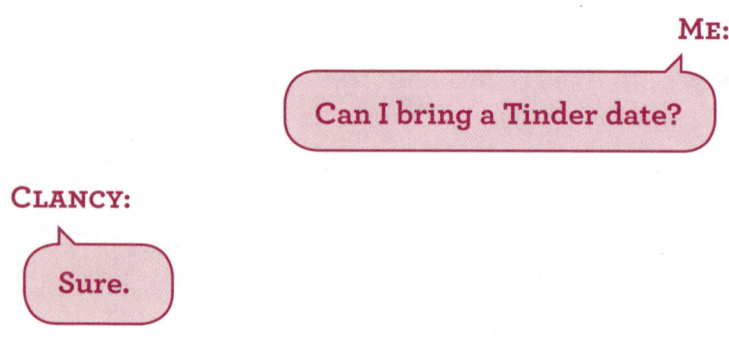

I arrived precisely at nine thirty, the first customer in the bar. Not even Clancy had shown up. I sat down on a plush velvet chair and pulled out my phone. Rich had texted that he was running late, so I called Clancy. Loud French music swirled around the art deco furnishings, and I watched the beautiful, waifish cocktail waitresses taste martinis at the bar. He finally picked up.

"Babes, I'm around the corner getting a pizza. Be there in three."

It had been more than a year since I had last seen Clancy. On that night he had dropped by my place with dinner. To feed thirty-five people. No joke: bags and bags of filet mignon, mac and cheese, crab cakes, asparagus—a veritable feast. And five bottles of wine. Typical Clancy. He had lost a lot of weight since then, and I could feel it when he hugged me.

"You look amazing as always. Let me get you a drink," he said, and sidled up to the bar.

We sat down on a couch and caught up for a few minutes before Rich arrived.

I went out to fetch him.

"He's with me," I said to the doorman.

They both smiled, and Rich followed me in. He didn't look quite like his photos, but that wasn't necessarily a bad thing. He was cute, sort of Seth MacFarlane-ish, if not a bit short.

"Rich, Clancy. Clancy, Rich."

They shook hands.

"Do you want a drink?" Rich offered. I pointed at my sauvignon blanc. "I'll be back in a second."

He disappeared to the bar, and Clancy looked at me after sizing Rich up.

"He's too short for you. And on the wrong team." I laughed. Clancy had believed I was a lesbian for years—in his mind, why else would I not want to sleep with him?

"Be nice," I commanded.

Rich returned. "So Amy told me a little about you, Clancy. Sounds like you're involved in some interesting things."

Clancy glared at me. *Uh-oh.* It was true; I had mentioned a few things to Rich—art collector, secret government official, international man of mystery—and Clancy would not like this.

"I just told him you were really into art, had some pieces at the Huntington," I quickly interjected.

Rich picked up my vibe and went with it. "Yeah, what kind of art are you into?"

We discussed sculpture, painting, Picasso, and interior design. Rich confessed he collected some art as well: black-and-white photographs. This was a natural outgrowth of his job: he was a photographer and a documentarian. He'd spent thirteen years traveling around the world filming skateboarders and surfers, and the last year shooting original content for Fandango.

At some point, Clancy disappeared to do whatever he does, and I was grateful. We'd all been getting along, but I wanted to get to know Rich one-on-one. It'd been difficult to determine what sort of chemistry we had with a third member. The conversation meandered a bit, and somehow the topic of near-death experiences arose. Rich told me he had had a bunch.

"Seriously? Tell me everything!"

"Well," Rich began, "I almost got killed by a bunch of thirteen-year-olds in Antwerp when I was twenty."

"What?" I laughed, disbelieving.

He proceeded to tell me about a group of twenty or so punk teenagers who accosted him and his friend. It quickly escalated into an all-out brawl, with Rich punching kids left and right. Then his friend pulled out a set of brass knuckles. The kids weren't too pleased with this new development, and whipped out knives. Rich saw the tunnel of light when one of them started charging at him, blade shining, two bloody holes in his forehead from the knuckles, eyes ablaze. And then suddenly out of nowhere—deus ex machina style—a huge, burly Irishman swooped in and tucked Rich under his arm.

"That did not happen." I stared at him in awe.

"It definitely did. Then there was the time I was in a coma for a month when I was seven. Car accident. And I was also in an airplane that dropped a mile in a second. Our plates of food all hit the ceiling. The first time I ever experienced a panic attack."

I felt the brussels sprouts I'd had for dinner ping-ponging their way around my stomach. I *hate* flying.

"Well, I flipped off the freeway once," I said, confiding in him my own near-death experience. "I was going seventy, and a car pulled up beside mine. The passengers glared at me, and then they swerved in front. I fishtailed and lifted into the air, rolling three times. What was crazy, though, was how calm I felt. Like, I said my good-byes, said thank you for the eighteen years I'd been gifted, and told my parents I loved them. When I landed upside down I thought I must be dead and it was like in *Ghost* or something. But I wasn't. I actually didn't even have a scratch on my body. The paramedics were floored. Probably karma, because the car that had tried to hit me was actually stolen, and the police report said it was an act of gang violence. So I guess we've both been victims of random acts of violence!"

These tales of dangling off the precipice of life brought us closer together. Literally. Rich had made his way onto the couch, and had his hand on my knee. I liked it. *This is how you do it, Ainsley. Work up to it.* Clancy popped in and out, as he always does, and I finished my second glass of wine. The waitress came over.

"One more round," Rich said.

"I don't know if I can drink anymore." I looked at him, feeling a bit tipsy.

"It's fine. You don't have to finish it."

She came back with the wine, and I took a sip, staring at him. I was definitely more attracted to him than I had been at the beginning of the night, but was that the sauvignon blanc speaking? Or was it because things had been thrown off initially by the presence of Clancy, and then once I'd actually started to get to know him we'd had chemistry? *Shit*, I thought. *I have no idea. No more wine for Amy.*

We talked and laughed a little while longer, and it wasn't until I'd pulled out my phone to gush over pictures of my parents that I realized how late it had gotten. (Side note: I'm totally going to be that mother posting nine thousand baby pics a day and stopping every stranger in the street to ogle at them.)

"Oh man, it's almost one, and I have to work in the morning. We should go." Rich settled his tab, and we found Clancy.

"Really great to meet you," Rich said, shaking his hand, meaning it, before we left.

Outside, waiting for an Uber, he leaned in and kissed me gently. We separated, and I looked at him, still over-thinking everything. I definitely felt something, but it was so hard to tell what. It had been a mistake to meet a Tinder date with Clancy hovering over us like an executive producer. *Screw it*, I thought, and pulled him back into me, kissing him more deeply.

The Uber arrived.

"Let's do this again," Rich said, and smiled as I got in.

"Absolutely," I said. If there was one thing I felt sure about, it was that I needed a second date with him to figure it all out. A proper date, with just him, me, and maybe a cup of coffee. Thank God for callbacks.

DATE NO. 19

That Awkward Anniversary

ECHO PARK

I was predictably tired on set the next morning, and considered rescheduling my evening date with Ben. Not that I wasn't excited to go to a haunted house with the guy; I just feared for his enjoyment in the face of my weariness. Plus, I could afford a rain check; I was still ahead of schedule.

Then the Cab Driver messaged me.

COLIN:

> I'm thinking New York for date three. Leave Monday or Tuesday.

I reread the text slowly, making sure my hangover vision

wasn't blurring things. Nope, it said New York. *Holy shit. Holy shit holy shit holy shit! NEW YORK! And so soon!* There would be no rescheduling of dates now.

However, I definitely needed to cancel my date with the Duck on Sunday. After my nights with Colin and Rich, I felt 100 percent convinced that my attraction to Justin just wasn't strong enough, that I would be leading him on by accepting a second date. I considered telling him I'd met someone else, then opted for the truth.

Me:

Hey Justin! So first of all, I think you are great, and I would totally love to be friends, but I'm not sure I really felt a romantic connection, and I don't want to lead you on...

Justin:

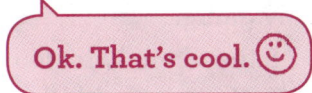

A smiley face! *So he doesn't hate me for not being into him like that! What a revelation!* Not that I had expected it to devastate him, but for some reason I always had such a hard time communicating to guys when I wasn't into them. Especially when I liked them as people, like the Duck. But why would he be upset? It had only been a first date; it wasn't like we lived together. Or had even kissed. Sure, it might be a tiny bit of an ego bruise, but at the end of the day it really wasn't that big of a deal. I smiled, and tucked this bit of acquired knowledge in my back pocket.

I rode the excitement of New York through the day, but by the time I left my house to go meet Ben at Taix at 8:30 p.m., I really wished I'd canceled our date, too. I was in pretty bad form. Those three hours of sauvignon blanc sleep + Wendy's until 7:30 p.m. = Tired Mess. I barely had time to throw on a Halloween-themed orange sweater and black jeans combo, brush my hair, and pound my head against a wall.

Somehow by God's grace I found a parking spot right in front of the venue, and I took this to be a good omen for things to come. But from the second I stepped out of my car and heard horrid, blaring music, I knew I was wrong. Some sort of heavy metal festival raged in the parking lot and within Taix's bar and miscellaneous rooms. Black Sabbath T-shirts swarmed every nook and cranny. Not what my headache needed.

I met Ben on the sidewalk. He didn't really look like his photos, mostly because of his new beard, but he had forewarned about it in his profile. Our energies immediately clashed, but I attributed that to my overall state of exhaustion and made a mental note to step up my game.

Ben suggested we get a table at the French restaurant to save our eardrums, and so we walked back to the hostess stand. I'd been here once for dinner several years ago, a rather disappointing Groupon purchase, and I hoped it had changed.

It hadn't. Well, maybe the furniture was more worn, and the tables less filled, but otherwise the same sort of sickly ambience. Like van Gogh's *Night Café*.

We sat down in a booth at an awkwardly comfortable distance, and the waitress came over to take our drink order. It was only her sixth day on the job, and she was effervescent. I wondered what she would be like after six months under the unsettling lights of the dining room. *Probably cut her ear off.* Ben ordered a cocktail, and I ordered a six-dollar glass of pinot noir, rightfully concerned by the low price tag.

"I'll definitely need to see your ID," our waitress said. *Hell yeah!* I beamed, pulling out my driver's license and handing it to her.

"Flattery will get you everywhere."

She and I both laughed. Ben didn't.

I pride myself on being an excellent conversationalist, but at that moment I just really didn't have the energy. My game was way off, as exemplified by our one running joke the whole evening: Ben being a serial killer. Our next stop was a haunted house, so it seemed appropriate enough at first, but by the seventh time I revisited it, the joke was dead in the trunk. And I started to believe it might be true.

He asked me a few questions about Portland and acting; I asked him about where he went to school and what he did (Sarah Lawrence, producing).

"I'm just wrapping up a season of a show on Adult Swim," he said, blasé.

"Which one?" I inquired, as if I knew any of them.

"*Mr. Pickles.*"

"No shit!" I almost fell out of my seat at the synchronicity of life. *Mr. Pickles*—the exact same TV show the *OkCupid Show* contestant had worked for! Yup, the nerdy cartoon editor who inspired my entire project. *Maybe Ben should be the one doing 40 Dates & 40 Nights,* I laughed inwardly.

"You know it?" he asked, clearly surprised by my reaction.

I nodded, trying to figure out how to explain my dramatic response without drawing too much of a parallel between awkward OkCupid guy and him, awkward Tinder guy. I pretty much failed, and quickly tried to segue into something else.

"How's your Tinder experience been?" I asked.

"Is this, like, being filmed or something? I feel like I'm being interviewed, like I'm on *Candid Camera* or something."

My breathing stopped. *Does he know? Has he read my blog?* Or maybe I was just that transparent. I mean, the Cab Driver had sensed it, too.

I tried to save face. "Sorry, that was an awkward question. Moving on ... What was the last book you read?"

And just like that, we went right back into Stiltedconvoville as we waited for our French onion soup to arrive.

Several teeth had been pulled by the time we finished eating, and Ben asked for our check. We needed to be at the haunted house by nine thirty. *Has it really been less than an hour?* Oy. Two minutes later, our darling waitress reappeared, chocolate mousse with candle in hand, flanked by two elderly Latino busboys.

"Happy anniversary to you, happy anniversary to you...," the three of them sang in perfect dis-unison. Ben and I exchanged looks of great confusion (horror?), and the waitress made a face that said *shhh, just go with it.*

The singing stopped, and the five of us glanced around in awkward silence, the candle flickering on the table. I blew it out, and the busboys scurried away, relieved of their duties.

"I wanted to give you guys something because the soups took so long, but I needed an excuse so my boss wouldn't find out," our waitress said, smiling. God, she was precious.

"Thank you, you're too sweet," I said, and she disappeared.

I started laughing uncontrollably. The lack of sleep, the

ridiculous level of irony in the anniversary present, the look of misery on Ben's face—it was too much. Tears of laughter poured down my cheeks, and he looked like his cat had died.

"I'm sorry," I said, wiping my soggy cheeks. "I'm just delirious. Let's go to the haunted house."

♥

We arrived at *The Purge: Breakout* at 9:28 p.m., just in time for our 9:30 tickets. Except not.

"I'm sorry, but you guys needed to be here ten minutes ago," the guy on duty frantically explained. "I'll try to fit you in later, but we're fully booked for the night."

I'm sorry, what?

"But we're on time," Ben stated.

"Yeah, but you're late," Nerves McGee responded. "If you wait, I might be able to squeeze you in."

And so we waited. For forty-five minutes, we sat under horrible fluorescent lighting with a teaser of *The Purge* running on repeat. It was a nightmare, only I wasn't scared, just numbed out and irritated.

"This is why coffee dates usually work best when you first meet; that way you know if you want to go on a real date," Ben said.

I glanced around for a corner to crawl into and hide my embarrassment.

"I'm so sorry. I wish I felt better," I apologized. "And I wish we could get in."

But we couldn't. We finally left at ten fifteen, and Ben asked if I wanted to grab ice cream or a drink.

"I, uh ... think I just need to go home and sleep. I'm

sorry," I said. We drove back to his car and sat there for a second.

"Well, nice to meet you. Sorry the *Purge* thing didn't work out," I apologized for a final time.

"Yeah, well, we can reschedule it another night," he said. *Is he joking?* I couldn't tell.

He looked at me for a long, agonizing beat, like he maybe wanted to attempt the most awkward kiss of all time, then finally got out. The whole thing was so uncomfortable, I rolled down my window and attempted one last joke, trying to end on a positive note.

"Don't follow me home and try to kill me now!"

He turned back and looked at me, dead serious. "Don't worry, I won't."

I felt faint. *Is it possible to actually die of awkwardness?* I watched him get in his BMW, and then I pulled away. My phone buzzed a few minutes later. *Please don't be him, please don't be him.* I checked the message at a light.

COLIN:

> I randomly won $1750 at the casino tonight. The same price as your round trip ticket to JFK. Check your inbox.

An email ping. Forwarded tickets from Virgin America.

My jaw dropped. So this was real. New York would actually be happening. Energy surged back into my body, the excitement bubbling up and over. How quickly things had morphed from awkward to awesome!

DATE N.º 20

New James

WEST HOLLYWOOD, NORTH HOLLYWOOD

Last year's model broken? Bugs that need to be fixed? Never fear, Tinder's here! With just one right swipe, you can upgrade that worn-out prototype. Because not even geniuses like Stephen Hawking get it right on the first try!

♡

I couldn't wait for New York. We weren't leaving until Tuesday night, but I started packing Saturday morning, going against my usual travel protocol. *What am I going to wear? How will Tinder be different in the Big Apple? Will Colin finally kiss me?* A million questions raced through my mind, but I was getting ahead of myself: I still had two dates left in LA, one of them with New James.

We'd texted every day since he'd reached out, occasionally talking on the phone, too. He closely followed my blog, and we joked that he was my editor in chief. It was odd for him to know the ins and outs of my dating life, especially once we had planned one of our own. And yet it didn't seem to bother him at all. Nor had it curtailed my writing in any way. If anything, I'd been even more honest the past week. Somehow, knowing he was reading had helped me open up; I wanted to be that compassionate girl full of heart who had changed his mind.

I also wanted to impress him. I knew this wasn't the healthiest attitude, that trying to impress often had the reverse effect, but James was just so intuitive, so confident and witty. And if imitation was the sincerest form of flattery, then I had succeeded: he wrote his own essay on a first Tinder date, with a ballerina from his hometown. Reading it was...compelling, to say the least. Now I could understand what he felt reading mine.

As I selected an outfit for our afternoon outing, clothes strewn over every inch of my bedroom, I tried to suppress my nerves. Since Gordon, I'd successfully limited my expectations to something between zero and *run*! Not this time. I already felt close to James. And we knew so much about each other. Or so I thought.

A little after one in the afternoon I heard the grumbling of a Harley rolling down my street. It was James, and I was making Obvious Tinder Dating Mistake #4B: Meeting on a Motorcycle. I just hadn't been able to counter his argument that he didn't want our night to end with a walk to my Jetta, like every other date. Plus, I trusted him. All that buildup had created an intimacy worthy of him picking me up. I shut my laptop, grabbed my purse, and took a deep breath. This was it.

He was taking off his helmet as I approached. Right away my heart started to deflate: James was short. My height, maybe an inch or two less. Shit. I didn't want to be so shallow, but I'd never dated a guy under five-foot-eight before, and I didn't think it was something I could get over. I felt completely overwhelmed with déjà vu from my night with Gordon; once again, my expectations had bested me. *Stop it, Amy. This is James. Be open,* I commanded myself. *And just look at that beautiful face.*

His blue eyes sparkled as he handed me a helmet. I didn't know how to fasten it, so he helped, his fingers gently brushing my cheek. His face was inches from mine, and I could feel his gaze upon me. I felt weightless. Out-of-body. Out of breath. *Whoa.*

"There you go. You ready?" He motioned toward the bike, and I nodded. "Let's go."

We hopped on and off we went, cruising down Melrose to the Pacific Design Center, where we were attending a film screening. It'd been a couple of years since I'd been on a motorcycle, and I enjoyed it, the wind hitting my body, the feeling of being able to reach out and touch the world at thirty, forty, seventy miles an hour. No wonder dogs love sticking their heads out of windows.

We were forty minutes early for the showing, and this gave us time to talk to each other in the flesh. I realized he knew disproportionately more about me, and I wanted to know more about him. He started to open up.

"I grew up on a farm in rural Pennsylvania, and I never even saw the ocean until I moved to California." *What? How does that even make sense?* "Now I've been to seventy-two countries."

"Oh my god, we have a *lot* to talk about!" I grinned, excited to peel back the layers of his adventures.

They began at Penn State, where James had studied vertebrate physiology, prepping to be a doctor. He'd even taken the MCATs before realizing that as much as he loved the "whats" of the human body, he was even more fascinated by the "whys." *Why do humans behave as they do? Why do we make certain choices, feel certain ways? Why are each of us who we are?* He wanted to tell stories, follow in the footsteps of his role models—Mark Twain, Jules Verne, John Hughes—so he packed up his stuff and headed west.

His story was such a strange and intriguing one—so full of luck and eagerness and right time, right place, preparation meeting opportunity—that it was hard to believe.

"A lot of people think I'm making it up," he told me. I could understand that. I mean, *I'd* never met someone who had chin-balanced a wheelbarrow on *The Tonight Show with Jay Leno*!

"Are you?" I studied him. He gave me a mischievous smile, and shook his head.

We found our seats in the theater and settled in. I didn't really want the movie to start, because that would mean James would stop talking. It did anyway. The lights dimmed, and as the opening credits began, he gently reached for my chin and drew me close, lightly kissing me.

I'd written an essay a couple of months prior, before I'd begun my project, called "The Kiss." In it, I depicted my experience in Vienna of standing in front of Klimt's masterpiece of the same name, and then detailed my own feelings about searching for that perfect embrace, physically, spiritually, artistically. I described it as a hunger, a longing to consume and be consumed, to merge with another. And in that moment, in a fully packed movie theater in the middle of West Hollywood, I felt my hunger being satiated. Or maybe starting to grow.

The film was incredible. A hilarious, tragic, touching, thought-provoking look at the cult of celebrity, purpose, mental instability, artistic integrity, and the difference between being appreciated and being loved. It felt so poignant and spot-on, some lines hitting home so directly that I wondered if there was some sort of special star alignment happening. Not that I'd ever bought into astrology, but …

From the movie we headed to my friend's housewarming party in the Valley. Riding over the 101, sun setting, cars speeding across the pavement, I felt a stunning sense of rightness. A sort of mise-en-scène: everything in its place. I rested my head against James's shoulder and closed my eyes. I was flying.

My choice to bring a first Tinder date to a social gathering with all of my friends easily could have backfired, like with Rich and Clancy, but I could have brought James anywhere. He was so comfortable in his own skin, so adaptable, so interested in everyone. Especially me. After chatting with my friends for a while, we ended up on a couch together, and the rest of the universe just sort of disappeared.

"Do you want to go somewhere we can make out?" I finally said.

"Yes," he responded affirmatively.

I invited him over. Not something I would normally have done on a first date, but with James it seemed natural. Anyway, I knew I had enough control not to break Rule #5, the big one. There was a reason that rule was in place, and I didn't need to be reminded.

Back at my place, I welcomed him in shyly. As open as we'd been in our conversation the last nine hours, the past week, bringing someone into your home often reveals more than words ever could. I watched as he took in the pieces of my tiny sanctuary: the books, the photos, the hand-me-down furniture, the stuffed Stanford cow wearing a Disney princess birthday hat. All of these things held memories, signified a part of me. *What does he see in them?*

I offered him a beer, and we took a seat on my couch. I relaxed, no longer worried about being judged for the space I'd created for myself. He was comfortable in it, and so was I. We talked, we kissed, we talked some more, we kissed some more.

"Where did you come from?" I asked, that rhetorical question that shows all of your cards and yet is still somehow acceptable.

He smiled. "A farm." *Ugh, am I already falling? Jumping? What is happening?* We stared at each other in silence for a long time.

"Am I what you thought I would be?" I asked him tenderly,

thinking back to my initial reaction regarding his height. If it hadn't been for my blog, I would have dismissed him based on this. But just as pole dancing had taught me to see past the damaging constructions of the female figure presented by the media, Tinder was helping me break down my socially formed ideas of what constituted the perfect man.

"Not exactly," he replied. "There's a girl on my kickball team, right? And she's cute and fun. Amazing body. And she's been trying to date me for a while now, and I keep turning her down. And one of my friends thought I was crazy. 'Why aren't you hitting that?' Then he hung out with her a couple of weeks ago, and he called me and told me he understood why I hadn't. She was just missing that thing, that spark. And what I didn't expect from you, from only having read your writing and talked on the phone, was just how big your spark would be."

I wanted to cry, but I didn't. I kissed him instead. Passionately. Desperately. I wanted more, my body betraying my mind, but I knew my heart needed to wait. This was enough for our first magical date. He left at one in the morning.

DATE N° 21

The Near-Death Experience

WEST HOLLYWOOD

*A*re you there, Tinder Gods? It's me, Amy...

I woke up in the clouds of romance, and almost ended up in the heavenly ones a few hours later. I was thinking about New York, texting New James, and walking through the crosswalk on the way to my brunch date with François, Suitor #21, when I almost died. A white Lexus took a wild left turn and screeched to a stop a foot away from me. I jumped, making eye contact with the concerned witnesses around me, and made a note to message Rich about my latest near-death experience.

François was at the bar, almost finished with his first

mimosa, when I arrived, rattled from the crosswalk and jazzed by everything else.

"Hi, hey, sorry I'm late. I'm a bit of a mess." I hugged him.

"No worries. Should we grab a table?" I nodded and he signaled the hostess.

We sat down, and the gorgeous waitress greeted us immediately. We ordered a mimosa carafe and coffees.

"So, I know nothing about you. Tell me about yourself." François smiled warmly. *Well, let's see. I've been on twenty-three dates in twenty days, all through Tinder, and I'm totally into one guy, absolutely crazy about another, and going to New York on Tuesday with a third. Oh, and I'm writing a blog about it, too.*

"I'm an actress and a writer," I responded. "It's really typical and boring. Tell me about you!"

He worked peripherally in education, helping "rich, dumb kids" from foreign countries find their way in the US university system. "I deal in human trafficking," he joked. He himself was a transplant from Paris; having studied at UCSB, he then floated around California for a bit before landing in Los Angeles.

"Do you love what you do?" I asked.

"No, but it's a job and I'm good at it. And I'm passionate about music and spend a lot of time with that."

We talked about LA nightlife and traveling and our favorite TV shows (pretty much everything on HBO). He had one of the calmest dispositions of anyone I'd ever encountered in LA. *Perhaps he was a monk in a past life,* I thought. *Although then he probably would have come back as another monk, a step closer to enlightenment, not a human trafficker. I should* ask him if he's read that book about the French father and son, The Monk and the Philosopher. *Holy shit, that was good. Christ, am I al*ready drunk?

"Wow, I just realized I haven't eaten anything since yesterday. And I didn't even really have dinner last night. And I went running this morning. I'm hypoglycemic; I'm starting to shake." I looked down at my hands. They were shaking (Obvious Tinder Dating Mistake #7: Not Eating When Hypoglycemic). "I wonder where our food is. It's been forty-five minutes."

He looked at me, concerned but still calm. "Want me to check?" he replied.

"No, it's fine. I'm sure it's coming. I'll be okay."

But I wasn't. My blood sugar was dangerously, pass-out-level low. The coffee had been a horrible idea, and I felt my anxiety building.

"If I faint, well, I ... it's my fault. God, this is really bad form. I'm so sorry. You must think I'm insane. I'm feeling really dizzy. Shit." I rested my head between my hands and took a few deep breaths.

"Do you want to go for a walk? Should I get a paper bag?" He was so unfazed, it would have been disarming were I not already disarmed. He reached for my hand across the table and massaged it lightly.

"Honestly, I'm really sorry. This is the worst first date; you must think I'm awful."

The food finally came, and I ripped straight into the burger. Avocado and egg yolk splattered my face, but I didn't care. I just needed food. If I could have mainlined the bacon directly into my bloodstream, I would have. I inhaled a quarter of the burger in six seconds. Then froze.

"You okay?" François studied me with his third eye.

"Yeah, I, uh, just feel like I might throw up." I stared at the burger. The bacon, the tomato, the slightly pink ground beef. My blood was saying yes, but my stomach was saying no. "Can you excuse me for a second?"

I disappeared into the bathroom and kneeled on the floor. *Please, God, let me keep it together.* Throwing up on a brunch date would be a first. Back in my early twenties—my twentieth birthday, to be exact—I had vomited on my date's shoe. But at least I had had an excuse: seven shots of Patrón. (Apparently this did it for him: we ended up dating for a year.) What was my excuse now? Too much Tindering?

I texted James.

> **ME:**
> I've really fucked myself over with this one. Having hypoglycemic episode, trying not to faint/pass out/have a panic attack. If I don't respond, don't worry, I'm prob at Cedars. Not in a ditch. Chat soon!

Somehow I managed to keep it down. I picked myself up off the public restroom floor and headed back into the dining area. François was walking toward me.

"Oh, wow, this is awkward. I was going to leave," he said stoically.

"I totally get it, François. Don't feel bad. I deserve that," I said, embarrassed. "I'll pick up the check. Don't worry about it."

He smiled. "I'm only kidding. I'm just going to the bathroom. Be back in a minute."

I ordered a ginger ale from the waitress (because ginger ale cures dating mishaps, right?), and François remarkably returned a minute later.

"Seriously, if you want to leave, I understand."

He came and sat next to me. "I actually think you're awesome, very different from the other girls in this city." *Wait, what? This was working for him?* "I don't know what you are doing later, but if you wanted to see a movie or hang out or something ... "

I told him I needed to go home and lie down. *And take a Xanax.*

"You're welcome to lie down with me," he said. I stared at him. Some guys really are attracted to crazy, aren't they?

"That's sweet, but I just need to be alone. Do some meditating. Deep breathing. That sort of thing." *Pack for New York. Get ready for an East Coast Tinder-bender. Hang with the guy I made out with all night.* "I should probably go," I said, my anxiety once again escalating.

"It was really nice to meet you. I had a great time," he said, hugging me good-bye.

I stared at him in awe. No way could my hypoglycemic episode and all-around loopiness have been interpreted as a great time. *Is he serious? Joking? Stoned? Hmm, that might explain his Dalai Lama-like zen-ness.*

"I, uh, had a great time, too," I replied. "Next time I'll try to actually pass out!"

James, James, and more James

HOLLYWOOD

I got home from my date with François and lay down. *What the hell was that?* I'd tried to make light of it in the moment, but I knew I needed to take better care of myself. There was no excuse for that sort of obvious neglect, especially with my family history of manic depression and chemical imbalance. "Guard your mental health," my mom was always saying. Particularly important advice right now, as I felt myself becoming unhinged by all of the excitement.

I took a nap, my body recalibrating, and when I woke up I attempted to put my life in order. Between now and my red-eye, I had production coordinating, my acting class, a Kmart background job, and improv. Luckily I didn't need to do any more first dates until I arrived in New York, so I could relax on the Tinder front for a moment. And see James.

He came over that night after his softball game (so cute in his pink uniform!), and we just talked. He massaged my back and told me not to worry, that I was doing great. Was I a little nuts? Sure, but that's what he liked about me. It was also what I liked about him. His quirks, his wanderlust, his fearless outlook on life. His kiss.

"You know what sounds perfect?" he said, his arms around me on my bed. "Me, you, Paris, Barcelona, Hong Kong. Just traveling and writing around the world together. Waking up in different cities, having sex, writing, sex again, write some more." We still hadn't had sex, but we both knew it was coming, and we both knew it would be great.

"God, this feels so weird," I whispered. Part of me wanted to say screw my project, screw New York, screw everything. But I also knew that I didn't actually know James. Not really. Not after two days. That's why I'd made the rules ... "Right?"

He shook his head. "Nah, it's awesome. Just embrace it. You'll figure it out."

I smiled. "Yeah, hopefully."

I saw him again the next day in the afternoon. Like the night before, it wasn't really a date; he just came over and hung out. Not exactly the magic of Saturday—more like the routine of a couple a year into a relationship. I told him about the awesome cinematographer we'd locked down, and he told me about his meeting that morning with a production company. But my mind kept wandering, distracted by my upcoming week. So much was about to happen, and I had an epically long Tuesday in front of me.

"I'm sorry, I should probably finish packing," I told him, feeling bad for kicking him out, even though I needed the space.

"I'll stop by tomorrow before you leave?" It was sort of a question, sort of not. I hesitated. That would be four days in a row. Another rule down. *Should I do it?*

"Sure, why not?"

My alarm sounded at 4:30 a.m. Tuesday. I made it to Torrance by six, and promptly got ushered to set, where I walked back and forth in a parking lot for hours and hours while Cris Judd danced with a shopping cart. *Just livin' the dream.* When we wrapped at four in the afternoon, all I wanted to do was sleep. A red-eye and a weakened immune system would not be a good way to start New York. But there was no rest for the weary. I got home and put the final items in my suitcase just in time for James to drop by and say good-bye. And break Rules #4 and #5.

I didn't mean for it to happen like this. I honestly didn't want to have sex before monogamy this time around. I'd done that enough times; I didn't need any more casual sex. And I really didn't want to sleep with James right before leaving for this trip (at least, not emotionally). I knew it would only complicate things, especially since I did have interest in the Cab Driver, and still wasn't entirely sure how I felt about James. Yes, our first date had been wonderful, and he seemed like an awesome guy, but we had barely scratched the surface. *Don't dive into the deep end, Amy.*

And yet I couldn't resist his kiss, his hands, the way his hips pressed into mine. It awakened my exhausted body, brought feeling back to my fingertips and down my spine. I gave in to the tidal wave slowly washing over me, overriding any logic I'd constructed to the contrary. And so it happened.

We kissed good-bye on my doorstep, and I shut the door, sinking into it. The fairy tale was over. Not that the sex had been horrible; just that it had shown me how little we actually knew each other. It had lacked that intimacy, that indescribable connection that great love produced. *How can I expect the earth to shatter when I don't even know his middle name? Or the name of his first pet? Or his most precious memory?* Hopeless indeed.

Did I regret it? No. I tried not to regret, but rather to learn. But I did feel a slight sadness. Because for a second, on that motorcycle, wind in my hair, I'd really thought James might be the one.

Maybe it would still develop into that, but as I laced up my boots and threw on my jacket, I couldn't shake the feeling that some inextricable truth had been exposed. That we'd both been playing into a fantasy, a sort of rom-com version of life. And it wasn't hard to see how that might have happened.

DATE N⁰ 22

The Broken Umbrella

Bushwick, Brooklyn

I've always been a sucker for experiences. Probably one of the reasons I fall in love so fast. Definitely why I ended up in Morocco for New Year's of 2010 with my friend Clara and a French guy she had been out with three times. And beyond a doubt why I was boarding a plane with Colin, this American Man of Mystery. *Pourquoi pas?*

"This is crazy!" I grinned over a massive glass of wine at the airport bar. "You're crazy, you know that. Totally crazy."

Colin smiled. "And that would make you ...?"

"Also crazy." I laughed. "Shit ... But whatever, this is going to be so much fun!" I was totally reverting back to Wild Child Amy, but I didn't care. The magnetic pull of

New York and spontaneous adventure had me sucked in. And the stories it would produce! It was too much.

"I can't wait to see what Tinder is like for you in Manhattan. It'll be a whole new ball game." He smiled slyly. Ever since I'd told him about my blog, he'd been fascinated by the sociological aspect. As someone who'd gone on around two hundred Tinder dates himself, he enjoyed seeing things from the female perspective. Did I find his interest in my dates with other men a little odd? Of course, but he was odd, so I didn't think much of it.

"Oh god, I can't even think about it yet. I can't think about anything. I'm taking a Xanax—you want one?"

He shook his head. I have pteromerhanophobia, a fear of flying, and I needed the drug to keep my mind from playing horrific images of airplane shrapnel piercing my liver while my left arm was on fire. Panic attacks at thirty thousand feet aren't pretty; just ask the flight staff on Air China who had tried to comfort me over the Pacific.

By the time we boarded our plane, I felt as light as a supermodel. I took the window, pulled out the itchy blanket and scratchy pillow, and rested my head in Colin's lap.

"Good night," I mumbled happily. "See you in the Big Apple."

I guess you could technically think of this transcontinental journey as our third date, especially since it culminated in breakfast at Allswell in Williamsburg. It looked like I would be breaking Rule #4 again, but how could I not? I mean, Colin had flown me to *frickin' New York*. Even if he was intent on seeing me Tinder while here.

"Don't worry, it takes a few hours for matches to start coming in. We just landed," he reassured me, as I swiped right to no avail over chorizo hash.

"Okay," I said nervously, wanting to believe him. *What if I'm not what guys like in New York? What if I can't get any dates while I'm here?* I took a sip of my Bloody Mary. "Oh wait, I got one!"

"See," he said. "You'll do just fine."

I smiled. *Let the New York Tinder adventure begin!*

I kicked things off that evening by exiting at the wrong subway station. Google Maps had told me to take the L, but my girlfriend Molly, who I was staying with in Greenpoint, had recommended I hop on the G and transfer. "Less walking in this shitty weather." *Fabulous.* I didn't want to show up to the Narrows for drinks looking like a drowned rat.

I descended the steps of the Greenpoint Avenue stop and passed through the turnstile before realizing I didn't actually know what I was doing. I've always had a really good sense of direction, an asset I attribute to long-distance running, but sometimes it results in overconfidence. Like right then. I pulled out my phone: no service.

I glanced around for a map, and found one near the platform of the Church Avenue–bound train. *Hmm.* I stared at it, trying to remember what Molly had said. I noticed a stop on the G for Flushing Avenue. That was the street the bar was on. *I'll just take this the whole way. Perfect!*

But it wasn't. When I emerged from the station, I discovered I was 1.1 miles away. An eighteen-minute walk, according to Google. It was seven fifteen, and I was supposed to meet Brian at seven thirty. I could take a cab, I thought. Or I could just hoof it.

I decided to walk. I didn't get to do much of that in LA, except from dates to my Jetta, so I busted out my dollar-store umbrella and strode confidently eastward. *I mean, who really cares about a little rain? I'm from Portland! And I love the streets of New York!*

I made it halfway before the wind and rain really started to pick up. It blew from all directions, so I couldn't figure out which way to point my umbrella. My feet and shins already started to ache from my heeled boots, and I still had hours to go before I would sleep. *Come on, Amy. Don't be a wimp. You're the new Carrie Bradshaw!*

I was two blocks away when the umbrella broke. It flipped inside out, and the metal snapped. I held on to the limp fabric and tried not to cry. But I was starting to crumble. *What on earth am I doing here? Three days ago I nearly fainted at brunch in LA, and today I'm falling apart on the streets of New York! What am I trying to prove? Who am I trying to become?*

I wanted to turn and run, screaming in the rain, but instead I tossed the umbrella in the trash can outside of the bar and coached myself under an overhang. *You have to do this, Amy. You've come too far. Like, more than two thousand miles.* I took a deep breath and walked in.

Things started off as awkwardly with Brian as they had with Ben. I ordered a Scotch cocktail with "penicillin" in the title, and made a terrible joke to the bartender. "There's no actual medicine in this, right? Because penicillin is the only thing I'm allergic to." *Fail.*

Brian and I stared at each other for a long, uncomfortable moment. He was definitely handsome—tan skin, dark hair and eyes, Latino—but had that brooding artist thing going on. Emphasis on brooding.

He finally broke the silence. "So ... how are things going?"

"Good ... good," I responded, trying to ignore the sense of dread spreading out to my extremities. More uncomfortable silence.

He tried again: "You been in New York long?"

Shit. I'd been thinking about how I would answer this question all day, but I still hadn't figured out my strategy. I didn't want to say I was just visiting, because I was afraid guys would think that a) I wasn't serious about finding Mr. Right and b) this was just a hookup. But I also didn't want to say I lived here and then be exposed based on my limited knowledge. I'd visited New York numerous times, but I was far from being a local.

Not that I didn't want to be. I'd dreamed of living in New York since the first time I'd come here with my mom at seventeen. *Maybe if I just practice the Secret, and put out into the universe that this is what I want ...*

"I actually just got here. I'm trying this bicoastal thing," I half-lied.

"Oh yeah?" He smiled. "So how long you been here? A year?"

I shook my head, my cheeks flushing. "Two weeks," I fully lied. *More like two hours.*

"Oh wow, you, like, just got here." *You could definitely say that.*

Maybe it was the lack of sleep, or the pressure I was

putting on myself to churn something out of this, or the fact I'd turned into Pinocchio, but I suddenly felt very ill. *Not this again...* I tried to keep my feet on the ground and the food in my stomach. *Stop making this about you, Amy. Or a blog entry. Remember what this is actually about. Put your focus on him.*

"So what kinds of things do you paint?" His profile had said he was a painter, and I figured art might be the one thing that could connect us. The one thing that we could both relate to.

I figured right. And wrong. Because once the ball got rolling, it turned out Brian and I had way more to talk about than I could have imagined. As soon as I began to really engage with him—asking him questions about his journey, his creative process, his view of the world—he blossomed like a passionflower. And so did I.

We jumped around from ancient Egyptian art to his side job in truck delivery to the struggle between genuine creative expression and selling out.

"Have you read Lewis Hyde's *The Gift*?" I asked, excited.

"Not yet!" He pulled out his phone and wrote it down. The first of many notes we both would take.

The more we talked, the more I remembered why I'd always wanted to move to New York: the people. I'd spent years in LA having the same shallow conversations over and over again about carbs and the 405, but every time I was in New York I was blown away by the depths people plumbed night after night, in one great restaurant and bar after another. This evening was no exception.

We finished our drinks, and the bartender asked if we wanted another round.

"How you feeling?" Brian looked at me. I checked my phone. I didn't have to meet my friends for dinner until ten thirty (yes, eating at ten thirty; Oprah would not approve).

"I'm feeling really good, actually. How about you?"

He smiled. "Wanna hit another place? There's some more cool spots right around here I could introduce you to." While I didn't feel Brian was a third James, I also wasn't ready to stop talking about Lena Dunham and Basquiat.

"That'd be great."

As we walked out, heading to the Pine Box Rock Shop for more laughs and book recommendations and unexpected trivia night madness, we passed by the broken umbrella. I stopped and pointed at it.

"So yeah, this was my umbrella."

He laughed. "Oh, shit."

I smiled. "I know, I was pretty upset when it happened, but you know what? I don't even need it. I'm an Oregonian. We don't believe in umbrellas."

He laughed again. "That's right. Just stay true to yourself and you'll be okay." More genuine words have never been spoken.

DATE N°. 23

The Doctor without Borders

Greenpoint, Brooklyn

"I still feel like I'm doing something wrong here," I said to Colin as I swiped through Tinder profiles. We were having lunch in Brooklyn, our fourth technical date. "Like the rules have changed and I can't figure out the game."

He laughed and poured me some more Sancerre. "Maybe you need to switch things up," he offered. "Swap out some pics, change your About Me."

I nodded. He *was* the cross-country Tinder expert.

I sifted through Facebook photos, nixing every one of them. *Too many people, too much smiling, different hair color, not enough spark.*

"Go with that one." He pointed at a sultry photo from a shoot I'd done a couple of years back. "New York can be really superficial. Sex sells." *Ugh.* I didn't love this, but I made the change.

"What should I say about myself? Portland native, just arriving via Los Angeles?"

He shook his head. "No, no. Hmm...wait, I've got it." He grabbed my phone and typed.

Amy, 28
I'm looking for a finance douche to take me to dinner.

"Oh my god, that's too perfect!" I said, rolling over with laughter. "And you know what? I feel so confident, I'm going to make a dinner reservation right now for nine p.m. at Glasserie."

I'd heard about the Greenpoint restaurant from Tim, the ultrahip creative exec I'd fallen in love with in London. We'd met at a barbecue in Chelsea, and spent the next four days together before I left for Barcelona. He was easily one of the coolest human beings I'd ever encountered. Almost as cool as the Cab Driver. And eerily similar in his sexual advances (or lack thereof): we'd only kissed once, at one in the morning on a street corner. "Some things are better done slowly, given time," he'd said. It was exquisite. *Shoulda remembered that before sleeping with New James.*

Anyway, Tim knew every cool restaurant and every cool bar in every cool city, and I knew this because he had given me recommendations for each of the places I'd visited that summer: Barcelona, Cannes, Paris. It was like he was dialed into this cool kids club, where the qualification for membership was being super fucking cool. I felt cooler even when I was just texting with Tim. And if he told me to go somewhere, you better believe I went there.

The profile changes worked, and I started winning again. Messages were streaming in from all types of guys: architects, musicians, real estate brokers.

GEORGE, 34:
I'm not a finance douche but I'm douchey in other ways. For example: I'm rich like a finance douche.

OLIVER, 31:
Unfortunately, not the finance douche bag you're looking for. What's your take on product strategy managers? We can be pretty douchey if need be ☺.

AYDIN, 28:
I am unfortunately not a finance douche, but I'm sure with a little prep time I could approximate the experience ☺.

I ended up choosing Aydin to join me at Glasserie, mainly because he had the most amazing cheesy smile I had ever seen and was "out of med school, into the world." I'd yet to go out with anyone in the medical profession, and had a lot of questions about Obamacare I wanted answered.

Before my date, I had a drink with Molly and her friend Maddie at Nights and Weekends.

"Molly told me about your project. It sounds insane," Maddie said over our pepper coconut milk cocktails. I confirmed the insanity of it, and they asked to see photos of my upcoming dinner date. I showed them Aydin, and they both cracked up.

"You can't be serious! You're going to eat him alive!" Molly cackled.

I smiled. "I'm being open." I closed out my tab, and they wished me luck.

Aydin and I both arrived at the restaurant exactly six minutes late. It was in an empty, industrial part of the borough, seemingly removed from all things cool. Which of course made it cooler.

"So nice to meet you!" Aydin greeted me warmly, big cheesy smile plastered on his face.

"You too!" I responded in kind, my energy rising to meet his.

"We officially have Ebola now!" he said cheerily. The disease had just made its way to New York, and was residing at Bellevue Hospital.

"I know! I'm terrified!" It was a weird way to begin the evening, but oddly appropriate, considering his line of work.

A hostess sat us at our table, and I excused myself to the restroom.

"I'm not leaving, I promise!" I assured him.

There was a short line, and the girl behind me struck up a conversation. "It's this Mariah Carey song. Everyone wanted to duck into the stall so they could secretly dance." I laughed (Reason #83 I Love New York: fantastic small talk). "I'll make sure I press myself against the fogged glass so you can see all of my moves."

I returned to the table and Aydin beamed. "How much are you loving this nineties music right now? This place is awesome!" he gushed.

"Wait until you've tried the food; I've heard it's incredible!" I said a silent thank you to Tim.

I put the focus on him right away, learning from the night before. He had just moved to New York as well (I decided to stick with the bicoastal/Secret thing) and was loving the city.

"There's no place like it in the world. The diversity, the extremes, the people," he said excitedly. I agreed, of course.

I probed further. "Where were you before?"

Aydin was born in Manila (half Filipino, half Turkish), but grew up in the Midwest. He'd gone to med school in Ohio and lived overseas for a while in South America and Istanbul. I quickly realized he was a much better person than me.

"I worked in a small fishing village in Ecuador for five months, helping patients within a three-hour radius. The first week I was treating anthrax, the second week delivering babies, the third performing surgeries. It was pretty intense. Then I lived outside of Buenos Aires for a while, working for an orphanage." *A fishing village and an orphanage?* I was impressed.

"Wow, you're like a saint!"

He smiled. "Hardly."

Our waiter, Dylan, came to take our order, and we decided to go omakase style. "You choose for us; we trust you." It was almost impossible not to. He was like a big, happy teddy bear.

With fantastic taste. Dylan started us out with the foraged

mushrooms in some heaven-sent broth, paired with rosemary flatbread (I died). He chose a Croatian bottle of red wine for us, with a cool minimalist label and an earthy palate. "It'll go perfectly with your entrees." And it did.

"I think this is the best chicken I've ever tasted," Aydin said after his first bite.

"Ditto this lamb," I practically moaned over mine. Two words: "food orgasm."

I'm not sure which part of the date I enjoyed more, the epic conversation about Turgenev and the Russian greats or the delectable combination of fresh mint, roasted garlic, and perfectly cooked lamb that constituted my entrée. It was really a toss-up.

Aydin made me laugh, cry, and seriously feel bad that I hadn't actually moved to NYC (yet). *How is it possible I'm meeting so many interesting, cool guys through Tinder?* I thought as he walked me the mile back to Molly's. He had just destroyed me with a story about a gardener he had treated one night in the ER.

"We were looking at an image of his interior, when suddenly there was this reptilian eye."

"No!" I shrieked. He grinned.

"Yes, apparently one of his hobbies on his breaks was letting these tiny snakes wriggle up through his penis, and this time he'd accidentally let go."

I pressed myself up against a graffitied wall, barely able to breathe.

We reached Molly's walk-up, and I turned to him.

"This is me."

He gave me a huge hug.

"This was such a great night. You're so cool," he said. *Thanks again, Tim.* "We should definitely hang out again sometime," he added.

"You know, I would really love that," I said, and ascended the steps to her apartment. *If only I lived in New York...*

DATE N° 24

The Ottoman Music Composer of the Opera

Williamsburg, Brooklyn

I spent the day at the Met, weaving in and out of ancient Egyptian sculptures and Greco-Roman wall paintings. It was one of my favorite museums in the world, along with the Musée d'Orsay, MoMA, the Louvre, the Guggenheim. *Which city do I prefer more for art and culture, Paris or New York?* I'd always thought Paris, but I was beginning to question this. One thing I definitely preferred about New York, though: the men.

My third NYC date was with a guy named Abel. We met at Passenger Bar for an early happy hour. He was tall, with a small ponytail on top and shaved sides. Definitely a creative type. We ordered a couple of seasonal brews and made our way back to the jukebox and pool table. A band was warming up at the front, and we wanted to still be able to have a conversation over the loud music.

Abel was originally from Chicago, but had been in Brooklyn the past year and a half after a twelve-year stint in Seattle. I could detect the influence of each city: the fine art of his hometown, the grunge of the Northwest, the edgy creativity of south Brooklyn.

"How do you like living here?" I asked.

"I love it. The best thing I've ever done. For my career, my social network, my life in general."

He was a musician, with his hands in so many projects I couldn't keep track. He had four or five bands (including one in London and another in Berlin), composed music for commercials and TV shows, produced for other bands, deejayed. He even specialized in Ottoman music.

"Last night I played at an opening for a gallery specializing in Ottoman art," he told me. *Only in New York.* "Oh, and I'm working on a sort of rock opera," he added, finishing his list of current endeavors.

"Seriously?" I laughed. "I'm going to be honest here, at the risk of sounding like a cretin, but I actually kind of hate opera." He smiled, not offended. "Although I will say, I read this book by Julian Barnes last summer, *Levels of Life*, and it made me understand why I haven't learned to appreciate opera yet. You see, he hated it, too, but then after his wife died, the loss was so great, the grief so complete, he finally understood it. The depths of those tragedies. When I read that, it made so much sense; it seemed so obvious. That's great writing."

We talked a lot about creativity and the current cultural

climate, particularly how technology was affecting the various artistic fields.

"The game has changed dramatically over the past decade. In some ways the Internet is the great equalizer, giving everyone a shot. But it's also almost impossible now to make a living in the traditional ways." He was talking about selling albums, but he just as easily could have been referring to TV and film or book publishing or journalism. Heck, he may as well have been talking about dating.

"So what's your favorite thing about New York," I asked as I finished my ale.

"The people," he responded without hesitation. "I had more substantial friendships within two days of moving here than I ever had in Seattle. And the diversity of my relationships. I never go into my local bar without meeting someone fascinating." He told me about Esteban the glass blower, and the big black finance guy who had encouraged him to invest in a certain chip. He had. The stock was skyrocketing.

I laughed. "Man, I simply do not have enough glassblowers or big black finance guys or Ottoman music opera composers in my life."

He smiled. "Well then, you've come to the right place."

And I had. I practically bounced up the crooked staircase of Molly's apartment. "All right, it's official. I'm moving here," I announced to Molly and her roommate, Cleo, removing my gloves and scarf. Molly gave me a sharp look as I danced my way across the kitchen floor.

"Don't you dare tease us again," she said firmly. "Don't go

getting a boyfriend back in Los Angeles!" I laughed, knowing exactly what she meant.

I had first seriously considered moving to New York in August 2012, after staying with Molly for a week that summer. I knew I had to move here, if only for a year. I could still remember walking through Chelsea with a high school friend I'd bumped into at the Guggenheim, and being so overcome by the city's magnetic pull that I stopped dead in my tracks. "I'm moving to New York."

When I returned to LA, I started formulating a plan. I would make the move in April 2013. I concocted all sorts of ideas for how I could afford to live in the city—SoulCycle instructor, bartender, professional dater—and began setting aside savings from a couple of commercials I still had running.

But it never happened. Because of a boyfriend. Whom I broke up with. It sounds counterintuitive: shouldn't I have wanted to move to New York *more* after a breakup? But it wasn't. I chose to stay in LA because I'd realized one of the reasons I'd wanted to leave was to get out of that relationship. I just hadn't known how. Once I'd gotten out of it, though, I started to fall in love with LA all over again, and really came to appreciate the life I'd built there.

That August, I once again stayed with Molly for a week, and once again I felt the pull of New York. I was twenty-seven, and it was the perfect time to shake things up, except once again I didn't. Because of another boyfriend. The terrible, possessive broke writer who barely managed to survive the one week I was gone. Thankfully that ended after five painful months, and I hadn't spoken to him since.

"So, great date?" Cleo inquired.

"Yes," I replied. "Well, yes and no. Yes, we had a great time; no, he's not the one."

I'd been experiencing a lot of that recently. The Doctor without Borders, the Broken Umbrella, the Duck. And while this had left me confused and remorseful those first couple of weeks—*what if I'm dismissing a guy because I'm too shallow? What if I led him on?*—I was finally understanding it differently. I'd had a meaningful experience with another human being—no more, no less.

DATE N° 24.5

The World is a Stage

Manhattan, NYC

After three dates with other Tinder men, it was finally time for my official "third date" with Colin, the whole *raison d'être* for this New York interlude. And I couldn't wait to see what sort of epic night he had in store. *A dinner cruise on the Hudson? A helicopter ride over the skyscrapers? Takeout Thai food?*

The evening started with the latter. While this was not epic, I was fine with it, because a) I loved Thai food and b) I'd eaten enough to feed a small village at Glasserie. We ate it in his large finished basement in Bushwick, in between guitar serenades (he took requests!) and yoga poses (he can do the splits).

After dinner, we made our way into Manhattan to begin

the real shenanigans. In the Uber, I was feeling a bit off (anxiety? Lack of sleep? Overly spicy Thai?), so Colin took my hands and massaged them. I briefly flashed back to New James massaging my shoulders. He'd barely crossed my mind since leaving LA. I wondered what that meant ...

"Feeling better?" Colin's kind eyes met mine. I nodded.

"I am."

Friday traffic made it a long car ride, but I didn't mind. I loved looking out at the lights, the throngs of people. At one point I was literally thinking about how many millions of strangers flooded these streets daily when I spotted a friend from high school. "Leah!" I called out to her. She came and gave me a kiss through the window. The New York circles were as small as the LA ones.

We stopped at Colin's friend Drew's place for a quick pregame drink. This was weird. Yet natural. Colin was weird, so of course his friends were weird. In the best way possible. Even though I couldn't understand what the hell they were talking about (future derivatives? Ripple effects? Anybody?), and the drinks we had were diet Gatorade and water, I appreciated this glimpse into his social circle. And Drew's puggle Bernie Madoff—absolutely adorable.

From Drew's we hopped the subway downtown for the evening's first "big" event: Rebel Bingo. We ordered real drinks, and then ran into my friend Brandon and his buddies at the downstairs bar at Irving Plaza (more serendipity). We chatted a bit before the game-playing began, and at one point Colin disappeared.

"He really likes you," Brandon said to me.

"You think?" I asked. "He still hasn't even tried to kiss me."

Brandon shrugged. "Maybe it's part of his strategy."

Colin returned and we headed upstairs. The venue was packed with a young, hip crowd of New Yorkers. A large screen with a countdown informed us shit was getting real in two minutes and thirty-five seconds. Thirty-four seconds. Thirty-three seconds. The ball finally dropped, and the crowd roared. Shit got real.

Rebel Bingo was just as awesome as it sounds. Kitsch, postmodern, ridiculous—this was not your grandparents' assisted-living-home pastime. Oh no. The emcee was a hot Brit, the ball girls spoke in slutty platitudes, and the prizes were, well, epic. A private bodyguard (a huge blow-up panther), a new best friend (a stuffed panda bear), an on-the-go party machine (a portable iPhone speaker). I mean, we *really* wanted to win the LED umbrella. (We didn't, but we won in fun.)

After Rebel Bingo, we flagged a cab and made our way to our final destination: the McKittrick Hotel. We were going to *Sleep No More*, a mind-bending production of *Macbeth*. Think *Eyes Wide Shut* crossed with Choose Your Own Adventure crossed with a David Lynch film. Easily the weirdest thing I'd ever experienced. Weirder than growing up in Portland. Weirder than being flown to New York by the Cab Driver. Weirder than doing forty Tinder dates in forty days.

Before we actually put on our masks and took our vows of silence, Colin and I grabbed drinks from the bar: absinthe for him, a Manhattan for me. We sipped them in a quiet corner, and started talking about relationships.

"What are you looking for?" he asked me earnestly, studying my face.

"I, uh ..." I thought of my blog, and all of the obvious things I'd laid out in my first entry. *Hot, funny, smart, emotionally available.* I looked at Colin. *Is it him? Is he looking for me? What is this between us?* I panicked. "I don't know." *God, Amy, terrible answer.*

"You'll figure it out," he said. This seemed to be the phrase of the month. *Would I?*

A coy blonde with red lipstick came up and encouraged us to pound our drinks and head toward the entrance. "Fourteen seconds—down the hatch, my pretties."

"See you on the other side," Colin whispered to me as we donned our *V for Vendetta*-esque masks. I felt my pulse quicken. A doorman waved us in, and we were off.

Surprisingly (or maybe not, considering the current culture of Facebook/Instagram/Twitter), my very first feeling entering the interactive theater was FOMO. People raced up and down stairs, in and out of secret corridors. Everyone seemed so sure of what they were doing, as if there were a correct way to play this game, but I didn't even know the rules. I looked around for Colin, but he had disappeared. Not that he would have done me any good anyway; I needed to experience it all for myself.

I took a deep breath, and entered into an empty room where I could center myself. It was an old-fashioned office, with a desk and chair, hanging picture frames, shelves of little bottles and knickknacks. *What do I do?* My natural inclination was simply to observe, like at a museum or a theater. But there were no rows of seats from which I could be passive. I could do whatever I wanted.

I opened up drawers and poured through books. I moved

from room to room, rolling along walls, my hands probing, searching, feeling. I felt freedom in my silence, my thoughts and experiences for my mind only. And then I saw a pair of actors in the woods.

I stood transfixed, watching their back-and-forth, listening to the pain in their voices without hearing any words. A group of strangers had gathered with me to watch. Voyeurs and yet participants. And then, suddenly, one of the actors began to run. My masked brethren and I quickly followed, tearing down a hallway, then up a passage of stairs. *This is amazing!* I thought, surrendering to the visceral excitement of my surreal surroundings.

The next two hours I followed my instincts. I danced through the forest, chased the pretty girl with the bloody gown, stretched out on a table as if to be etherized. I cherished my faceless anonymity and the freedom it gave me, but I also felt the pull toward being exposed. I wanted to be tearing through the hallways in a shimmering gown, hair soaked, blood on my face. *I'm a performer*, I realized as I twirled through the misty forest, pirouetting across the stage. *To watch or be watched?*

A group of strangers hurried past me, and I intuitively ran after them. We entered into a large, dark room and people began to assemble around the edges. I could tell something intense was about to happen, something dark and strange and twisted.

The music began to pulsate and deepen, the lights strobing faster and faster. Actors spilled into the middle, their bodies jerking in an insane dance, their clothes ripping off. *An orgy.* I watched their naked bodies writhe, entranced. Before pole, I would've been beyond uncomfortable. But nudity no longer scared me. Instead of shame, I interpreted power.

And then it was over. The actors dispersed, and we made our choice of whom to follow. They were all ultimately leading to the same destination, into the woods.

I found a balcony ledge to perch on to witness the final act: the hanging. A hand lightly touched my leg. *Is this an actor? A stranger?* I turned calmly to my left. It was Colin. I smiled and touched his arm. It didn't matter that we couldn't speak, because no words were needed. For just a moment, I understood everything.

And then the performance ended.

DATE N.º 25

The Glamorous New Yorker

West Village, NYC

Colin brought me coffee and a pastry in bed. I'd slept in his room, and he'd taken the blow-up mattress in the living room. There'd been no funny business, no hanky-panky, no casual sex. Still not even a kiss. I was beginning to think we were fated to be friends. Or maybe not. With him it was so hard to tell. At any rate, I was happy that I hadn't broken Rule #5, like I had with New James.

I left a short while later and walked the mile and a half back to Greenpoint. I didn't listen to Pandora, or call a friend, or pull out my phone at all (except to take a couple of pictures of Instagram-worthy graffiti). I just stayed in the moment, listening to the rumbling trucks, the birds, and the murmuring voices, trying to soak in as much of the

Brooklyn streets as I could. *Sleep No More* had left its mark.

Back at Molly's, I signed back into Tinder. Two guys had offered to take me out that night, one for happy hour, the other for dinner. I didn't have anything else to do but write and date and explore New York, so I confirmed both. *Pourquoi pas?* Besides, it would get me ahead of schedule again if I needed a day back in LA to regroup.

♥

I met my first date of the evening, Chris, in the West Village. We were going to go to Bar Sardine, but with people bursting out of the windows, we opted for Ofrenda instead. We sat down on the patio, and Chris started telling me about his job.

"I work as a writer for *Vanity Fair*, the *New Yorker*, some other publications freelance. I write about fashion, young up-and-coming starlets, bar and restaurant reviews. I did a sex advice column for a while for *Glamour*."

I stared at him, moon-eyed. I couldn't not tell him.

"So I'm just going to go ahead and tell you, since you basically do what I want to do, and yeah, I don't know, this might be weird, but I'm writing a blog called *Forty Dates & Forty Nights*. It's exactly how it sounds, all through Tinder, and you're number twenty-five." A pause. *Is he offended? Put off?* He seemed ... apathetic. "I'm sorry, did I just make things super awkward?"

He shook his head. "Nope. I just won't be having sex with you."

I laughed, relieved.

We ordered two jalapeño margaritas, mine with salt, his

without. They were strong. Thank God. My early confession to Chris hadn't completely torpedoed the date, per se, but it had colored it. I could tell he thought I might be a vapid LA mean girl, of the Strategist variety, and I felt myself trying extra hard to prove otherwise. Furthermore, I felt intimidated. Something about his experience as a working writer in New York, his impeccable fashion sense, his overall sophistication, made me feel silly and small. I began to project, especially when we started talking about sex.

"Isn't that kind of awful, not having sex for forty days?" he asked.

"No," I replied, "because I don't think we should be having sex within the first couple of dates anyway. It's such an intimate experience, and I think it can have a negative impact." I didn't want to tell him I'd already broken my sex rule, or that my encounter with James had proven my reasoning for that rule. What if Chris outed me in a column? I hadn't even properly processed it for myself, let alone for the Internet.

He disagreed. "In my column, girls asked me that a lot—when is it okay to have sex?—and I think it's whenever they're ready. There shouldn't be arbitrary rules put in place. What are you, like a Texan?"

I swallowed hard, stumbling in my defense. "No, I'm a pole dancer. I've had plenty of sex. I'm very sexually liberated." *Where am I going with this?* "It's not about arbitrary numbers. I just think personally, from my own experience, I'm too emotionally sensitive to open up like that with someone I don't really know yet. I don't know, this project is for me; I'm not trying to tell anyone what to do or not do." I suddenly felt five inches tall.

The floodgates opened. "You see, the last couple of guys I was with, I slept with them on the second date. And it was totally a mistake. One devastated me, and the other, well, it was just this horrible morning. I actually wrote this super personal essay about the experience, waking up next to him and the loneliness I felt, but …" *Shut up, Amy.*

He pushed further. "What'd you conclude?"

"I, uh, I don't know. It was relating to death, and this play I'm working on in my acting class …" *SHUT UP.* "Anyway, I can't have casual sex." *Even though I just did.* The guilt flushed my cheeks.

The subject finally changed, and Chris told me about these tattoo parties his friends threw. They put random words and phrases in a bowl; then everyone pulled out two and got a tattoo of whatever they were.

"My buddy got 'very fast' and 'pineapple,' so he designed this." He showed me a photo of a tattoo of a pineapple on a speedboat named *Very Fast.*

"That's a real tat?" He nodded. "This is why I need to move to New York!" I exclaimed, overeager.

"No, it's not," he stated. *Five inches tall.*

We finished our drinks, and Chris asked me what my plans were.

"I have a dinner at eight thirty. Wanna grab another drink?" Things had finally improved, and I was enjoying his company.

"Sure."

We wandered around the West Village in search of a not-slammed bar. Which didn't seem to exist.

"I want to go into that CVS and pick up a twelve-pack of Diet Coke. And you should include it in your blog." I laughed, assuming he was joking, but he walked straight toward it.

"Wait, are we actually going to the CVS right now?" We were.

"You cool having a drink at my apartment?" he asked. I thought about it. Probably not the best idea, but I trusted him. And he also didn't seem interested in me at all. *No fear of breaking Rule #5 here.*

"Yeah, why not?"

His studio was small and intimate.

"Sorry it's messy," he said, scrambling to tidy things up, his cool exterior slowly melting before my eyes. I remembered the vulnerability I felt inviting James in. Chris clearly wore his heart on his fridge like I did.

I sat on his bed and reviewed his impressive bookshelves.

"I'm judging you right now," I teased.

"Go ahead, but quite a few were gifts I haven't read. Like *Thinking, Fast and Slow.*"

I smiled. I'd read it last summer.

"It's actually fascinating. You'd enjoy it."

Design and architecture books peppered the stacks, Thompson and Vonnegut, several biographies, lots of nonfiction.

"Oh God, Bolaño," I said, spotting *2666*. Old James had recommended it to me during the summer, and I'd given up two hundred pages in.

"Yeah, that's one I haven't read. I attempted *The Savage Detectives* and hated it."

I told him about my similar failed attempt.

"The same thing happened to me with *Infinite Jest*," I admitted. "I adore David Foster Wallace's essays, but man, I could not get through that!" Chris came over and gave me a hug.

"I'm so happy you said that. You know why you couldn't get through it? Because it's terrible. And only pretentious douche bags claim it's the greatest thing ever. Because of all the footnotes."

I laughed. *Are we ... connecting?*

He made us some whiskey cocktails, and sat down across from me in an old chair, clearly a valuable piece. We'd been talking for about one minute when it broke, sending him backward.

"Oh no!" I gasped. He was fine, but the chair, not so much. I could tell he was upset, but he handled it coolly, with aplomb.

"This is probably my most prized possession. If there was a fire, first I'd take that box of photographs over there, then this chair."

I looked at him sympathetically.

He continued. "But it's an old piece, and that's what happens with furniture that's still being used. I'll get it fixed. Anyway, it's just a material thing."

I smiled, impressed by his serenity. I would have been sobbing.

"I was actually in a fire back in Canada," he admitted. "You learn what's really important." Impressed again.

Maybe it was *2666*, or the broken chair, or the whiskey, but all of the walls that had been put up by my early blog admission crumbled. We looked over photos from the box, listened to music, talked much more comfortably about sexuality.

"You're a lot prettier than your Tinder pictures," he said.

"Thanks?" I responded to the half compliment.

"When I first saw you on the street, I thought maybe it was part of your game."

I laughed. "Either I have bad taste in photos, or I'm not photogenic, but it's certainly not part of my game." Or maybe it was. I intentionally hadn't put up hot Vegas pics or glamorous headshots, because I didn't want to set up super-high expectations. So now the opposite was happening. *Oh well, better to pleasantly surprise than disappoint.*

My phone buzzed. It was 8:20.

"I should go. I'm going to be late."

He moved in close and I kissed him. I never would have predicted this two hours before, tripping over my words, but now it felt right.

"Are you sure you want to go?" He looked in my eyes. *Yes? No?*

"I can't cancel," I said. "But maybe we'll see each other in LA." He was flying in on Tuesday for a month.

"Maybe," he said, and walked me out.

"Call me," I trailed off as he shut the door.

"Good night."

As I stepped into the cool night air, I wondered what Chris thought of me. I had definitely liked him the more I got to know him, but I got the distinct feeling that I'd somehow ruined any real chance between us from the moment I mentioned the blog. I mean, he had still kissed me, but ...

I thought of the other guys I'd been dating. Colin, James,

Dan—they all knew, and they were all on board. Perhaps too on board. My project had introduced a strange element into the equation of true love. Was it making it impossible to come up with a solution?

I remembered something Ashley had said to me in the very beginning, when I'd been questioning if I should do this at all: "Amy, whatever guy you end up with will accept this journey, and admire you for it, because it's you. And you don't want to be with someone who doesn't accept you."

She was right. The right guy would call. In the meantime, I had another date.

DATE N° 26

The Breakdown

EAST VILLAGE, NYC

DRUNK AMY, 28:

Redhead, pretty. Like any good actress, Drunk Amy wears two separate masks: happy and sad. Most of the time, she spends her Dionysian nights in the world of comedy, tearing up dance floors, laughing until her cheeks hurt, spinning around stop signs and scaffolding. But every so often, she descends into tragedy. Sleep No More gets real, and Macbeth becomes her. And then sometimes, if you're lucky, Drunk Amy performs both.

I was tipsy. Very tipsy. I hadn't realized the strength of Chris's whiskey drinks until I stumbled out into the streets of the Village. And by then it was too late. Who knew which version of Drunk Amy would be coming out to play at my dinner date with Mark?

I pulled out my phone to inform him I was running late for our eight thirty reservation, but he'd already texted me.

MARK:

> Got caught up finishing a few things, be there at 9! Sorry!

I sighed, relieved. At least I'd be able to down a couple of glasses of water before he arrived. I ambled along briskly and showed up to Wasan a few minutes before nine, huffing, puffing, and buzzing.

MARK:

> 5 mins away! Order whatever you like and obviously on me, I think I walked past it.

I flagged the bartender for a water, and then chugged it. *Please stop spinning*, I ordered my head. Mark strolled in a minute later, much more relaxed and free-spirited than the profile of this forty-year-old suit-and-tie attorney suggested.

"Here, let me take that." He stretched out his arm, and I gave him my coat. Some men made this gesture feel awkward and dated. Not Mark. There was an ease to his maturity, none of the sugar daddy awkwardness I had occasionally encountered in the past.

"Let's order some sake. Are you hungry? You look hungry. We need to get this girl some sake and some sushi," he told the waiter. He had the excited energy of a six-month-old puppy. Our waiter brought over two sakes to taste, and we both agreed on the same one. He grinned. "Great minds."

The waiter returned with the carafe, and Mark's face fell.

"I thought we were getting that big bottle," he remarked. "Oh well, we can just order it after."

Oh boy, it's gonna be a long night, I thought as we clinked glasses.

"Cheers!"

I asked him about his career, and Mark informed me he was an entertainment lawyer who had just moved back to New York after a nine-year stint in Los Angeles. He was partnered at several firms. Or maybe his firm had several offices? I struggled to follow with all that sake. At any rate, he worked, like, a hundred hours a week, and I was in awe. I was barely holding down my full-time job of dating. I wanted to steal some of his octane.

In addition to working, he also loved basketball and comedy shows.

"You should do stand-up," he said, the third date to mention this. "You're really funny."

I made a face. "Oh no, it terrifies me. I'd rather jump into a bathtub of sharp knives." The *Macbeth* was emerging. "I'll stick to commercials."

"You got a lawyer?" he asked. I shook my head. "Then who does your contracts?" *Uh, who does he think I am? The actual Wendy's girl?*

"My manager."

He studied me seriously. "Is she a lawyer?" I shook my head again. "Send me them tomorrow. I'll take a look."

I almost laughed at the thought of him reviewing my stand-in contracts, but I held it in. He was so earnest and sweet.

Food runners graced our table with elegant dishes—miso soups, salmon sashimi, Japanese eggplant, toro—but while delicious, the portions were miniscule. Our waiter dropped two pieces of foie gras sushi in front of me (Mark was kosher), and I consumed them in twenty seconds flat. *So. Good.*

"We're going to need some more food," Mark informed him. "And that bottle of sake."

I got a steak bowl with asparagus and shiitake mushrooms, and he got a tuna bowl. I shoveled the rice into my mouth, attempting to line my stomach with every last carb in preparation for the painful morning that was sure to come. It seemed to be working. I didn't feel quite so drunk. At least, not until we stood up to go and grab another drink at a neighboring bar. Then there was a problem. And that problem was sake.

I've always considered sake to be the sniper of alcohols. Beer, wine, whiskey—I pretty much know exactly what I'm getting. One Blue Moon, I can still drive. Two glasses of sauv blanc, it's 50 percent more likely that I'll make out with you at the end of our date. Three Jack and Diets, I'm climbing an urban pole. But with a bottle and a carafe of junmai daiginjo? Oh no, there's no predicting what's going to happen.

We briefly popped into a gay bar to say hello to his very pretty friend who worked at Viacom ("someone you should meet!"), before making our way to Kingston Hall.

"What would you like to drink?" Mark asked.

A shot of liquid Advil? I thought, noticing the whole coconuts several people were sipping from.

I pointed. "One of those." *At least those'll have electrolytes, right?*

We took our coconuts and meandered toward the back. I twirled playfully, trying to keep it more Helena than Ophelia. Drunk Amy had officially taken center stage, and the night could go either way. The verdict was still out, so to speak.

Until it was settled. After about five minutes of light banter and an innocent game of truth, Mark unleashed the beast. He had no way of knowing, and neither did I, but he removed the floodgates with a single simple question.

"What happened to your last relationship?"

I honestly tried not to cry, but Mark wouldn't let me hold it in.

"I can tell you're still in love with him. I could tell all night." *He could?*

"Oh god, I'm sorry." I started to sob.

"Oh no, please, you're wonderful! I could just see that you were holding on to something. But you're unique, you have this special quality about you. Tell your parents thank you." More sobbing.

"You know what you should do?" he said, wiping away my tears. "You should text him. Tell him you're flying back to LA tomorrow and want to meet him for a drink. Go after what you want."

I nodded. Maybe I should text James.

"I'll give you some privacy," he said, and disappeared.

I composed a message.

ME:

> I just want you to know, I miss you all the time.

    I stared at it, my thumb hovering over SEND. *Who cares? Just send it. It's the truth: you miss him. He should know that.* I lowered my thumb a millimeter from the screen. *No! Drunk Amy, don't do it! It's the sake talking! Even if he is the one, he needs to come to you! Text Colin! Text Molly! Just don't text him!* I pressed CANCEL and shoved my phone in my back pocket. Mark returned.

    "You ready to get out of here?" he asked. I nodded. "Come on, I'll get you a taxi."

    He hailed a cab on the other side of the street, and we ran across. He took both of my hands and looked me in the eye.

    "Your life is going to be so great; just follow your heart and be true to yourself." He gave me a kiss on the cheek, then opened the door. Always the gentleman.

    The taxi took off. I pulled out my phone and unlocked it. I was still crying, but I also felt an overwhelming happiness.

ME:

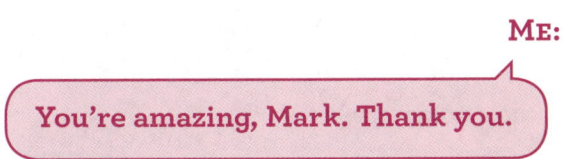

> You're amazing, Mark. Thank you.

    I pressed SEND. I rested my head against the seat, feeling grateful for the Marks of the world. And the Colins. And the Marvins. And all of the other great guys I had met that reminded me that my life was not a tragedy. Far, far from it.

… DATE Nº 27

The Hangover Cure

Financial District, NYC

*I*ngredients:

- 1 mimosa
- 3 eggs (organic, cage-free)
- ¼ cup smoked salmon (wild-caught)
- 1 chocolate mousse (calorie-free)
- 1 high school teacher (Tinder-sourced)

Time to prepare: 2 hours

The sushi rice lining failed. I woke up with the sun looking like Benjamin Button. And I don't mean the young version. The booze and the soy sauce had practically sealed my grayish blues shut. *Oh god.* I turned away from the mirror and sat back down on the pullout couch. Today was going to be *rough*.

I showered off the previous night's crusty tears and sake sheen, prepping for my final New York Tinder. Michael had asked me to dinner, per my profile request, but as I had my flight back to LA that evening, we arranged for a late lunch instead. I was hungry, but still dreading it. *Will I even be able to form complete sentences?*

An entire pot of eye cream and gobs of concealer managed to make me look closer to Julianne Moore than Judi Dench, and I curled my hair in an effort to distract from my face. *Oh well, you can't win 'em all,* I thought, as I grabbed a bottle of Emergen-C-enhanced water and headed out.

We were both late to Les Halles, a French restaurant in downtown Manhattan. I appreciated Michael's effort to be douchey by picking a place in the financial district, even though he turned out to be anything but a finance douche.

"How's your day been?" he asked as we settled into the dark brasserie.

I decided to be up front. "Uhh, I'm hungover." No point in trying to hide the obvious.

He laughed. "Long night?"

"More like long month." I smiled.

We ordered our food—smoked salmon omelet for me, steak frites for him—and I got ambitious with a mimosa. It would either help or hurt the cause, and I was willing to take the risk.

"The morning after is so much worse as we get older," he sympathized. "Not that it stops me from going out."

This ushered in the sort of drunkest-night-of-our-lives

conversation my previous twenty-six dates had been sorely lacking. It began with his legendary night the previous summer in Dublin, where he had his first drink at noon in the city and his last in a small unknown village with complete strangers. He woke up in a strange bed next to a strange man and for a moment questioned the night's events. (Both he and his bed partner agreed things had not taken a brief detour to West Hollywood.)

I countered with not one but *two* all-night-rager stories, probably the most hardcore partying I've done in my life (and remarkably sex-free ... well, sort of). One had been the Full Moon Party on Koh Phangan in Thailand with my brother and a rowdy group of Brits and Aussies. My bro, watching me go buck wild, yelled, "Amy, you're the craziest person I've seen!" (Photos confirm this.) The other? The previous summer's twenty-hour bender in Saint-Tropez. You haven't lived until you've danced on dinner tables amid filet mignon and sea bass at the restaurant Brasserie des Arts. *Highly* recommended.

Somehow, painting myself as a drunk party girl eased my nausea, and we finally moved into more civilized conversation. Like the fact that he was a high school social studies teacher.

"Really?" I felt bad again. About everything. My hangover, my blog, my tales of debauchery. I had an enormous respect for teachers. Several of them had changed my life. Continued to change my life.

"Yup, for three years now in Bed-Stuy."

He told me of the ups and downs of his job. The kids who were scared of him, the ones who looked up to him. The ninth-graders reading at a third-grade level. I got misty-eyed when he told me about Carl, a junior he'd had in 2013 who was on the verge of dropping out.

"These kids are good kids; they've just never had the right guidance."

Well, he'd given Carl the right guidance, and Carl had scored a 75 on his Regents. Up from 30.

"When I told him, he was so excited. I took him to lunch and told him to order whatever he wanted. He got a sandwich and chips. Then he told me he had never liked history until me. That affected me, you know?"

I did know. I told him about Mr. Halpern, my junior-year English teacher who had taught me how to actually learn, not just get straight As.

"*The Death of Ivan Ilych* was a revelation. I did my IB oral presentation on it. I wrote my first screenplay about it. I still talk about it. I'm talking about it right now!"

From that point on, I tried a little harder to show up for Michael. I stopped halfway through my mimosa (it hadn't helped anyway), and I focused on his warm smile and protective linebacker physique instead of my pounding headache. We ordered dessert, contributing another pound to my goal of forty, and discussed his current awesome living situation (across the street from his school).

After the chocolate mousse, he walked me to my train and gave me a big hug. Not even an attempt at a kiss. I couldn't blame him. Nor did it feel like there was anything between us beyond friendship. I pulled out my phone to check the message I'd received from Colin.

Colin:

> Call me before you leave. I'll swing by.

No service. I'd ring him back at Molly's.

I felt a tap on my shoulder. I spun to find Michael. *Has he returned for a kiss? That'd be pretty ... cinematic.*

"I forgot that the J doesn't stop at Fulton on weekends. I'm with you until the next stop."

I smiled and we stepped onto the train. We talked for a couple of minutes about my anxiety over my upcoming flight and the three lessons he had to prepare for the next day.

"Brooklyn Bridge," the automated voice announced.

"This is me. Have a safe flight. See you later."

I was pretty sure I wouldn't as the train pulled away, but I wouldn't mind if I did ... if I ended up in New York ... and if I were less hungover.

PART 3

Too many boys, not enough time.

What happens on date two stays on date two; not everything should be on the Internet.

When you want to see someone, you see them. Especially when they fly you across the country.

●●●●○ AT&T LTE   12:31 PM   79% 🔋
< Back

June 19, 2015, 12:31 PM

1. A date a day for 40 days.
2. A blog a day for each date.
3. All dates from Tinder.
4. ~~scribbled out~~
5. ~~scribbled out~~

I knew better. Now if only I'd known <u>him</u> better.

HOME IS WHERE THE HEART IS?

Colin stopped by with a bottle of wine. We sat in the living room with Molly and her boyfriend, and I sipped it slowly, lost in my own thoughts. *Where do I go from here?* Los Angeles, of course. But what would the final third of my dates look like? I was entering the home stretch.

"It's five thirty. I'm calling you an Uber," Colin said, pulling out his phone.

"Oh, no, you don't have to do that. I can call one," I said. He had paid for everything we'd done. And while I'd certainly enjoyed being taken care of, I also felt guilty, gambling winnings or not.

"I want to. I invited you on this trip." He smiled. That he had. And what a whirlwind it had been.

He grabbed my luggage, and we descended to the street.

"This has been amazing. Thank you so much for the chaos," I said.

He stared at me in a way he hadn't before. The silence hung there for a moment, and then I broke it. "What's ... what exactly is going on between us?"

He took my hand.

"Amy... I really, really like you. I don't think you realize."

I wasn't sure I did. Part of me felt it—I mean, *he'd flown me across the country for a date*—but then, he'd never made a move on me. Years of sexual conditioning had led me to believe this meant he wasn't interested.

"But I only have room for one more great love. When I commit, I truly commit. All of my passion, all of myself. And my heart can't take another failed relationship. It either needs to be everything or nothing. Do you understand?"

I nodded, his behavior slowly coming into focus.

"I think you're amazing. And I want you in my life, one way or the other. So I'm not going to take that risk unless it feels absolutely right."

The Uber pulled up. My eyes were welling up. I thought of my best friend Samuel, who had never tried once to hook up with me. Not in Vegas. Not at a wedding in Tuscany. "I want you to know that not every guy just wants to fuck you," he had told me in my early twenties. I finally believed him.

"Before you go, though, I need to do this." Colin lightly drew me into him, and kissed me ever so softly on the lips. He lingered there, taking his time, then drew back. "There. Now we've kissed."

I watched the sun set over the skyline. I didn't want to leave. Not yet. I didn't want it to be over. What a gift Colin had given me. And what a gift my Tinder experiences in New York had been. In fact, all of my dates. I'd come across such interesting people, with such diverse backgrounds and stories. Even those I hadn't jived with—the Strategist, Ainsley, the Anniversary guy—had added a certain texture I could now appreciate. Each encounter had been an opportunity to learn, to see things from a different perspective.

Whose perspective do I want to explore further? Colin's? Dan's? New James's? I'd been so wrapped up in the energy of Manhattan, the forward thrust of my project, that I hadn't really taken the time to seriously reflect. Now I had a moment to do so: I would be taking the next day off, thanks to doubling up with Chris and Mark. I desperately needed it, to regroup and recover. To be by myself. I was glad I'd eliminated Rule #1.

But I felt bad about breaking Rules #4 and #5. Well, sort of. Those two were tricky. Double-sided. On the one hand, my experiences with James and Colin had proved the importance of really getting to know someone before forging ahead in a relationship. This wasn't the movies: it took more than three dates to decide whether to spend the rest of your life with someone. Even when long-term relationships do start with those sorts of fireworks, it still takes time and effort to build the bonds that last for decades.

With Colin, breaking Rule #4 had been wonderful, deepening our connection. Our dates had been spaced out in a way that gave us room to breathe; the first had been more than three weeks ago. And we also hadn't escalated our relationship physically. We were still feeling each other out, getting to know each other. *Some things are better done slowly.* It made sense.

New James was a different story. We'd had a long, intense first date, followed by face time the next three days in a row, culminating in sex. I'd gotten swept up in the moment, in the romanticism of it, in an idea rather than the reality. Which was that we didn't know each other. That we thought we did, because he was reading my blog and I enjoyed his praise of my character. Of Jamy Madison. The sex and my week in New York had illuminated this: my heart had not grown fonder; the distance had just created distance, in which I could see things more clearly.

Not that I wouldn't stay open to New James, to our second "official date," scheduled for Wednesday. But I needed to get to know him. The real him. I wished I hadn't agreed earlier in the week to let him pick me up at the airport. It now felt like way too much. I was so tired already, and I wasn't even at JFK. My head started spinning again. My throat hurt. *Am I getting sick?* Anxiety bubbled up. We were pulling into the terminal.

Relax, Amy. You've just had an incredible adventure and very little sleep. You just need to center yourself. Breathe. Everything's going to work out just fine. Focus on your breath. That's it. The anxiety is all in your head. You're fine. Nothing's wrong with you. The plane will not go down.

I reached for my Xanax, then decided I'd try and go without. I'd put enough in my body. This wasn't a red-eye or a twelve-hour transcontinental flight; I didn't need it. And if I did, if the turbulence got bad, I knew I had it with me. I would be fine on my own.

My phone vibrated. I answered.

"Hey, Leah!"

"Hey! Oh my god, I have to tell you about this guy I just met on my doorstep!"

"I'm listening."

His name was Pete. She'd been eating Chinese food, and he'd been walking down the street with a carry-on. He'd stopped to talk to her, and *A* led to *C* and next thing they were making out. She'd asked him to stay, but he had a flight back to LA to catch.

"Ha, that's crazy!" I laughed. There was something to be said about meeting organically. "Wait, I'm leaving for LA right now, too. What airline is he taking?"

Mine. Leah sent me his photo, and I approached Pete at the terminal. We chatted for a few minutes, musing over the serendipity of life. What were the odds of him and her? Of him and me? Of any of this? I was beginning to think they were pretty high, as long as one was listening.

I slept on the plane without alcohol, without Xanax, without legroom or horizontality. My body ached for it. I couldn't wait to spend the next eight hours in my own bed, with its mountain of pillows and Teddy.

"How was your trip?" James gave me a hug at passenger pickup.

Transformative. "Great. Just ... great. Sorry, I'm honestly so tired. I'll talk to you more about it on our date."

I couldn't be on anymore. Not until I'd had some time for me. I let him do most of the talking on the way back to my house. He parked on the street, and I grabbed my bag from the backseat.

"I made you something," James said, pulling out a huge pot from his trunk. "My grandmother's homemade chicken noodle soup."

"Wow, that's so sweet," I said, totally overwhelmed by this gesture. He knew I hadn't been feeling well. "Thank you."

I started wheeling my suitcase up my driveway, and then *CRASH!* I spun around to see noodles and carrots martyred on the pavement.

"Shit shit shit shit." James bent down, scooping the victims into the empty pot.

"Don't worry about it. I'll get it tomorrow," I said gingerly. "It's the thought that counts. It was very kind." I gave him a quick kiss. "I'm sorry, I just really need to get some sleep."

I dreamed I was living in New York, working as a writer, living with Old James. Except it wasn't Old James. It was more like this amalgamation of all the guys I had loved, with the title James. Like dreaming of one's childhood home, only the building itself doesn't even remotely resemble it; it's just this feeling. I held on to the reverie as long as I could, but the morning sun was winning through the rust-colored shades. And my phone was buzzing.

JAMES:

> What are you doing today?

Was he really texting me at eight in the morning? It was much too early for this. And I had told him the night before that I needed the day to myself.

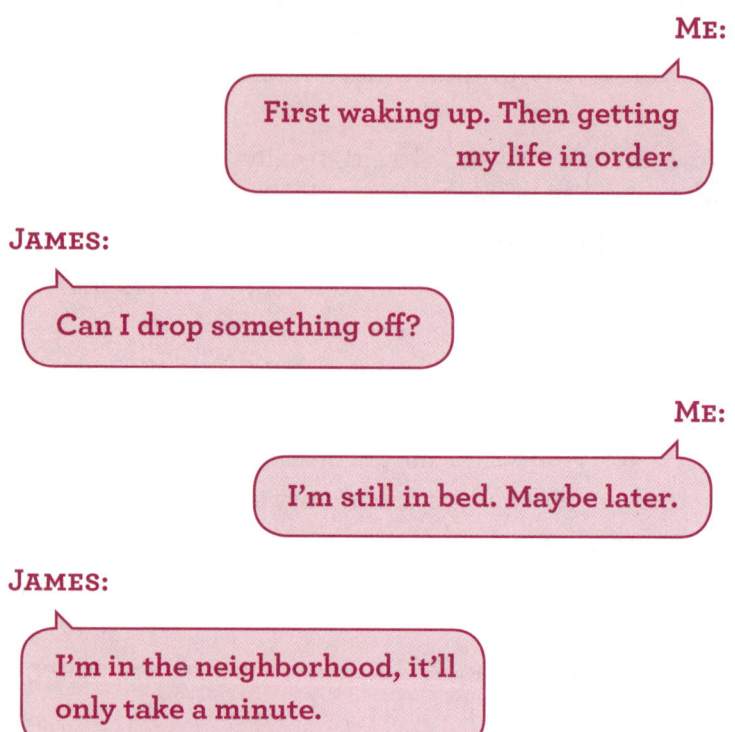

The last thing I wanted was to see anybody at that moment. I wanted to wake up slowly, make myself a cappuccino with sugar-free gingerbread syrup, read the *New York Times*, enjoy the solitude of my home.

Five minutes later came a knock at the door: James, with a brand-new pot of soup.

"This is ... wow ... you really didn't have to do this."

And he really didn't. I wished I could appreciate this token of his affection, but it felt smothering. Outsize. On an entirely different page.

I smiled. "Thank you, James. I'll call you later when I'm more myself."

DATE N⁰ 28

I hope they serve Chai in hell

STUDIO CITY

(Back in L.A.)

I felt like a new person. No wonder God had made a day of rest! My forty-day dating challenge had been pretty darn taxing, but that's why Lent only happened once a year. (Or it happened to prepare Christians for the sacrifice of Jesus by his Father to save everyone's sins. Maybe it was time to drop the religious analogy and stop offending the faithful.)

I was looking forward to my first date back in LA, at the Norton Simon with Garrett, the thirty-seven-year-old, glasses-sporting, impeccably dressed gallery manager. I needed a little dose of nineteenth-century European art to remind me why I hadn't skipped my flight and stayed in New York. (In fact, I had made this my new About Me: *Remind me why I'm here and not in New York.*) Instead, I got Chad.

Garrett canceled at the eleventh hour (literally 11:00 a.m.), so I once again went into desperation mode, swiping and typing with wild abandon. And that's how I came across Chad.

I had known from the moment I swiped right on him that he was going to be a total douche bag. Call it a sixth Tinder sense, or just call it blatantly obvious. For example, his good-looking shirtless profile pic, with his perfectly coiffed sandy blond hair. Or this:

CHAD, 32

What one has not experienced, one will never understand in print.

More blasphemous words could not be spoken to an artist. Or anyone who has ever read a book.

So why on earth did I swipe right on Chad? Well, two reasons. One, he was super hot. Douchey hot. And I'd pretty much been avoiding guys who were super douchey hot because I was prejudging them. And I felt this may have been unfair. Maybe they just couldn't afford shirts. Two—and more importantly—I needed a day date; I had improv that night.

We matched immediately, and I sent off the first message, a counter to his offensive About Me.

ME:

> But here's the thing—what about what one has experienced in the imagination?

CHAD:

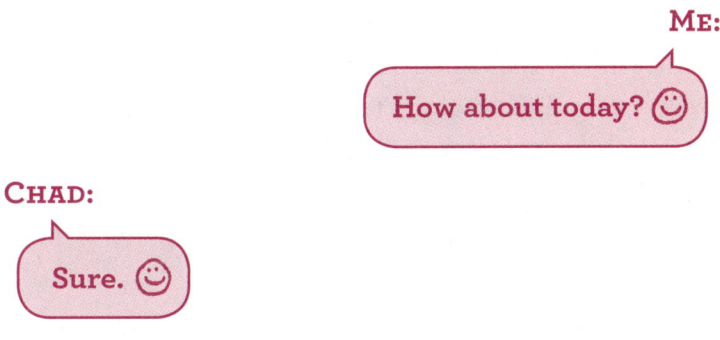

His response made no sense—Red Flag #3—but I still went forward, apparently hypnotized by that flawless hair.

ME:

CHAD:

Sure. 🙂

Perfect. Date #28 solved.

He told me to park at a residential address and that we could walk over to his favorite coffee shop (Obvious Tinder Dating Mistake #8: Not Meeting at the Coffee Shop). I parked and texted him that I was there.

CHAD:

Sweet buzz 103.

Alarms were going off. *Run, Amy, run!* No way should I step into his apartment.

Buuuuuut ... we did have seventeen mutual Facebook

friends. And he did have the cutest toy Pom ever. And how dangerous could a guy with exquisitely manicured eyebrows really be? Besides, I had my Taser (a gift from who else but Clancy).

I strolled up to a door with carved pumpkins in front. *How sweet!* Except it was 102. *Shoot.* I knocked on the door to 103. Chad was even hotter and douchier in person, wearing an Under Armour T-shirt and sweatpants combo.

I still felt uncomfortable with the whole scenario, so I came out swinging strong.

"Hey, I didn't realize I'd be coming to your place. I thought we were just going straight to coffee. But so we're clear, I'm not here to have sex. I'm not a call girl."

He half-laughed. "No worries, we're gonna go get coffee. I was just finishing this test for my company. I failed it miserably. Let me get ready really quick."

He disappeared into another room for a minute and talked to me through the wall.

"So, you been on a lot of Tinder dates?" *I usually ask that question.*

"Yeah, quite a few," I replied.

"And what's your experience been?" *Does he know?* I was already getting in my head.

"Really great actually. I've met some awesome people."

He reappeared. "Any sex on the first dates?" *Ugghhh.*

"Nope—that's a rule of mine."

"But what if the coffee's really good?"

I laughed. "Yeah, no. Unless it's seriously mind-blowing. Like, you-put-drugs-in-it kind of mind-blowing." He chuckled. (Probably a pretty off-color joke, all things considered.)

We left for coffee, and he told me he had just broken up with his girlfriend in Toronto. The day before.

"Are you okay?" I asked, already knowing the answer.

"Yeah, I'm usually pretty over it by the time things end." I nodded. He continued. "Long distance sucks. I was spending so much money. Even when she'd come here, I was dropping two hundred dollars on dinners, a hundred fifty on lunches."

I tried to keep it comedic. "So why are we going for coffee?"

No laugh—just, "Because I'm not getting laid." *Okay then.* We kept walking through the quaint neighborhood.

"I don't think I've ever been in love before," Chad said, in a moment of apparent self-reflection. *I believe that!* "Well, maybe with my ex a few years ago, but I cheated on her all the time." *Wait ... what?*

"Uh ... what?"

He nodded, nonplussed. "Yeah, I cheat on every girlfriend. It never starts that way, though."

I laughed. Loudly. *This has to be a joke.* "Are you serious?"

"Yeah, I'm in a very honest mood today. I don't know why," he stated calmly.

I suddenly felt very off-guard. Something was wrong. His forthrightness with cheating, the way he had punctuated "honest mood"—he *had* to know about my blog.

Things got progressively weirder once we got to Aroma Café (same place as Date #2; man, did I miss the Merchant Marine right now). In line, he told me he "just wanted to have sex with a bunch of random chicks." Then he ordered a Cobb salad and a dirty chai (appropriate), and I got a half-caff latte.

As I sat watching him eat, he told me he got Brazilian blowouts and that he worked in—you guessed it—banking.

"I love it: it pays great and I get to do whatever the fuck I want."

Sounds fulfilling. "Cool. So what do you do in your free time?" I asked.

"Go out—1 OAK, Warwick, Hooray Henry's. A lot of clubs. *I usually lie to girls and say, 'Oh no, I never go to clubs,' but no, that's me.*" *Is he on drugs right now? Am I on drugs? Where are the cameras?*

"So, UCLA, huh? What'd you study?" He asked questions in this overly direct way, like an interrogator.

"Art history."

"Smart lady." His eyes bore holes into mine. "And you've been on a lot of Tinder dates? Any bad ones?" *Is he asking this to verify my identity? Do I tell him about Ainsley? Or Steve?*

"I, uh, had one where the guy told me when we sat down it was his thirtieth birthday. That was pretty weird." I was hoping to gauge his reaction. He had none. Just the same creepy smile.

His phone vibrated. "Ugh, I hate this guy." He pressed "ignore." "Let's get out of here." *YES!* He charged outside and I followed. He stopped in front of a boutique clothing store.

"Do you think I should get this?" Chad pointed at a horrible long-sleeved hoodie. *More testing?*

"No, it's awful."

We kept walking.

"Zane just texted me I need to call him. I'm gonna put him on speakerphone. He's a douche," Chad said, dialing.

Zane picked up. "Hey, bud."

"Yo," Chad replied. And thus I became a fly on the wall to a conversation of dunces.

"So yeah, I thought about what you said, about those girls last night, and you're right. They're just young and dumb, you know?" Zane spoke as if he'd just had an epiphany on world peace.

Chad pressed mute so he could provide a running shit-talking commentary. "This guy is such an idiot. Doesn't know right from left."

Zane blabbered on: "... he's like the Great Gatsby, you know? Even when he gets a couple hundred grand, he's still not happy. It's like, I want nice shit, too—I love to ball—but he wants to be the Wolf of Wall Street. I want that, too, but it's like, without a yacht he's miserable. I mean, bro, you gotta start with a basic platform like I have ..."

Chad hung up. "He's fucking terrible."

"How long have you known him?" I asked.

He shrugged. "Eight years? Since New York. He's one of my closest friends. He was talking about our other buddy. Shit, he's calling back."

More absurd douchiness.

I knew I was being played. There was no way this could be real. *Did he text his friend to follow along in messing with me?* I was floored, and growing increasingly tripped out. The tables were being turned. Chad was serving me some of my own medicine for writing my blog. Punishing me for having not been up front and honest with all of the guys I'd been dating.

He was still on the phone when we arrived back at his apartment. I should have just peeled off into my car, but I really wanted to find out if he knew. It seemed like the only logical explanation. I sat down at the kitchen table and checked an email from Sascha while he finished the phone call. He sat down across from me.

"I'm producing this dance short—" I started to explain.

"I only watch reality TV," Chad cut me off.

I stared at him. "Uh, are you serious?"

He nodded. "Yup. *Top Model, Shark Tank,* that sort of thing." *Yup, there's a camera crew waiting behind the refrigerator. I don't need any more evidence.*

"All right, I should go. Sorry we're not having sex," I said, bringing the coffee date back full circle, trying to end on a joke.

Again, no laugh—just, "I'm not good at it anyway."

I turned around, ready for Ashton Kutcher to tell me I'd been punk'd. But he wasn't there.

Chad continued. "I just have this really big dick, and all I like to do is go in and out." He used his fingers to demonstrate. "I don't give a shit about pleasing anyone else. Then I like to kick 'em out. They usually end up feeling pretty bad." *What. The. Hell.*

"I'm in a *really* honest mood right now, Amy. You could ask me anything. Anything." *He totally knows!*

I took the bait. "What do you know about me?"

He smiled. "Nothing, Amy." *He's lying.*

I tried again. "What do you think you know about me?"

More smiling. "Absolutely nothing."

Finally: "Am I on a reality show right now?"

He stood up. "Yup, I'd have you sign a release, but we won't be having sex, so you don't need one."

This was too much. I had to get out of here. Interrogation was over—time to go.

"I'm leaving." I grabbed my purse and walked to the door.

"You're a good woman," he called out as I left.

I practically sprinted back to my Jetta. *What. The. FUCK. Am I dreaming? Do guys like Chad really exist?* I sat in my car and tried to work out what had just happened. It had to have been a setup. And if it was, it had worked. I felt sick, freaked out to the point of calling the whole thing off.

But maybe he didn't know ... It all seemed too surreal, too unbelievably *douchey* ... And yet I'd heard a lot of horror stories. Maybe I hadn't been punk'd after all. Maybe I'd just finally experienced the Darker Side of Tinder. I might never know. But at least I had learned.

LESSONS LEARNED

1. Don't swipe right on douchey, hot shirtless guys.

2. Don't stay on date if guy says things like "I cheat on all my girlfriends" or "I usually lie about clubbing," even if you're writing a blog about it.

3. Don't stick around to find out if douchey guy knows about your blog. Even if you're feeling guilty about not being honest with other wonderful guys you've been out with over the past several weeks. It doesn't matter. Just leave.

4. Always carry a Taser.

DATE No. 28.5

New James revisited

WEST HOLLYWOOD

When I got in my car accident at eighteen, my mom proved why she deserves the Amazing Parent of the Century Award. It wasn't because she held me in her arms all night and made me feel safe and protected, or because she let me skip school for a few days (although those things were amazing, too). No, it was because she forced me to get behind the wheel the very next morning. "If you don't do this right now, you might never be able to again." Well, I did, and thus I'm still driving cars to this day.

After my horrible date with Chad the Real American Psycho, I wanted to swear off dating. After twenty-seven mostly great dates in a row, I was ready to throw in the towel because of one run-for-the-hills douche bag. I felt so shaky and rocked by the experience that I considered calling James and canceling our dinner. *Didn't I put myself through enough yesterday? Over the past month?* Maybe I just needed another night to myself. Or to join a nunnery ...

To hell with that. I channeled my mother and pulled myself together, ready to get back behind that wheel. I was no virgin, and I needed to figure out where things stood with James. Even though the soup incident had been A LOT, he was still a decent guy, and I owed it to both of us to give it another chance and get to know him better. Plus, my Groupon to the restaurant we were going to expired that night.

Yes, I said Groupon. A couple of years back, I'd been the queen of daily deal coupons, even going to China on one. I'd since fallen off the bandwagon, except when I'd come across this one to Fig & Olive—a fantastic four-course meal, including wine and cocktails—and had bought it to take Old James. But I didn't want to think about him right then. This night was about New James.

He arrived promptly at seven thirty on my doorstep, sporting a blazer and dress shoes. Although I had also enjoyed his T-shirt and leather jacket ensemble on our first date, I preferred this sophisticated look. He flashed me a winning smile and gave me a quick kiss. Then revealed a huge bouquet of flowers. *Whoa.*

As I filled up a vase with water, James told me about the meaning behind each one.

"This one's native to my hometown in Pennsylvania; this one is my grandmother's favorite."

Like the soup, it was sweet. Too sweet. I stiffened, my

thoughts turning inward. *This is moving too fast; it's way too much.* I needed to communicate with him.

We sat down on my couch, and I word-vomited.

"I like you a lot, James. I just want to make sure that we're on the same page. I've had a tendency in the past to jump in too quickly, like with my emotionally abusive ex, Pat, who was always buying me flowers, and I want us to really get to know each other, you know? Not that I don't love the flowers, or that I think you're in any way emotionally abusive; I just ..." *This sounds terrible, Amy.*

He touched my arm gently. "I understand," he said. And I could tell he did. I let out a deep sigh.

The flowers had definitely triggered me. Things with Pat had moved maglev-train fast, and ended horribly. We'd been in a show together, playing an engaged couple, and I'd allowed the romance of the theater to sweep me away. One night in tech week he told me he had loved me and wanted to marry me before we'd even kissed. He seemed so sincere, and I was so flattered, I just ran with it, sleeping with him the following night after his profession of love, spending every day with him, accepting weekly bouquets from him. Only to suffer terrible verbal abuse for several months after the run.

But James was not Pat. Pat would have flipped out right then, instead of listening to me. Nor was he Old James, or Cameron Daughters, or anybody else. He was just himself, and that was who I needed to show up for, to be open to, to get to know. It was time for our second real date to truly begin.

We took his Dodge Dart to the restaurant, a car that I learned he had won on a game show.

I laughed. "Me, you, and the Duck!" He told me how he'd become a Lyft driver to subsidize the hefty taxes on the prize winnings, and to learn more about people.

"Whoa"—my head was spinning from the coincidences—"you mean *you're* a cab driver, too?" He grinned.

We got to the restaurant, and the hostess seated us on the back patio. James's farm boy roots quickly revealed themselves as he perused the menu. He knew how to grow tomatoes and make chicken soup, but he didn't know the first thing about fine dining. I ordered for us.

Our first course consisted of three crostinis: one mushroom with truffle and scallions, one manchego and fig, and another prosciutto, Marcona almonds, and Parmesan. Unfortunately, they contained two of the three foods he detested most: nuts ("they taste like dirt") and mushrooms ("they taste like dirt"). However, being the adventurer that he was, he took three bites of the mushroom and ate one half of an almond. The third food, which was at the very top of his "most hated" list, was olives. Good thing I had brought him to Fig & Olive. This was not boding well.

For our salad course, I got the house specialty, which contained, you guessed it, figs and olives. James didn't touch it. However, I did help him out with his burrata, beet, and heirloom tomato salad—first, by informing him what burrata was (not exactly the foodie I'd been hoping for), and second, by eating it.

For entrées, I'd selected the Chilean sea bass for him ("trust me, it's awesome") and the lamb chops with gnocchi and eggplant for me (not quite Glasserie, but still very good). I ordered a glass of pinot noir to go with mine, and he gave it a swirl and a taste.

"It's ... red wine." He smiled, clearly not a sommelier. I would have preferred a more refined palette, like the Mondavi I'd dated when I was twenty, but as long as he was willing to go to Napa with me, this was not a deal breaker.

As the night progressed, I discovered more about James. He'd learned to cook from his grandmother. He hiccuped daily like a minion from *Despicable Me* (so bizarre!). He told great jokes, and sometimes super corny ones. He'd taken odd jobs to learn about people, like being a grocery deliverer. He'd gotten in a horrible car wreck when he was eight that had stunted his growth. He liked thinking about space and colonizing Mars. His eyes lit up when he smiled. He was a good guy.

But I definitely wasn't feeling what I'd felt with him that first day, when I'd prematurely cried Romeo. And not just because of the flowers, or the burrata, or the sex. The sparks were just no longer there for me; the chemistry had cooled. Back at my house, when he kissed me, all I could think was, *He's not the one; something's missing.* Sadness and guilt coursed through me. How could I let him down without hurting him?

DATE No. 29

The Hero Friend (or, the Meta-Date)

HOLLYWOOD

Another day, another date canceled. *Ugh*. What was going on here in the City of Angels? As if I needed one more reason to go back to New York, the Tinder flakes just kept leaving me hanging. And even though I'd gotten back on the road with James after the debacle with Chad, the wounds from the previous day were still fresh. I had some pretty major PTDD (Post-Traumatic Douche Disorder). I no more wanted to act in desperation than I wanted to experience Chad's "really big dick." So I Tinder-messaged Darren.

ME:
Can we please go on a date tonight?

Darren:

> As long as you start your blog post like this: "Darren is a friend. He's too short and fat for me, but he helped on my web series for free so I decided to let him take me out."

Me:

> LOL!!!

I literally laughed out loud. God, I loved Darren. We met back in 2010 on a commercial. I was a background actor; he was a production assistant. We were both living out the dream. We didn't talk too much our first several encounters, mainly because he was too short and fat for me. ONLY KIDDING. It was because I'd been too busy being a blur in an office building and he'd been running around filling Starbucks orders.

A couple of my girlfriends from set told me Darren had a crush on me, but I never gave it much thought since I had a boyfriend at the time. I did, however, give it some thought when I was crewing up to shoot my web series and needed an extra hand. Darren had gladly stepped in and saved the day. Just like he was doing right now.

Darren:

> Pick you up at 8?

ME:

> YES! Thank you! ☺

But wait, let me rewind just a tiny bit, because the story of how we got to these Tinder messages is actually pretty cute. You see, early on in my forty dates, I had sent Darren the link to my blog. I had kinda sorta maybe wanted to tease him. And it had worked.

DARREN:

> I will swipe furiously to find you, Jamy Madison.

And he did, to no avail. A week went by.

DARREN:

> I've been Tindering a lot… It's never gonna happen ☹

ME:

> It will!!

DARREN:

> Maybe I'll be "Number 41: Real Life Wins."

I didn't hear from him again for a couple of weeks, until he messaged me about coming to New York (we were missing each other by an hour). Neither fate nor Tinder seemed to be on our side.

Then, one day during my swiping frenzy, Darren popped up. "Yes!" I vocalized to Teddy, and immediately texted him.

Me:

I just swiped right on you!!! 😊😊😊

Darren:

Shit I already swiped left.

Damn. Not meant to be.

Darren:

Can we just date in real life?

I thought about this ... *No.* If he was going to be one of the forty, we had to match through Tinder. It was the only rule I hadn't broken.

Finally, an hour after my disaster date with Chad, we matched. (Apparently his earlier statement had been a lie.)

Darren:

You should just go to New York

ME:
You found me!!!

And thus Darren could officially be part of my project, and Suitor #29. Cute, right? Now for our date.

He picked me up a few minutes before eight, and I gave him a huge hug.

"Oh my god, you have no idea how happy I am to be going out with you tonight and not another Chad."

He smiled. "That's what friends are for. I've already got the title for this entry: 'The Hero Friend.'"

I laughed. This actually worked on a lot of levels. For instance, there was a great pic of us from a couple of Halloweens ago with him as Superman. And then there was the fact that we called principal actors and featured objects "heroes" in our industry. And finally, he had just come back from saving someone's life in New York.

"You did what?" I looked at him incredulously.

"Yeah." Darren blushed, forever modest. "I donated my bone marrow to a sixty-six-year-old man with cancer."

I beamed. Darren was the best.

We parked at his place and walked up to Lucky Strike. I hadn't been bowling in ages, and it was exactly the kind of fun, brutally competitive date I needed. We warmed up with a Blue Moon and Rebel IPA at the bar, chatting about our jobs, our Tinder experiences, and, of course, my blog. It got *super* meta.

"I'm excited to see what you say about me," he said. "What's my name going to be?"

I laughed. "You can choose it if you like!"

"Sweet!" He grinned. "And let's see, what should we do for our second and third dates? How many is this gonna take?"

I looked at him, confused.

"To get laid," he clarified. More laughing.

"God, I love that you know my rules. That you literally know everything."

We got our shoes and picked our balls.

"This is gonna be tough, since my fingers are so fat," he said, showing me how they were sticking.

"Uh-huh, likely excuse for the fact that I'm gonna kick your ass."

"Nope, I was on a bowling league in high school," he boasted.

"I was on a bowling league in middle school!" I exclaimed.

"Well then, we're both nerds."

I disappeared to the bathroom, and when I returned, the screen displayed Darren's chosen name: Alphonse. For ex-leaguers, we both played pretty horribly the first game, me going nine for nine (I literally couldn't pick up a spare to save my life). I didn't even break a hundred, and he won the first one. But in the second game, I hit my stride, bowling an impressive 157. At least, impressive when compared to the board of celebrity high scores:

1. *Common* *147*
2. *Bode Miller* *138*
3. *Ne-Yo* *133*
4. *Avicii* *129*
5. *Gary Cole* *125*
6. *Jocko Sims* *124*
7. *French Stewart* *121*
8. *Rusko* *114*
9. *Shooter Jennings* *97*
10. *Dave Navarro* *92*

I mean, I beat frickin' Common, okay? And slaughtered Dave Navarro. Celebrities must never do normal people things, like play on bowling leagues.

We played two more games. I stole the third one from him in the tenth frame, and he won the last one (my fingers usually max out after three, and I was kind of drunk). We decided to end on a tie, so we could both walk away winners (although I clearly was the victor, with the evening's best score).

We walked back to his place, and Darren let me judge him on his book collection over a couple of bottles of water.

"See, it's as good as the Glamorous New Yorker's," he said proudly. I laughed.

We talked about kissing on first dates, and how he agreed with the Cab Driver—he didn't usually like to do it. I told him I agreed with James: that it should only happen if it's organic. He nodded.

We finished our waters, and then headed out to the car. As he was shutting the door to his place, Darren grabbed my waist.

"Screw it, I'm just gonna do it."

We kissed for a minute, and it was nice. Sort of how you'd expect it would be, kissing a friend you just went on a Tinder date with as part of a blog he knows about.

"That's organic as shit!" he proclaimed as we pulled apart.

I laughed. "That's definitely going in the blog!"

We drove back to my place, and he came in for one more drink. We talked and laughed a while longer, and then he got up to go.

"Time for some *Walking Dead*," he announced, giving me a hug.

"Drive safe," I called from my doorstep as he walked down my driveway. "I'm glad we finally got to go on this date!"

He turned. "Me too! And let me know if you need any help on your pole shoot."

"Oh, you're the first person I'll call." I smiled, then shut the door. It was nice having hero friends.

DATE Nº 30

A Stand-Up Guy

WEST HOLLYWOOD

It was Halloween. And for me, Halloween is like New Year's Eve and my birthday: better left unplanned. Just like Tinder first dates, these holidays all come down to managing expectations. If I am trying too hard to find *the best* thing to do, chances are I'll miss the thing that's happening right in front of me.

I definitely wasn't looking for the best party this Halloween, as I'd done some years in the past, but I was looking for a good story. Yes, *story*. For the first time since I'd started my dating experiment, I was less concerned about the merits of the suitor and much more interested in the evening's activities. This was clearly the absolute wrong way to go about finding my husband, but if I found my husband Tindering on Halloween, well, chances are that we'd both be really into role-playing. Enter: Mason.

Mason and I had matched before I'd gone to New York. In fact, our first exchange occurred at LAX as I hopped on my flight. We touched base again the day before I got back.

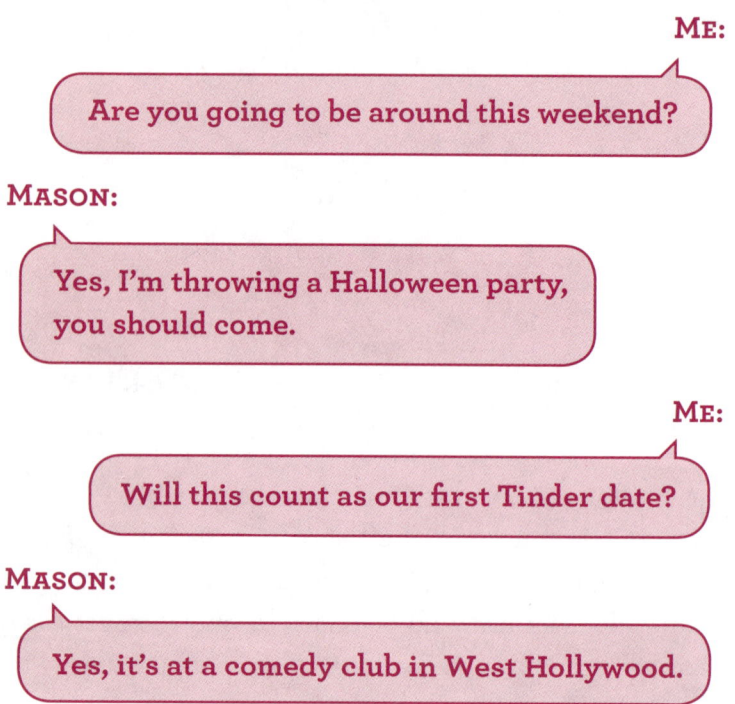

ME: Are you going to be around this weekend?

MASON: Yes, I'm throwing a Halloween party, you should come.

ME: Will this count as our first Tinder date?

MASON: Yes, it's at a comedy club in West Hollywood.

Sweet! This would definitely make for an interesting story. And if nothing else, I could take notes for my future career.

The show started at eight. I figured that I would have plenty of time during the day to shop for my costume—the Wendy's girl—but I figured wrong. The day got away from me with writing, and it was now almost seven. I finally accepted that I would not be finding a blue-and-white striped blouse and buying a Frosty and chicken nuggets, and thus went digging in my closet for a past costume. I'd dressed as a race car driver last year, I no longer had the blond hair to pull off the Girl from *American Beauty,* and my Ice Cream Parlor Girl outfit had blood on it (*hmm, Dead Ice Cream Parlor Girl?*). So I went with the Slutty Eskimo.

 Mason texted me that there was no rush to get there by eight, so I dropped by my girlfriend Clarissa's place to wish her a happy birthday. She was dressed as Xena, Warrior Princess, and was helping her boyfriend gay up his Spartacus costume. (She cut his velvet skirt shorter than mine.) They were heading to the West Hollywood Halloween Carnaval, aka Lady Gaga's Utopia, with a bunch of people, and part of me wanted to bail on Mason and join them. But I had a job to do.

 Clarissa only lived a mile from the venue, so I walked. My buddy Ryan looked at me like I was crazy—"Walk? In high shoes? *In the rain?*"—but I assured him I had it under control. My broken umbrella experience in New York had thickened my skin.

 I enjoyed watching the freak show on the streets and dismissed the catcalls from the deadlocked cars on Santa Monica Boulevard. (Not that they angered me; just that I didn't need anybody to tell me I looked sexy. I already knew that.) By the time I'd climbed the long, steep blocks up to the club, I was drenched—partially by the rain, but mostly in sweat. I'd become a Drowned, Slutty Eskimo Rat.

 I spotted Mason right away in his Scarface costume, and he seemed as harried as me. It took him a second to process who I was—the Tinder girl—but he figured it out.

"Hey, good to see you. Thanks for coming."

"Of course." I smiled. "I love comedy."

He introduced me to a White-Trash Pregnant Chick (costume), and then we stood there in uncomfortable silence, watching a White-Trash Asshole (not costume) bomb on stage. *This is gonna be fun.*

Mason disappeared to introduce the next comic, and returned to chat with me briefly.

"I give you guys a gazillion kudos for doing this. I've been thinking of trying stand-up, but I'm terrified," I said.

"You totally should!" He grinned. "And let me know when you do; I'll get you up." *Score!*

I took a seat near the front by myself and watched the show. It was ... painful. *Note to future self: do not perform stand-up on Halloween in West Hollywood.* The audience may as well have been zombies. (A couple actually were.) One comic even referred to us as the Zombie Apocalypse. It was brutal. If Mason's offer to take the stage had brought me one step closer to doing stand-up, watching each performer slowly join the ranks of the dead shoved me right back in my comicoffin.

That's not to say there weren't a few bright moments, or that these comics didn't have talent. Some of them definitely did. It was just a "tortured souls" kind of night. When Mason thanked the audience at the end for spending Halloween supporting artists, I felt an overwhelming amount of respect for everyone who had braved the stage. It took guts to get up there.

Or cocaine.

"Is he your boyfriend?" the sixty-year-old stripper cum

stand-up asked me after the show, while Mason performed his hosting duties.

"No, we just met on Tinder," I replied.

"Oh," she said, concerned. "He's a really great guy. But he has some problems, you know?" She put a finger to her nose and sniffed. I glanced around, uncomfortable with this incriminating information.

The crowd thinned, and Mason and I finally had a chance for some one-on-one. Up until this point, it had been about as un-datelike as possible. I mean, he'd given me his half-finished beer midway through the show, and shot his fake gun at me a couple of times, but our exchanges had been limited. Now, he actually took the time to look at me.

"You look really great. You're really pretty," he remarked, somewhat surprised.

"Thank you," I replied, neither flattered nor offended; just ready for some actual conversation.

He read my mind. "Wanna come back to the greenroom with me and talk?"

"Sure!"

He grabbed my hand and led me back.

"Is it okay if I hold your hand like this?" he asked.

"Why not?" I said, promptly releasing it.

Two other guys were in the greenroom, and Mason started chatting with them. I watched as he pulled out a little baggie of white powder. *Wait, is he really about to blow this in front of me?* I guess it *was* Halloween, and he *was* dressed as Tony Montana, but *really*? We'd barely spoken twenty words. The older woman had been right.

I was ready to leave. I'd seen more than I needed to (or

should have seen). And I'd already made Obvious Tinder Dating Mistake #9: Looking for Story and Not Person; I certainly didn't need to repeat my Ainsley mistake by staying with him an extra hour.

"I have my friend's birthday party downtown. I should probably get going," I lied.

"Aw, you have to go already?" He looked hurt. "Well, can I take you out on a real date sometime?" he asked.

"Yeah, maybe..." I smiled sort of sadly. He was a funny guy, and nice enough—just ... no. "Good to meet you. Great job up there tonight," I said, and took off.

My phone died on the walk back. Chris, the Glamorous New Yorker, had texted me earlier to see if I wanted to go to a party down at the Ace Hotel. *If only I'd done that*, I thought. *Or stayed with Clarissa. If only I'd just let the night take me instead of trying to force this thing to happen.* Not that I could have predicted how Fear and Loathing the show would be. Or that Mason would be so in character as Tony Montana. But I'd known better.

It was past midnight by the time I got home and charged my phone.

CHRIS:

> Come! This space is AMAZING.

He sent photos of the venue. It did look amazing, and I felt some pretty serious FOMO. The irony was Chris hated Halloween, and hadn't planned anything. *Sigh.*

I crawled into bed, exhausted and sober, and turned out

the light. *Hey, at least I won't have a hangover tomorrow!* I thought optimistically. And sure, maybe I hadn't hobnobbed with Oompa Loompas this Halloween or spun around a pole with Paris Hilton at her house, but I had learned an important lesson, one that I could take with me into the New Year:

Don't first-date-Tinder on holidays.

Birthdays included.

DATE No. 31

My Match Match

WEST HOLLYWOOD

NAVID
36-year-old man / Los Angeles, CA, USA

His details:

"Creative professional seeking smart, sophisticated woman"

Relationship: Never Married
Height: 5'10"
Have kids: No
Faith: Agnostic
Want kids: Definitely

Smoke: No Way
Ethnicity: Persian
Drink: Moderately
Body type: Athletic and toned

I matched with Navid, my thirty-first Tinder date, five months before I started my project. How was this possible, when I'd only just signed up on Tinder the week before my journey? Well, Navid and I initially matched on Match. That's right—the same online dating site where I met Old James. And well, I had met Old James, so I hadn't met Navid. Until now.

What was funny about my date with Navid was that it never would have happened if it hadn't been for Match. Had I not recognized him from our previous connection, I would have swiped left on his profile picture without hesitation, because a) it did him zero justice and b) he didn't look like my type. But since I already knew other details about him that Match did a much better job of providing (education, career field, income, preferences in mate, interests, favorite books, music, movies, etc.), I swiped right.

I sent the first message on Tinder.

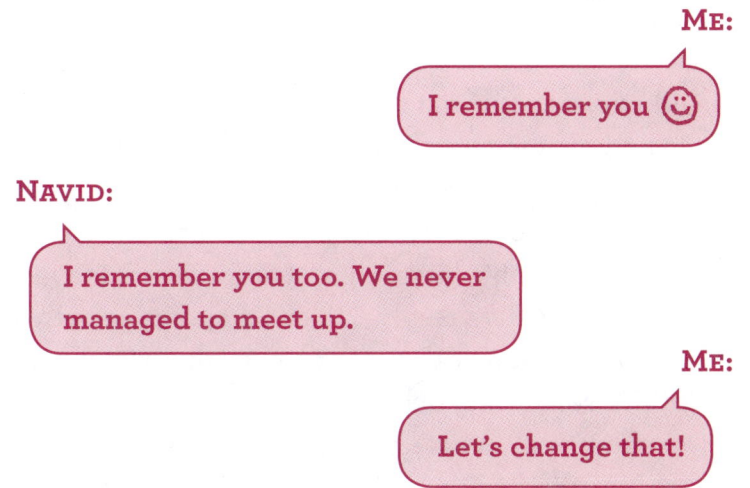

ME:
I remember you 😊

NAVID:
I remember you too. We never managed to meet up.

ME:
Let's change that!

And so we did. (This, to me, is one of the major selling points of Tinder. Sometimes you can spend a month emailing back and forth on Match, getting to know each other, because everyone's more serious—you're paying twenty-five dollars a month! Since Tinder is less precious, it just makes actually meeting in person a lot simpler.)

We met at the Village Idiot for a post-Halloween happy hour, and we seemed to be the only ones not hungover (the entirety of the very attractive staff had gone to the same party until the early hours). I was hardly surprised: the first thing in his About Me section read, *Not into: Club girls*. After Chad and the Stand-Up Guy, I really appreciated this.

"Did you dress up for Halloween?" I inquired.

He showed me a picture of his costume: a fox mask he had printed out and folded from his computer. I laughed.

"I'd say that's the laziest costume ever, but I guess you did actually have to make it," I said.

He smiled. "The thing is, with my job, that's pretty much what I'm doing every day. So I don't feel the need to do it for a holiday."

Navid explained to me that he worked as a production designer and art director for huge studio films. He told me about the tentpole picture he was currently working on, as well as the passion projects that he'd been directing. He showed me some stills from his latest short. I was riveted. I loved his work ethic and creative resolve. Plus, I'd always secretly had a thing for production designers—at least, the straight, good-looking, thirtysomething ones.

"How about you? What's your story?" he asked me.

I told him the basics: actress, writer, Wendy's stand-in.

I wanted to tell him about the blog and pole dancing, but decided against it. Something told me that with him I should wait. His vibe, his authenticity, his maturity, his dislike of club girls. I wanted to get to know him better before dropping any bombs. I steered away from my writing and sexuality.

"I'm actually considering moving to New York."

"Do it," he said confidently (Reason #1,236 to Move to New York: Navid says to do it). "I lived there for a year for a job. If it's something you want to experience, which clearly it is, you should make the leap."

I told him one of my friends had a room opening December 1, but I was thinking I'd wait until after the holidays.

"No, go now. Why wait?"

I loved his enthusiasm, his easy confidence. Not that he didn't turn around and sell me hard on LA.

"No one really lives in New York. It's not a real place," he said.

I thought of my experiences there over the years, the collective chaos, the constant flow of energy. The Cab Driver and his rootlessness. I knew what Navid meant.

He continued: "But in Los Angeles, you can actually live a normal life. You've got all of the cultural components, but you can have a yard, and there's nature, and the weather, and you can maintain a healthy lifestyle."

Ah, a healthy lifestyle. I suddenly craved a fresh-pressed juice and hot yoga. Then finished my sauvignon blanc.

"I'm really glad we finally met," I said. "It's funny that it took Tinder to make it happen."

I explained to him why I'd dropped off before. He understood.

"What's your experience been with Tinder compared to Match?" I asked.

"Oh, they're all awful," he sighed. "I'm starting to enjoy just being alone. It's like, we've all been sold this idea on how our lives should go, but once we realize that that's not the way things actually are, it makes it much easier to accept where we're at."

I looked deep into his eyes, trying to harness some of his Zen wisdom.

"It's just one big comedy of errors," I remarked. "This whole life thing is utterly insane when you think too much about it. But I sure am glad I'm along for the ride."

He smiled warmly, then: "I hate to cut this short, but I should probably get going." He had plans to see a movie that night with a friend.

The temperature outside had dropped and I hadn't brought a jacket, so I let Navid drive me to my car.

"This is it." I pointed to my Jetta. "The poor man's version of yours."

He drove an Audi A7.

"Oh, it's all the same thing," he said. Somehow he made the most basic statements sound profound. *Teach me your ways, O enlightened one.*

"Let's do this again," I offered, perhaps the first time I had pushed for a second date.

"Absolutely," he said, and leaned toward me. I couldn't tell if he wanted to give me a hug or a kiss, so I gave him a kiss. He'd been going for a hug.

"Ugh, sorry, that was awkward." I blushed.

"No, it's fine. It's hard to tell how these things should end."

I felt embarrassed, but it didn't last long. His energy was too calm for me to be frazzled. I opened the door and stepped out.

"Enjoy the movie!"

Navid smiled. "Chat soon," he said, and drove off.

I hoped he meant it. Just being around him made me feel more relaxed, more stable, more evolved. And besides, we had matched on not one but *two* online dating platforms. And that alone deserved at least a second date.

DATE N° 31.5

A New York Reminder

SILVER LAKE

I'd missed the Halloween party downtown, but I wasn't going to miss a second opportunity to see Chris, the Glamorous New Yorker. I met him and his best friend in Franklin Village, and he looked just as adorable and East Coast as ever. We popped into La Poubelle to grab a drink.

If he had exuded an air of pretense our first encounter, it evaporated in the darkly lit French bistro. The more I listened to him talk and laugh, the longer I observed the way certain subjects animated him, the closer I wanted to be to him. This was one of the only second dates where I found myself actually more attracted than with the first. It didn't hurt that his art school friend added plenty to the conversation, nor did watching their interaction, their friendship.

From La Poubelle we headed to Cliff's Edge in Silver Lake, about as close to a Brooklyn vibe as one could get in Los Angeles. We ordered a couple of whiskey cocktails, then grabbed a table. Twenty minutes later, two friends of theirs joined us—female comedy writers. One worked on *The Mindy Project*, the other *Parks and Recreation*. I attacked them with questions, beyond thrilled to hear their journeys to the writer's room.

Chris only got cuter and more lovable as the evening progressed. He was obviously most comfortable around those he knew and cared about; his guard was completely dropped. He lost none of his intellect, sophistication, or New York sensibility; simply gained this warmth and playfulness. Like when we had gone back to his place in the West Village. This was his element. And I yearned to be a part of it.

I drove him up the winding streets near the reservoir to his Airbnb.

"Do you want to come in?" he asked. It was nearly one in the morning, but I did. I wanted to see where he had chosen to live for the next month.

The space was small but charming, not unlike my own bungalow, except with a view. Built in the twenties, it donned original furnishings and possessed a rustic quality.

He put some music on his iPhone, and we talked on his bed. Talking led to kissing, which did not lead to sex—I'd learned my lesson. We fell asleep sometime around two.

Or at least I did. Chris could not sleep at all. I woke up sporadically to him pacing, or reading. Around six o'clock, the light began to pour through the French doors that opened onto the deck. I turned and looked at him, a sort of mutual agreement passing between us.

"Should I go?" I asked gently.

"I'm sorry, I just want to try and get at least an hour or two of sleep," he replied.

"Oh no, I totally get it. Happens to me all the time," I assured him. I had a notoriously difficult time sleeping in the same bed with a man, unless we'd been dating for months, so I understood. I put on my boots, grabbed my purse, and gave him a quick kiss. "Text me later."

Carving back down the hill, I was struck by the heaviness of the morning, the thick fog of night taking its time to lift above the palm trees. The sun ached to break through, her promise of light and warmth thinly veiled, barely out of reach. I could still feel the softness of the sheets, the smoothness of his skin, and I longed to be back in his bed. I hoped he was finally asleep.

DATE N.º 32

The Texan Snowflake

FAIRFAX

I needed coffee. Lots of it. Straight to my veins. Good thing I was meeting my thirty-second date for Sunday brunch, where there was sure to be an endless flow of it.

I'd actually suggested a caffeine meet-up when Justin and I had both swiped right a few days prior.

ME:
> Can I buy you a coffee? Or frozen yogurt?

This had been my opener and generous offer in response to his request for *no hookups, ladies—buy a guy dinner first*. He had admired my brevity, and so here I was, pulling up to

BLD to meet the "connoisseur of fireworks and whistling."

I liked him from our very first hug on the street corner. He'd moved out to LA from Texas eight years ago, and had not lost an ounce of his Southern charm. I put our name in at the host stand, and we dove right into conversation as we waited outside for our table.

I learned Justin was an art director (two in a row!) and a Burner (two not in a row!), a far cry from his mechanical engineering and small farm town beginnings.

"I wasn't sure exactly what I wanted to do when I moved here; I just knew I wanted to make movies." It all sounded very familiar.

And yet it wasn't. Tyler Durden was wrong. People are unique snowflakes. Sure, we might share 99.9 percent identical genetic code, but my god if that 0.1 percent doesn't make for some incredible variations. And even if we are all decaying matter, it doesn't mean we aren't still beautiful. And Justin was both unique and beautiful.

After telling me about his current job on a TV game show, I told him about my ever-more-likely transition to New York. "Sometimes it's really good to shake things up," he said. "That's how I ended up at Burning Man in August."

Of course I wanted to know more, so he told me about the huge installations, the unusual social system, the king of the desert.

"This one guy was so popular. Dreads down to his waist, cataracts for days. I asked him where he was from, and he said he was transient, moving between California, New Zealand, and Mexico, working at marijuana farms. 'I make, like, nine grand a year,' he told me."

"What's his number?" I joked. "Think he's on Tinder? I wonder if I have a shot!"

We got seated inside and placed our order: French press coffee and frittatas with chorizo home fries and brioche (only thirty-five pounds until I reached my goal!). I learned more about his upbringing and his move out west, including the month he ran out of money at twenty-two years old.

"My dad finally got to say it, 'I told you so.' I felt horrible. But it's the exact same story as everyone else out here."

"Au contraire!" I interjected. "My mom is an artist, so she was unbelievably supportive of me. Even though I was a straight-A student, when I decided I wanted to be an actress at fifteen she was like, 'Do you want to graduate early? Go down for pilot season next year?' That's probably the reason I've been so unsuccessful. I've never had anything to struggle against!" Justin laughed. "I'm only kidding," I added. "I've been in a Pepsi commercial, so I've definitely made it."

Commercials led to my Honda yoga TV ad, which led to pole dancing, and I told him about "Why I Dance."

"It's a feminist piece, showing the beauty of every woman's body. We're trying to change the dialogue about female sexuality. In our current culture there's so much exploitation, and we want to shift this to celebration."

He listened intently, nodding his agreement.

"I don't think there's anything more beautiful in the world than women," he admitted.

"Well, that makes two of us!"

Delving into femininity and sexuality opened the doors to all other topics, rendering nothing taboo.

"If you can't talk about sex, politics, and religion, what's the point?" Justin grinned.

"Love it!" I exclaimed, then went straight for it: "Do you believe in God?"

"Well, my father used to be a pastor, so I grew up Christian, and it was just a given," he replied. "But then when I moved to California, and everybody had differing views, and believed in them as strongly as I believed in my own, I started to question everything. For a while I was agnostic, but it didn't really feel right, so now I'm in a more complicated space of spirituality. How about you?"

"Agnostic." I smiled. "I grew up Christian like you, but then some point around junior or senior year of high school I realized I didn't actually believe in it, more just felt a strong nostalgia for it. But we all have those moments. Standing in the middle of Chartres, up on a mountaintop, looking out over a foggy lake. Even Sam Harris has finally admitted it. But I respect people's beliefs, if it helps them feel better about life and be a better person. My only problem is if you're so focused on the possibility of an afterlife that you neglect this life right now. Because really, this is all we know for sure."

We hopped straight down a rabbit hole into the cosmos, and the brilliance of Hubble and Einstein and outside-the-box thinkers, and quotes from Neil deGrasse Tyson. I could've asked for no better conversation over breakfast, and we were both sad to have it end.

"Let's put a pin in it," he said, "and pick it up another time."

I nodded eagerly. "Totally."

He walked me to my car, and we hugged good-bye.

"Thanks for being so willing to meet," Justin said.

"What can I say, I like people!" I beamed.

"Well, you're definitely personable." He waved good-bye. "Until next time!"

I turned on the engine and sat there for a moment. I just felt happy. As with the Duck, I hadn't felt sexual chemistry with him. In fact, he looked so much like my brother it was kind of eerie. But I loved the deeper connection I'd experienced with Justin. The human connection. What more could one really ask for on a first date?

DATE Nº 325

A Refill of the Stein

HANCOCK PARK

It had been exactly two weeks since I'd first met Dan, and a lot had happened. Eighteen different guys, New York, the beginning, middle, and soon-to-be end of my relationship with New James (I still needed to officially break it off; I'd been avoiding it). I had no idea what to expect in round two with the closeted nerd from Bromosa.

He showed up at my place with a bottle of bubbly, an entire cheesecake, and champagne flutes from Ralph's.

"Wow! It's like a celebration!" I laughed. "What are we going to do with this whole cheesecake?"

He shrugged sheepishly. "I thought maybe you had roommates."

"Nope. But breakfast for the next week." (Or not. I had

zero calories to spare on store-bought desserts. But it was still sweet.)

I poured him a glass of wine from the sauvignon blanc I had just opened, and we sat down on my couch.

"So tell me how it's all been going! This has been crazy, huh?"

I nodded. "One of the weirdest, best things I've ever done."

"Yeah, I've read a few entries, but I stopped because I'd rather get to know you in person, not through your blog. I want the real Amy, not Jamy Madison."

I smiled. This was refreshing.

We finished our glasses as I caught him up on the past couple of weeks.

"You hungry?" he asked.

"Starving." I hadn't eaten since brunch, and it was nearing nine o'clock.

"Let's go grab dinner."

♥

We ate at Osteria La Buca, one of my favorite Italian restaurants in the city. I'd had my twenty-first birthday here, when it was just a hole in the wall that sat eight tables. Now it had expanded up and out, with more than thirty tables. *People change, restaurants change, everything changes.*

Our pastas were fantastic, the upstairs fireplace romantic, the wine tannic. Dan was still Dan, and we still had a great conversation, but it wasn't the same Fourth of July explosion we'd experienced down at the beach.

"I feel like I keep having a lot of great first dates, sometimes even second, but then they just sort of fizzle out," he confessed over the last of our Super Tuscan. "I don't know why it keeps happening. If it's something I'm doing wrong."

I looked at him, sympathetic. I knew why.

"It has nothing to do with you. It just takes time to get to know someone. And not every person is a perfect match. Or even a halfway decent one. First dates can be really exciting—it's brand-new! It's this human being in front of you with a lifetime of experiences and stories! And that's great. But then on second, third, and fourth dates, you really start to assess if this is someone you can share your life with. That's, like, a massive thing. Of course there will be a lot of dead ends. But that doesn't mean they are failures. As long as you're just showing up as your wonderful self, being open and honest, then you're on the right track. I have faith. It'll come."

He smiled. We both knew where this particular road was headed—a cul-de-sac—but we were both all right with it.

DATE N° 33

The Thirty-Third Time's a Charm

SILVER LAKE

I didn't have a ton of patience for dates canceling (obviously—look how I'd ended up with Chad). So when Daniel, the suitor who had bailed on me not once (Date #1) but twice (Date #16), asked me if I wanted to grab a drink Monday afternoon, I was pretty reluctant to meet with him. But something in me told me to give him one more chance. Like the fact that I still needed my daily date. I rather appreciated the irony of him leaving me high and dry and then flying in for the save, so I agreed to meet him at Barbarella for happy hour.

"Wow, you, like, ran in here! You must have been really excited to meet me," Daniel remarked as I smoothed down my hair. Just moments before I'd tempted the Grim Reaper as I jay-sprinted across Hyperion Avenue.

"Yeah, the anticipation's been building for so long, it just got to be too much," I confessed. *More like the opposite.* My expectations for the cinematographer had dropped into the negatives.

With such little to live up to, it would have been hard for Daniel to disappoint. But as it turned out, he was a pretty solid guy. Sweet, down-to-earth, great smile, hardworking. He currently spent most of his time as a DP (director of photography), but had started off in nature photography. That was still his passion.

"The best job I ever worked was this wildlife documentary we shot around the world. I got to shoot penguins in Antarctica, warthogs in Africa, monkeys in Southeast Asia."

I stared at him, beyond jealous.

"Wow, I'm beyond jealous."

He laughed. "Yeah, it was pretty amazing. Except I got booked, so last minute I didn't have time to get all of my shots. So here I am, three feet away from cobras, recording baboon fights, and all I can think is how terrified I am of getting rabies. But I didn't."

Daniel had gone from filming one sort of harsh reality to another: reality TV.

"Yeah, I pretty much hate the show I'm on right now. Following these awful D-list divas who have no business controlling the sets. But they're producers, so they have the final say. It's exhausting. I'm thinking of just opening a bar."

Well, that's a change of direction! After a decade of working his ass off, simultaneously pursuing his dreams and sacrificing his soul to the machine to pay the bills, Daniel was ready to switch it all up.

"Sometimes you just get to this point where you've been doing something for so long, and it's been eating up all of your time, and you have to ask yourself, what do I really want? I mean, this is what I truly enjoy." He gestured to us, sipping specialty cocktails, shooting the shit. "It's too much, wrapping at midnight and being recalled at six a.m. I want to have a life. And sleep."

I thought of all the things going on in my own life, the transitions I had been envisioning: finding a husband, moving to New York, being a paid writer. In no way could I compare my own self-imposed dating/blogging regimen to his legitimate career—especially since part of my job entailed the thing he said he would rather be doing—but I was starting to feel really exhausted. Some things are meant to be temporary. Like reality TV shows. And do-it-yourself bachelorette blogs. In fact, everything.

He started telling me about a game show he'd been working on, and I stopped him.

"Okay, I'm sorry, I just can't get over how many people have connections to game shows in this city."

"Why?" He laughed. "Have you been on one?"

"Three, actually."

I told him about my experiences on *The Rich List*, *Who's Still Standing?*, and *5th Grader*, and how I'd Tindered with another guy who had also been an elementary school dropout.

"You know, it's funny. I recently had a Lyft driver who had won his car on a game show."

My mouth dropped. It was too much of a coincidence.

"Was it a Dodge Dart?" I inquired. He had to be talking about New James.

"Yeah, actually, it was. He was this super wholesome farm boy. From Pennsylvania, I think. Said he liked driving Lyft because it gave him ideas for stories."

Yup, my thirty-third Tinder date got a ride from my twentieth Tinder date. And then it came up in conversation. Small, small world.

"Really nice kid. Seemed super innocent," Daniel commented. *If he only knew.*

"He's not. It's all a facade." I laughed, still enjoying the synchronicity.

"Why, did you go out with him or something?"

"Yup." I nodded. "Tinder! Further connecting the world, one swipe at a time."

I made a mental note to call New James back. I'd been avoiding the confrontation, but clearly the universe was telling me to just face it.

We finished our drinks, and I had to get going. I had a production meeting for the dance short, and a million other things I needed to take care of, like setting up my remaining seven dates and figuring out the rest of my life.

"It was great to finally meet you," I told him, sincere.

"You too," Daniel replied, giving me a hug. "I'm glad you gave me a third chance."

I was, too. Our date reminded me of several important things. One, people deserve second chances. And sometimes third chances—because life happens and things go wrong, but then they sometimes go right, and if you aren't open to it, you could miss out on something great. Two, nothing is ever set in stone. (Well, ancient Egyptian hieroglyphs are, but even those one day will morph into a different configuration of sand, worn down and dissolved by time.) And three, we are way more connected than we could ever imagine. *You, me, and everyone we know—we're all just a Tinder apart!*

DATE Nº 34

How to be myself
(or learning to handle rejection)

MELROSE

> "*The snow goose need not bathe to make itself white. Neither need you do anything but be yourself.*"
> –Lao Tzu

I found myself in an unusual position the next morning: between writing up Date #33 and getting ready for Date #34, I had fifteen minutes to kill. Not enough time for a workout or an episode of *Girls*, but just enough to check out one of Navid the Art Director's short films.

As predicted, the production quality was superb, especially considering the budget. Watching it upped my interest in Navid at least 15 percent. I pondered whether to text him, then decided to just go for it, committing Obvious Tinder

Dating Mistake #10: Not Allowing a Gentleman to Make First Contact after Your Initial Meeting.

ME:

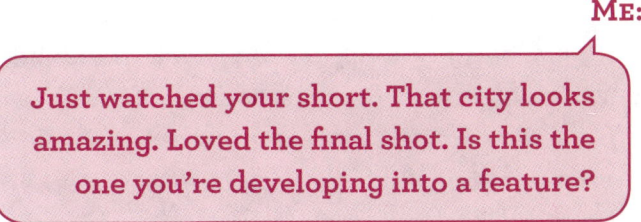

Just watched your short. That city looks amazing. Loved the final shot. Is this the one you're developing into a feature?

I put Chef'Special's "In Your Arms" on repeat and did my makeup. Fifteen minutes later I got Navid's response.

NAVID:

Yes.

Well, it's direct, I thought, *if not a little ... completely over it.* I texted him back.

ME:

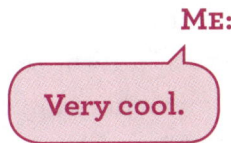

Very cool.

Which of course was met with nothing. I didn't feel hurt, exactly; more like...not enough. In an overwhelming way. I began to question my entire self-worth. *Is it because I'm too immature? Too shallow? Too much of a party girl?* I mean, I had worn a black and gold shirt that could have been construed as "clubby." Or maybe it was the awkward kiss. It had to have been the awkward kiss. *Dammit, why did I do that? Why did*

I ruin everything with the intelligent, successful, totally stable art director?

I positioned myself on the diving board, and was about to jump into the deep end when I took a step back. *Whoa, Amy, it's just one guy. Who you don't know at all. Who probably isn't even right for you. In fact, who DEFINITELY isn't right for you, because he doesn't even want to date you. And it doesn't even matter, because you're dating, like, five other guys who are great and do want to date you. Remember what you told the Full Stein the other night?* I nodded, seeing my point.

And you know what else? my inner dialogue continued. *You are a party girl. And you're also smart and funny and kind, and worthy of love, and totally enough. Perhaps a tad bit manic, but it's you, and you're wonderful.* I smiled and finished getting ready. *Thank you, self. You're right. On to the next.*

Adam was running late due to traffic, so I spent the extra few minutes becoming more acquainted with his profile. *Explorer, adventurist, traveling the world.* He had a picture with an elephant instead of a tiger (the latter were all the rage in the Tindersphere), a motorcycle, and one in front of a bay that looked like a Boudin painting. I liked him already.

I closed out his profile and started to do more Tindering. Most of my remaining dates were already set, but a couple of slots remained to be filled. And there was always the possibility of a flake. Adam showed up mid-swipe, and I quickly shoved my phone in my purse.

"Hi!" I gave him a hug. He looked a little older than I'd

expected. But he was thirty-eight, at the top of my age range. *Distinguished,* I decided.

I ordered a soy latte, and he got a mocha shake.

"Love it," I remarked. *See, youthful spirit!*

We sat down outside, the weather a perfect seventy-five degrees.

"You look like you're dressed for winter," I commented, noticing his sweater and jeans combo.

"I am. I'm heading to Utah after this," he replied.

"Oh yeah? What for?" I asked, assuming an epic ski adventure.

"Finishing up this shoot, actually." *This could be promising.*

"Are you an actor, or ...?"

He shook his head. "Producer." *This* was *promising.* "I used to act—well, I sometimes still do—but for the past six years it's been mostly about producing."

He told me about the film in Utah, and it sounded great. Right up my alley. It was based on the true story of a guy who got fired from a big bank for speaking up about their bad behavior. When no one would hire him, he ended up in North Carolina working as a server at a Waffle House.

"I love this kind of thing," I told Adam, and launched into a diatribe over wealth addiction and greed.

"Have you seen the movie *I AM*?" I was getting super animated, the way I always do when I'm passionate about something. And have had too much caffeine.

"I have not," he replied.

"Oh my god, you need to watch it. You'll love it. It's all about the corruption of the lie we're being sold as the

American Dream. Yachts, billions, celebrity—none of that will fill right here." I gestured to my heart. "It's about recognizing our shared humanity and responsibility to each other, this collective 'I am.'"

We spiraled into eight different conversations at once, switching between scripts and travel and police shootings and his ridiculously famous stepsister. I now had one knee pulled into my chest, the other on a nearby chair, sprawled out like a four-year-old. I learned that Adam had starred in a Lifetime movie, been an Olympic-level skier, and visited twelve countries in 2014.

"My goal is to travel less this year," he boasted.

I laughed.

"Well, I'd say you're winning at life if your goal is to travel *less* and you love traveling."

"It's great seeing the world, but it affects my career," Adam explained. "And my ability to have a relationship." I nodded. *Very promising.* "But I am itching to go somewhere," he added.

I laughed again. "You're going to Utah! In literally two hours!"

"Oh, right." He smiled. "I should probably be taking off."

We did the obligatory walk to my car, and he told me about his desire to get a Jeep for his outdoor adventures.

"It just gets such terrible mileage," he lamented.

I stopped in front of my Jetta.

"That's why I got a TDI, so I could save the environment. Fifty miles to the diesel gallon at a time. Tapping into those ol' Portland roots."

Adam gave me a sly look.

"What?" I asked.

"You're such an LA girl."

I scrunched up my nose, sheepish.

"I am, aren't I?"

Maybe it had been all of the crazy confidence I'd gained from being rejected, or the coffee, aka truth serum, but I had been unapologetically myself for the last hour. And now Adam was calling me out. *Shit.*

He drew me in for a platonic hug. *I should really grow up if I ever want to date a man,* I thought sadly. He pulled back, still holding me.

"God, you are so ... adorable." His eyes twinkled. "Can I kiss you?"

He did, ever so lightly. *Wait, hold on! I hadn't ruined it by being myself! Woo-hoo!*

"Have a fun time in Utah." I sort of curtsied, then pirouetted away to have some fun times of my own running errands.

I was halfway through my Trader Joe's shopping list when Adam texted me.

ADAM:

> **I hope I get to see you again soon. This weekend?**

I smiled. *See. Now aren't you happy you were just yourself, self?* I grinned, putting blueberries in my cart. *I am.*

In fact, I was so happy just being myself that when I got rejected a second time later that day, this time by Chris, I didn't drown myself in a pool of cabernet. He texted that he didn't feel comfortable dating me because of my blog, and I simply accepted it. No tears, no crumbling of self-worth. Just acceptance. Was it unfortunate? Sure, because I liked him and would've liked to go out with him again. But did it mean there was something fundamentally wrong with me? Of course not. I was going to be just fine, Chris or no Chris. And hey, at least we didn't have sex.

Unlike New James. *Ugh.* As educated as I was becoming on the art of rejection, I still was having a hard time communicating my feelings to the Pennsylvania boy. It was one thing being rejected or rejecting guys I knew I wasn't going to marry after one or two dates, but James and I had *slept together.*

He'd been calling and texting, and I'd pretty much been ignoring him. For all the wisdom I'd been espousing to myself and others, I couldn't seem to woman up and face him. I felt awful, but the situation completely overwhelmed me. I was usually on the other side of this equation post-sex, and I just didn't know what to say. "You're really great, but I don't see this working out"? Okay, fine, but then why had I slept with him? It seemed impossible to say something without hurting him. I wanted it to just gently fade away. Maybe it would ...

DATE N⁰ 35

The Guy Next Door
HOLLYWOOD

Tinder changes the way you look at people. For instance, I now wondered if every guy I passed on the street was on it. Cute bartender who served me a drink? *I bet he's on here!* Weirdo staring at me while I pumped gas? *Immediate left!* Hottie with the body next to me in SoulCycle? *Ohhh, I'm swiping till I find you!*

It's funny, but in a lot of ways, Tinder makes it easier to meet people than in real life. On the surface, this might seem pretty tragic—do we really need an interactive version of Hot or Not to talk to a guy?—but hey, in the Facebook Era, it's where we're at. And if my last month or so of dating had taught me anything, it was that a lot of great people were using Tinder. People I otherwise would never have met. Or maybe I would have, without getting past hello.

Take Jeff.

Jeff and I matched on Tinder a couple of days before Halloween. Our exchanges were the sort of standard, run-of-the-mill messages that you didn't write home about. But suffice it to say, he went to a house party with a keg for the holiday, and my weekend was "mellow." (How does one describe a Tinderbender to a potential date?)

Two days passed after All Souls' Day without any communication, and then something unusual happened. I ran into him. And in the most unlikely place: the loft downtown where we were location-scouting for "Why I Dance."

I recognized him instantly, but it took me a few seconds to remember from where. When it dawned on me he was a Tinder match, I hesitated before calling it out. After all, we were in a room with several other people, including his friends, who owned the space, and my girlfriend, the director, and it might have been uncomfortable for him.

"We've been talking on Tinder," I blurted out. He stared at me for a long moment, processing. *Oh god, this is embarrassing. I'm not wearing any makeup, and I don't look like my picture. Efff.*

"Oh, wait, you're the girl I was talking to this weekend! The redhead." He said it in a way that made me question even my hair color. *Does it not look red enough, like my pictures?*

Everyone found this coincidence quite amusing, and Jeff and I shared in an awkward laugh.

"Well, nice to meet you," I said, and then followed my friend out. I waited until the stairwell before turning to her. "Um, that was *crazy*. I swear, since I started these dates, this kind of thing has been happening *a lot*." *Hellooooo, universe.*

Later that evening I received a message from Jeff.

JEFF:

> Well, now that the ice is broken, would you wanna grab a drink sometime this week?

I thought about it. He was friends with Greg, which meant he could easily find out about my blog. He might even already know about it.

ME:

> Okay, now that the ice is broken, I should tell you I'm in the middle of this: fortydatesfortynights.com.

JEFF:

> That's definitely being in the middle of something.

No kidding. I told him I would still be up for getting a drink if he was, because hey, it could be interesting. He waffled, on the fence, then decided he was down. We settled on drinks at Sassafras on Wednesday, and thus he entered the books as my thirty-fifth date.

We met at nine in the evening. To be fair, I'd known from our fortuitous run-in that there would probably be no romantic connection between Jeff and me. His somewhat ironic floral hat, his Tom Selleck-worthy mustache, the fact that he was friends with Greg—none of these were bad; they just weren't for me. Just like my blog hadn't been for Chris.

However, this knowledge didn't bother me. After all, I had accumulated such a wonderful array of potential suitors by this point that I was considering hiring an assistant to handle my schedule. Worst-case scenario? Jeff ended up being beyond awesome and I added him to the list.

My initial instincts turned out to be correct, but that isn't to say Jeff wasn't a good guy. Or beyond awesome. He just wasn't my type. And he was not really ready for a serious relationship. Like marriage with kids.

"I never meet girls on Tinder; it's more just a game I play when I'm bored," he told me up front.

He originally hailed from the East Coast, a soccer player who moved out to Los Angeles without much idea of what he would do. Luckily, his father was in the business of flatware, and thus Jeff benefitted from some serious nepotism: he'd been hired to do deliveries to a high-end store on Rodeo Drive. (Perks included seeing Larry King.)

It hadn't taken too long for Jeff to find some direction, though, and he ended up at Chapman, receiving his master's in film. He was now working as a cinematographer and doing well—the only guy from his class to have worked on a feature so far—but he was still very fresh on the scene.

"My best gig was on a Nick show. They were passing out these parfaits. It was great." *Oh, the draw of craft services.* I sent Diego a telepathic wink.

We spent a sizable amount of our old-fashioned sipping time discussing my insane dating schedule (Jeff: "I'm flipping this around; we're talking about *you*"), and I gave him the inside scoop on the process.

"Yeah, I'm really impulsive. I joined Tinder, saw this UCB show, went out to the desert for my parent's anniversary, and told them I had this idea. They thought it was crazy, obviously, so I did it. Thank God they've been busy in Europe this whole time, and not in Cali worrying I'm in a ditch."

We finished our cocktails, and Jeff walked me to my car.

"Well, good luck with everything. I'm glad we got to do this," he said.

I smiled and gave him a hug.

"Yeah, me too. Look out for your write-up!" I teased. *Gotta love the meta.*

♥

I got home and spent some time reflecting on our conversation. I thought about the past month of my life, the guys I had met, what my drink with Jeff had meant. *Did it even mean anything, in the grand scheme of things?*

Of course it did. Even if he wasn't "the one," it still meant something. They all meant something. Because while the end goal of all of this Tindering and dating was to find my partner, the journey itself had proven to be incredibly rewarding.

You never know who you're going to meet when you put yourself out there: a partner in traveling crime like the Cab Driver, a fellow game show contestant, the happiest med student on earth, who you can get down and dirty with on Chekhov. Maybe it's even the guy on your friend's couch downtown, who can make you laugh over a whiskey. There's only one way to find out.

DATE Nº 36

Close Encounters of the Hollywood Tinder Kind

I like people. This is a fact. Hearing their stories, learning about their varied experiences of this world, seeing different topics from another perspective—these are all reasons why I love meeting new people. And dating. But sometimes, you just want to be around people you know. And who know you. Like your parents. And today was one of those sometimes. Today I was seriously homesick.

Maybe it was because I had brought them up to Jeff the night before, or maybe it was because I'd broken Rule #7B: No Facebook-Stalking Parents, but I woke up desperately missing my mom and dad. I usually talked to them at least every three or four days, sometimes daily, depending on the time of the month (my mom suffered the brunt of my emotional calls), but now all I could do was peruse their stunning pictures of the Mediterranean. While I'd been throwing back whiskey and sauvignon blanc with strange men, they'd been exploring the moonlike city of Cappadocia, catching waves on the beaches of Greek islands, and getting spiritual at the Hagia Sophia. *Why can't I be there with them?*

I had an audition in the afternoon that only strengthened the pangs of separation. In the world of the film, I was an alien, Princess Lahara, from a distant galaxy who had left my home and my family after my king father had turned everyone but us into emotionless beings. It was too painful for me to stay, so I discovered Earth, which I loved and found fascinating. But I also missed my parents.

The audition actually went great. I felt more dropped in and connected than I had in ages. It didn't matter if I booked the part; it just mattered that I told Princess Lahara's story. *My* story. For those ten minutes, I *was* Princess Lahara.

But when I left, I was me, and I longed for my own family even more. *Sigh. Life imitates art.*

As I walked through the warm, dusky air later that evening on my way to meet John, my thirty-sixth date, all I wanted was to bury myself in my mother's arms. I felt tired, overwhelmed, anxious. If only she could stroke my hair and tell me everything was all right… But alas, she was probably playing mini golf aboard their transatlantic Celebrity Cruise, and I was about to have happy hour and then go to space. *C'est la vie.*

I should just call and cancel, I thought, only yards from the

Well. *You don't have to do this; you can just go home and curl up with Teddy and cry.* I paused, seriously considering it. *No, Amy, you're so close. Literally ten feet away. And five dates. Plus, he already bought the movie tickets. Just do it.*

The cavelike bar was surprisingly crowded for six o'clock on a Thursday. John arrived a minute after me. He was taller than I'd expected, and somehow...nicer. Not that he had seemed mean over text; it's just that his personality hadn't really come through—one of the pitfalls of online communication.

After twenty minutes and a Heineken, my shoulders finally softened. I kept reminding myself of the Broken Umbrella: *Put your attention on him.* Once again, it worked.

We spent most of our time at the bar talking about writing. John was a screenwriter whose first feature film had been made a couple of years ago. It had done the festival circuit, and even made it to Netflix. He and his writing partner were currently working on a more whimsical drama about a struggling poet. I loved the idea.

In the meantime, John still had his day job: waiting tables at a chichi restaurant on Sunset Boulevard.

"It's weird to think that the majority of my life's income has come from other people's donations."

"I know all about that!" I laughed. "I waited tables for six years. The day I finally quit my last restaurant job was glorious. But I gotta say, sometimes I still miss it, that sense of family. I met some of my best friends working in the service industry." I gazed off, suddenly nostalgic over my waitressing past. It was *really* one of those days.

We finished snacking on the surprisingly decent fries

and Caribbean chicken kabobs, then made our way over to the ArcLight.

"You're my first Tinder date," John admitted shyly as we waited for the light to turn.

"I am?" I smiled, feeling both flattered and like a criminal. His first Tinder date, and he ended up with a girl writing a blog. I was like a rock musician taking a Texan girl's virginity.

We met up with his writing partner, Marshall, and his girlfriend, Jezebel, in front of the theater—both on Zooey Deschanel's level of quirkiness—then found our seats.

"You ready to go to space?" they asked us from several rows down.

"Let's do this!" John enthused.

I pulled out a stick of gum and prepared for the ride. *Three ... two ... one ... lift off!*

Interstellar was ... ambitious. Though far from a perfect film, it moved me. The score alone made my heart beat out of my chest several times, and many of the shots were (horrible pun) out of this world. And as for the story? I cried. Oh, did I cry. It didn't matter that I was sitting next to a first Tinder date. It wouldn't have mattered if I were next to the Queen of England. Nothing could have stopped my waterworks when so much of the film's drama centered on family being separated. I was the only person in the theater silently sobbing, but I didn't care. It felt good to have that cathartic release, to see the very same things I'd been feeling all day heightened to the heavens and then reflected back. Why else did we go to the movies?

"It was like *2001*, without Kubrick," Jezebel commented afterward.

"Yeah, Nolan was just blatantly ripping things off," Marshall added.

"He can't write a first act to save his life," John concluded, "but I still enjoyed it."

I smiled, thinking of my own experience of it. My own experience of the entire date, which was no doubt different from John's.

Jezebel and Marshall split off, and John walked me to my car.

"I had a really nice time tonight. I'm glad we did this," he said, standing on the sidewalk. I thought of where I'd started at the beginning of the night, and where I was at now. It felt like another planet.

"Me too. Thanks for taking me to space. I really needed that." We both smiled, and he gave me a gentle kiss into that good night.

DATE Nº 37

The Spiritual Juggler

SILVER LAKE

Sick of spending hundreds of dollars a month to visit a psychologist? Tired of still calling your mother to solve all of your emotional problems at twenty-eight years old? Feeling down and out and not sure where to turn? Then join Tinder! That's right, the onetime hookup app now offers a wide range of services, including drinking buddies, on-call comedy show attendees, and super-effective untrained therapists. You're just a swipe to the right from having all of your worries whisked away!

♡

I went into Date #37 feeling one thing: stress. My trip to another galaxy the night before had relieved me of my homesickness, but it hadn't absolved me of my dating and producing duties. There was camera equipment to be picked up and burrito boxes to be ordered from Chipotle. But first, coffee with Tony.

Confession: I swiped right on Tony because of the photo of him chin-balancing three folding chairs stacked on top of each other. I couldn't resist. Before meeting New James, I hadn't even known such a talent as chin-balancing existed, and now here was yet another Tinder match performing this incredible feat. I had to meet him. (Plus, he looked darn good in a vest and khakis wielding a croquet mallet.)

During the course of our messaging, Tony revealed he was an ultimate Frisbee player, and this immediately set things in motion.

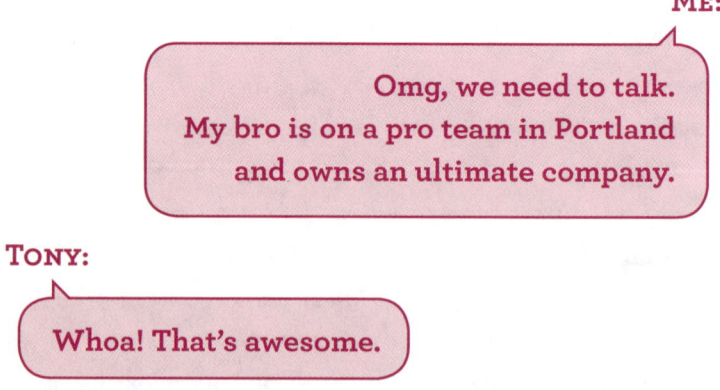

Me: Omg, we need to talk. My bro is on a pro team in Portland and owns an ultimate company.

Tony: Whoa! That's awesome.

With such a strong connection as Frisbee, coffee at a hipster hangout had clearly been inevitable.

I stepped into Cafecito Organico in Silver Lake and immediately felt at home. And by home, I do mean Southeast Portland. The inside looked like a taco shack from the nineties, and the outside was filled with Bohemians on MacBook Pros. There was even a small crew shooting an indie movie. *Doesn't get more hipster than this!* I thought as I made my way to the bench where Tony sat, delicious fair-trade decaf latte in hand.

Right away I knew Tony would not be interested in dating me. Not because I wasn't awesome—I'd already learned that lesson—but because we were prettttty different. He reminded me a lot of my brother, which was a huge compliment, but Kevin and I had always been on opposite ends of the spectrum. Sure, we'd been cut from the same cloth, but I wore Topshop while Kevin rocked Patagonia.

I started off the date in the most logical place: asking about his chin-balancing skills.

"Are you like a circus performer or something?"

"Yes, I'm a juggler," he replied.

My eyes went wide. "Ooh, tell me more."

I wanted to pull out my iPhone and record Tony as he spoke about his craft. It was that poetic. He described to me the usual chaos in his mind, the million thoughts racing by every second, the information superhighway of his cerebral cortex. But then when he juggled, everything stopped. The focus required to keep afloat five, six, even seven objects meant that all other concerns receded into the distance. Even more than François or Navid, Tony was a true Zen Buddhist, achieving enlightenment through the repetitious task of juggling. I was obsessed.

"I can juggle three scarves, but that's about it." I laughed. "However, I have found something to help me overcome my worries and fears and just be completely present."

I told him about pole, and how my dance had been

evolving the more I allowed myself to embrace where I was at.

"Like the other day, I went out with this guy who I felt too 'party girl' for, right? And at first I felt bad about it, but then I realized, screw that, I do like to go to a club and dance my ass off every once in a while. So my next class, I danced to M.I.A.'s 'Bad Girls' and had the best time ever."

He smiled calmly. "You gotta do you."

We snaked our way from hobbies to travel to New York to my summer semester abroad in Paris, studying French. Tony told me about his complete deficiency in learning other languages. Except, of course, sign language.

"Wow, you are like a completely kinesthetic learner, aren't you?" Another calm smile. (I hadn't made him laugh once. Not sure if this was a reflection on me or him.)

We talked about the education system in America, and the necessity of a learning curriculum based on the majority.

"But then we're letting some bright, potentially even brilliant kids slip through the cracks," I said, bringing up children with Asperger's and autism. We agreed it was a shame, and lamented the shortcomings of our current system and the nearly impossible task of fixing it.

"I received a great education, but I feel like in a lot of ways I've just been wasting it," I remarked. "I could have done anything out of school, I was an amazing student, but of course I chose to become an actress and an alcoholic."

He almost laughed.

"I'm also an alcoholic," he commiserated.

I did laugh.

"But you shouldn't say that about yourself," he continued. "Don't measure your success against anyone else's. It's about your own personal journey. Finding that focus and being able to stick to it and create."

I studied him. *Does he have some sort of special access to my mind?*

"You need to be able to strike a balance. God or the bottle, you know?" I didn't know, so he explained. "People turn to religions to find meaning and community. To feel that connection, a sense of something greater. But it can lead to complacency. On the other hand, without that, people often turn to the bottle. If there's nothing else, then what's the point? It's about finding that spiritual space where you can stay both grounded and productive."

I wanted to hug him.

He tied up the whole discussion perfectly with a personal story involving juggling, teaching, focus, and gratitude. Again, I wanted to capture his elegant storytelling on camera, as he told me about his current day job, working children's parties as a clown and juggler. Was this his dream job? No. But he made the best of it. He described how he managed to transcend the stale clichés of the birthday performer, and interact with the children in a way that created value: building games together, teaching them important lessons through his craft.

I could have listened to Tony's words of wisdom for several more hours. Days even. But we both had to get our Fridays started.

"I really enjoyed talking with you," I said. "You know, my birthday is next week, and my brother is in town. You should come. You guys should meet."

He smiled (still no laugh). "Definitely."

I left my coffee date with Tony feeling a thousand times calmer than I had going into it. As I drove away, I couldn't stop thinking about him. Did I want to date Tony? No. No matter how much I respected his enlightenment, I 110 percent needed someone who shared my sense of humor. Did I want him as my new therapist? Abso-frickin-lutely. He was better than any professional I'd been to—although I couldn't see him jumping on weekly sessions. So would I settle for him being my brother's friend? *Mais bien sûr.*

DATE No 38

The Guy with the Best Biceps

MID-WILSHIRE

True Player: *Baller of the highest magnitude. Forthright and all-encompassing in his skill with the ladies. Divinely marked with the ability of pure domination.* –Urban Dictionary

How did players do it? How did they wake up every morning, next to Monica or Erica or Rita, then ball all day and fall asleep next to someone else? I wanted to call up Usher or John Mayer or Tiger Woods and hear their strategy. It took major dedication to balance so many sexy significant others. And my resolve was finally crumbling under the weight of thirty-seven guys.

I went ahead and did another first date that night in order to leave the following day completely free for our shoot.

Needless to say, I was suffering some major player fatigue. Like Michael Jordan taking on baseball, I was beginning to think I'd overstretched my gaming ability. I could no longer keep up with the text messages and phone calls, the guys who'd advanced to the second and third rounds and those who'd fallen to the wayside. Did I really need to add one more to my roster?

Yes. Because from the moment Scott sat down across from me at Rascal, I knew I couldn't say no to those biceps. They. Were. Perfect. Like Ryan Reynolds in *The Proposal.* Or Channing Tatum in *Magic Mike.* In fact, Scott had done gone and Henry Cavill-ed me—in no way had I been prepared for that body by his demure pictures. Pleasant surprise indeed.

Now, I wasn't so shallow as to be completely swayed by the physique of an Olympian God. Oh no, Scott had to prove he was more than just a chiseled six-pack of abs, or a pretty all-American face. And thank the hot Jim Caviezel Jesus he was.

"Thanks for meeting me. Sorry about last week. I was just slammed with this new job," Scott said, apologizing for unknowingly leaving me with Darren.

"Don't worry about it! It's all working out." I smiled, wondering how much he could bench-press. "So what's this new job?"

Scott told me he'd just started assisting a director. I hadn't heard of him. He listed off several big studio comedies.

"Yeah, I should probably know who that is." I sighed, regretting having bombed out my film minor with pinot noir. "My writing partner actually just began working for a director as well, Jonathan Demme."

"Who's that?" he asked. I suddenly didn't feel so bad.

My phone buzzed: Sascha. I looked up to see her waving from outside.

"Sorry, my girlfriend is here to pick up this camera for our shoot this weekend. I'll be right back." I waved at her. "Actually ... " I waved her inside.

"Hiiiii!" Sascha flashed her effusive smile and gave me a yummy hug. She and Scott shook hands, and we chatted for a minute.

"Okay, let me get you the camera."

We walked outside and she turned to me. "He seems great! What date is this?"

"Thirty-eight!" I said excitedly. "He's kind of wonderful, right?"

"Yeah, such a sweet energy! Oh my god, I can't believe you're almost done."

"I know!" I smiled. "I'm so ready! Forget raining—it's flooding men! See you tomorrow!"

I skipped back into the restaurant. Scott was gone. I stood stone still. *Did I take too long with Sascha? Was he upset I didn't know who his boss was? Is it actually possible I've been ditched?*

The bathroom door swung open, and Scott strolled toward the table. I laughed as he sat down.

"So, I actually thought you left."

He started cracking up. He had the best laugh. I made a weird self-deprecating face. More laughter. *Yay, he thinks I'm funny! Take that, Spiritual Juggler!*

He asked me about what we were filming, and I showed him our Kickstarter video.

"Wow, incredible," he said, meaning it. I could tell he

was just as supportive as Matt Two—if not financially so, spiritually so.

We started talking shop, and he told me he was directing his first film in the spring. A character piece, driven by a wicked badass heroine.

"Who wrote it?" I asked.

"Me." He smiled. I felt warm and fuzzy.

"Awesome."

We continued chatting about film and writing, and I continued making weird faces. It was becoming harder and harder to talk about what was going on in my life without saying a single thing about what was going on in my life. I couldn't take it anymore.

"So this backfired on me last time, but I like you, and I'm almost done, and it's kind of important, so just ... whatever." I took a deep breath. "I'm doing a blog called *40 Dates & 40 Nights*, and you're number thirty-eight."

Scott looked like I'd just told him Santa Claus wasn't real. *Dammit, Amy, why'd you drop that so quickly? Ughhh.*

"No way. I think I've heard of that."

I lit up. "You have?"

"Yeah! Wow, this is so surreal. So you're going to write about this?" he asked.

"Mm-hmm. You can even choose your name." I grinned.

He asked me more questions, and I gave him more answers. He didn't seem fazed, just curious.

"I probably should've left you. That would have made for a better story, right?"

I shook my head.

"Oh no, a better story would be me and you falling in love,

making this into a movie, then using the money to go to Italy." (He'd never been—tragic!)

"That would be good!" He laughed.

"Okay, we have to talk about something else," I said, changing course. "I want to get to know more about you!"

He caught me up on a few more details—like the fact he'd been living bicoastal(!)—as we split a mac and cheese, kale salad, and burger. All I wanted to do was keep making him laugh.

"Want to come with me to my friend's show at Molly Malone's?" *Please say yes.*

"Where's that?" he asked.

"It's this Irish pub on Third Street. Or maybe Fairfax. I mean, duh, it's an Irish pub, Molly Malone's. Hello, Captain Obvious. I can't remember where it is. God, this is boring. Am I boring?"

He laughed. "Any other night I would come. I have a Skype call at seven a.m., and with this new job ..." I understood.

He walked me across the street to my car.

"Wow, you got an awesome parking spot. I'm in a lot illegally. Hopefully I haven't been towed," he said, as we stopped in the middle of the street.

"Wait, you risked being towed to hang out with me?" My voice had suddenly jumped an octave.

"Of course."

I leaned partway in, and he met me. We kissed in the glow of headlights. More warm and fuzzy ... And oh my god, his biceps. Even better when kissing.

We finally pulled apart.

"I'm gonna title this 'The Guy with the Best Biceps.' Cool?"

He laughed. "Let me know when it's posted."

"Oh, I will." I smiled. "I will."

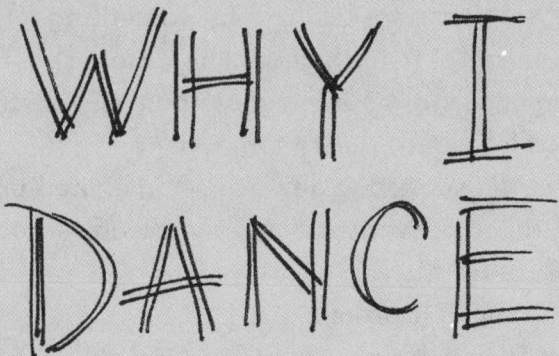

WHY I DANCE

It had finally arrived. The weekend of our dance shoot and my final two dates! It hardly seemed an accident that the two most important, personal projects of my life were culminating at almost exactly the same moment.

As I watched each of the dancers bare their bodies and souls, the camerawomen capturing them, Melanie directing, Sascha supporting, I felt a deep gratitude for their willingness to share themselves, to share this story. It took strength to do what we were doing, far beyond just the physical might to pull ourselves up the pole. Vulnerability isn't easy, but it's essential: to dancing, to writing, to acting, to dating, to life.

When it was my turn to dance, I could feel my heart pounding in my chest. There was so much I wanted to say about my journey in these four and a half minutes, I struggled to contain it. My hands trembled as the first few drumbeats of the score sounded. I stepped out into the light, and my body began to move. Hesitantly, almost painfully. I thought I might cry. I could feel everyone's eyes on me, waiting to see what I would do. Suddenly the camera terrified me. *What if I look silly, or graceless, or unsexy?* I'd only ever danced in class, in that dark, cocoonlike space. Never in the naked sunlight, being captured for the world to behold.

"Just breathe, beauty," Melanie tenderly encouraged. "Be yourself."

I reached for my chest with my hands, my hair cascading over, then tossed my head back, letting go. *This is me! This is who I am! This is the love I want to give!* I dropped down to the floor, prancing, writhing. I crawled to the windows, reaching for the sun's rays, feeling the coolness of the windowpanes.

I pushed off of the column and shed the diaphanous white sweater I'd been hiding under. The layers off, I leaped toward the pole, grasping it as if it were a long-lost lover, and swung around. I climbed toward the heavens, then dropped back to the earth. I felt timeless, joyful, free, me.

The music decrescendoed, and as I walked slowly, deliberately, powerfully toward the camera, I felt more exposed and more honest than I ever had in my life. I collapsed in my girlfriends' arms, thrilled, crying, laughing. This was what I wanted to bring to my art, my relationships, the world. This expression of acceptance. This feeling of community. This gift of love.

DATE Nº 39

My Weekend of Love

BEVERLY GROVE

I could barely lace up my favorite boots, I was so happy and fulfilled and bruised and tired from the past two days of female empowerment. I reclined on my bed, one boot on, and closed my eyes. Images of remarkable women danced across them, the raspy lyrics still playing: *And who shall wear the starry crown? Good Lord, show me the way...*

I had passed gently through the alpha and theta stages of sleep when I heard a lovely little chime: my phone!

CHARLIE:

> Running a tiny bit behind. Would 7:15 or 7:30 be okay?

ME:
7:15

There was no way I could stay awake that extra fifteen minutes. Or even one minute. I finished my other boot and left.

We met at Fat Dog on Fairfax, right next to one of my favorite five-dollars-a-cup coffee shops, the Coffee Commissary (I would have paid ten dollars for a latte right then). We finagled a high-top table inside, and I immediately started showing him pictures of my seminude body. Something about his heather purple V-neck sweater made me feel unusually comfortable.

"Wow, you're stronger than me!" he exclaimed, clearly focused purely on my athleticism.

"Honestly, Charlie, it was one of the most magical, special, important weekends of my life," I gushed, flipping through photo after photo of stunning women exposing their essence. "I still can't believe what this turned into. It started with such a simple concept, and then grew into so much more." I was talking about the short, but I may as well have been discussing my blog.

"I can't even tell you how much strength it's given me. To love and accept my body for what it is. To live authentically. Also, I had no idea how much I missed gymnastics!"

After a fifteen-minute women's studies lecture on female empowerment, I finally opened up the date to discussion. (Also, my food had arrived and I was starving. Charlie had had an early dinner, so I got to eat solo.)

"So you're a yoga instructor?" I asked through a mouthful

of Caesar kale, vaguely remembering his Tinder profile.

"On the side," he replied. "I also have a day job in TV as an assistant in post. But I'm a writer."

I smiled. *How do I attract so many writers? I mean, it must be like a sign or something ...* "Fantastic! What are you writing?"

He told me about his pitch meeting coming up in a few days, by far the most important of his career thus far.

"Great! Pitch it to me right now," I said.

And he did. The pilot sounded great: a one-hour sci-fi drama dealing with space and global economics and family dynamics. The production company was already interested, but now they wanted to hear the bible for the rest of the series.

"I keep telling myself it's not a big deal, that it's not even happening. But it's a really big deal," he said, fighting nerves.

"You'll be great. Just be yourself and focus on the story you're telling," I said. "Do what you just did with me and you're golden."

We stopped talking about work and moved on to other topics. Like drugs. Maybe it was because I felt so open from all of the women and dancing, or maybe it was because I was nearing the end of my Tinderbender, but I had zero inhibitions with Charlie. He felt like an old friend.

"MDMA was probably the best thing I've ever done. So much love, so much happiness," I rhapsodized, reliving that night in Vegas, still feeling those same emotions from this weekend. Charlie had never tried it—too much anxiety.

"It was important to me as an artist," I continued waxing. "I compare it to having a stroke, where suddenly you're functioning entirely with the right brain. I'm pretty sure

I took too much and nearly died, but it was incredible. I no longer identified myself as a separate entity from the world. Everything was one."

He laughed.

"Oh god, you must think I'm nuts! Pole dancing, mind-altering drugs. Why am I telling you this stuff?"

"It's okay." He grinned. "I just think you're a crazy party girl."

"I am!" I laughed. "But I also read! And see tons of movies! Did you see *Interstellar* yet?" I asked, seamlessly transitioning the discourse down a more normative first-date path. Not that I regretted sharing any of my experiences. Not in the slightest.

The check came, and I put down my card. Charlie threw in a twenty, more than enough to cover his glass of pinot noir.

"Wait, what am I doing?" He placed the bill back in his wallet and pulled out his card. "Let me buy you dinner. Chivalry is not dead."

"Are you sure? You really don't have to. You didn't even eat. Plus, I talked about feminism half the time." *Plus, we're just going to be friends*, I wanted to add. But I wasn't feeling quite *that* open.

"No, I want to. Really, it would be my pleasure," he said. He was sweet and kind and gentle. Another Tinder win, only steps from the finish line.

"Okay, if you want to," I said, taking back my card. "But you're gonna have to deal with me sending you more pictures from the shoot. And a link when it's finally finished."

He grinned. "Great!"

He paid the check and then walked me to my car, further reinforcing his chivalrous nature. We hugged good night, and

I thanked him once again for dinner and sharing his evening with me.

I drove home, blissful, exhausted, overwhelmed, grateful. I couldn't wait to share with Charlie the love I felt this weekend. I couldn't wait to share it with everyone. ♥

DATE N⁰ 40

The Nice Guy Finishes Last HOLLYWOOD

Before there was New James and the Cab Driver and Best Biceps, there was Old James. And before there was Old James, there was Josh.

Josh and I went to Lincoln High School together in Portland, Oregon. I didn't know him well my freshman and sophomore years, but I always had a secret crush on him. He was too smart and nerdy to have a public crush on—those were reserved for the jocks and bad boys. So I swooned from my corner of the library.

Sometime toward the end of junior year, I had a major crisis of identity, and completely changed social circles. This finally gave me the opportunity to get to know Josh, but my crush remained secret: he had a girlfriend. I remember spending a day together in Laurelhurst Park, talking for hours in the warm sunshine. All I wanted to do was kiss him. To talk to him forever. He was so smart, so attentive, so handsome, so ... *nice*.

All through senior year I imagined myself together with Josh, but I knew it would never be possible. He was too good of a person; he would never fall for someone as wild and vain and flawed as me. Even if I hung out with theater kids and IB students, I still had my dating roots in the football team.

One particular incident right before graduation captured it all perfectly. It was the senior awards assembly, and they were distributing the Harvard Book Award, the highest honor for academic excellence. When they called Josh to come and receive the award for the men, I was sitting next to the quarterback and wide receiver, wearing a trucker hat and Abercrombie miniskirt. When the principal called my name to receive it for the women, the quarterback turned to me and said, "I didn't know you were smart." I grinned and made my way to the podium to stand next to my Prince Charming. Even if I never got to actually date Josh, we would always share this very public moment.

That summer I moved down to LA, and Josh and I talked periodically on the phone. If he hadn't found me wild and vain and flawed before, now it would have been impossible for him not to. I was on such a roller coaster. I'll never forget a conversation we had during that first year, as I sat on Santa Monica Beach watching the sun go down. I was talking a mile a minute, telling him all of my silly Hollywood stories, dazzled by the boulevards lined with palm trees. He must have thought me ludicrous, sitting in his dorm at Stanford, studying neuroscience. We were back at square one.

Several years passed with hardly any communication. I fell in love once, twice, fifteen times. I dated and dated and dated some more, not unlike the past forty days, maybe just less ... purposefully. Then I heard from Josh out of the blue on Facebook:

JOSH:

> I have our best chance yet for a much needed reunion. You should come to a wedding with me in LA! I'm going to be a groomsman at what should be a wonderful afternoon and evening. The date is Sunday, May 1st. I'd love your accompaniment. Send an update when you have the chance, and I look forward to reconnecting.

Two months later, I went to the wedding with him in Palos Verdes. It was perfect. Like, beyond perfect. The most romantic, beautiful, "can I marry you right now, that's how perfect this is" kind of perfect. As we wound through gorgeous coastal streets in my worn-down '99 Z3, top down, Josh even said, semi-seriously, mostly perfectly, "We should get married at twenty-seven." My first proposal.

He lived in San Francisco at the time, and I made arrangements to see him the following month. A game show thwarted my first attempt (I was literally at the airport when the producer called to tell me I would be needed that weekend), so I drove up the next Thursday.

The weekend was magical. He introduced me to his world,

and we connected emotionally, intellectually, physically. We even went out to Napa and stayed a night at my great-uncle's barn. More magical perfectness and Rule #5 breaking.

But something happened on my drive back down Interstate 5. I freaked out. *I can't do long distance! He hates Los Angeles! He wants to raise a family in Portland!* I went from zero to one hundred, the asphalt burning beneath my Z3 and the June sun.

I got back to LA and successfully talked myself out of having a relationship with Josh and into having one with the writer/director of the small film projects I was producing. Josh found a girlfriend shortly thereafter, and from their pictures on Facebook, they looked happy together. Really happy.

Over the next couple of years, I thought about Josh often, and the mistake I had made in letting him go. I would listen to Katy Perry's "The One That Got Away" on repeat while running up and down Bronson Canyon, telling myself I'd meet a new Josh. A better Josh. One that lived in my city and didn't want to move to Portland. And who was maybe a little wilder. But still just as smart and kind and compassionate.

Then one day last year out of the blue Josh messaged me. He was moving to Los Angeles in the summer to work for UCLA. I called my mom.

"How fantastic!" she said, always a huge fan of his.

"Yeah, but he's still with his girlfriend," I lamented.

"Well, they're not married yet," she replied, always the pragmatist.

When I got back from my month in Europe in July, Josh was officially living in Santa Monica.

Josh:

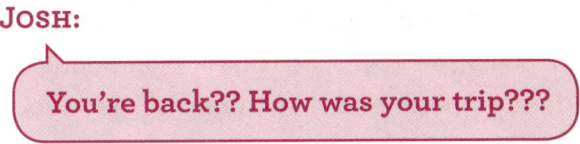

He'd clearly done a bit of Facebook-stalking.

Me:

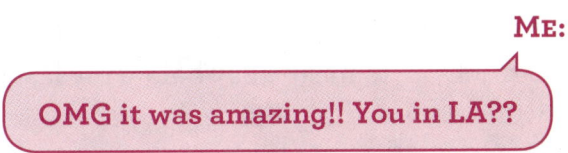

We arranged to do some story-swapping over sushi at Sugarfish.

Obviously I'd never been one to fret over what I wear or how my makeup looks (sorry, Marvin), but I put some pretty serious thought into both that night. I wanted to look perfect. I hadn't made a big deal of it to any of my friends, but inside I felt like a Jackson Pollock. He arrived a couple of minutes late, looking sharp as ever, and I melted.

We ordered two Trust Me drinks. It didn't take long before the topic of relationships popped up. He was still with Taylor.

"We had a serious talk about it in Mexico, whether we were going to break up or plan to get married, and we decided to stay together."

My heart sunk. I tried not to let it show, expressing enthusiasm for their happiness, but I was disappointed. Crushed, actually.

And then a week later I met James. It was like the universe felt sorry for me and delivered a Josh 2.0 into my Match inbox. In fact, he reminded me so much of Josh that that was how I described him to my mom.

"He's in Mensa, he's athletic, he just spent a year in Kenya working for an NGO, he loves art history and music, he's passionate and empathetic and driven and so good looking, and he's just like Josh!"

My mom told me to take it slow. We all know how that worked out.

If I'm being honest, a huge part of me had hoped James would reach out to me the day before my last date and tell me he'd worked everything out and loved me and wanted to be with me again. Even if it didn't happen in real life, I'd already decided that that was how the rom-com would end on screen. A perfect happily ever after.

But what I'd never prepared for was Josh.

Just like with Darren, when I'd started this blog, I had sent him the link. He had always loved my writing, and again, I kinda maybe sorta wanted to make him jealous (I told you! I'm not a good person!). He thought it was great, and shared it with his coworkers. This thrilled me.

Then, sometime between brunching with Justin and supping with Dan, he sent me a text.

JOSH:

Hey! So when are we going to meet up again?

ME:

Swipe right on Tinder and I'll squeeze you in ;) But maybe after the 40 dates.

JOSH:

> Oh yeah! We should give you 40 days off first.

ME:

> Are you and Taylor together? I'm assuming and hoping yes. [Horrible big fat lie.]

JOSH:

> On a break, long distance just breaks people... I actually am on Tinder, coincidentally.

I began to cry.

ME:

> Start swiping right. I want you to be my 40th date. But first we need to match.

For some reason, even though I'd broken every other rule, I couldn't let go of this one. Maybe it was *because* I'd broken every other rule. I wanted to prove to myself that I could keep just one.

I swiped for several days before he finally popped up: Josh, 28. (There are a lot of men between twenty-eight and thirty-two years old in LA, apparently.) "Yes!" I yelled out loud in my bedroom. But nothing happened.

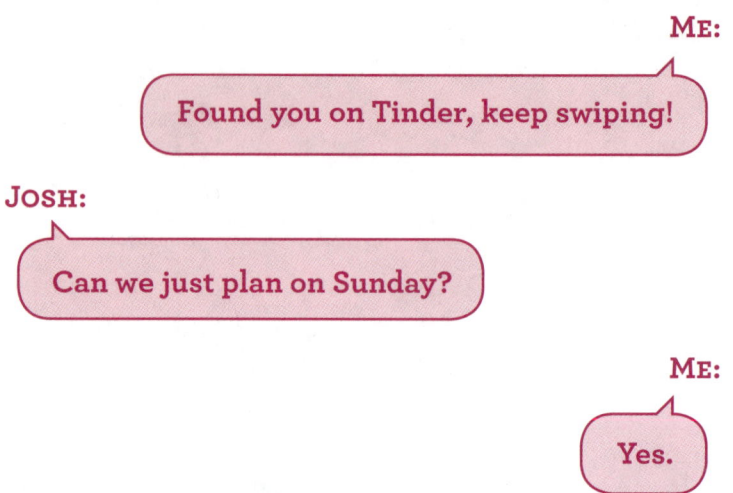

Rules truly were made to be broken (Obvious Tinder Dating Mistake #11: Refusing to Date Guys Not Met on Tinder).

Josh wanted to do something that hadn't been done yet, so he asked if he could cook me dinner at my place.

"That sounds amazing," I said.

I couldn't remember the last time a guy had cooked me dinner. Maybe Valentine's Day 2007?

He showed up at seven fifteen in dapper attire.

"I love that you're dressed up and I'm essentially in pajamas!" I laughed, absolutely not loving my choice of UCLA stretch pants and American Apparel tank at all. *I should have put on one of my hundred adorable cocktail dresses*, I thought, considering a quick change.

Josh smiled. "You're fine! It's your house! I'm here to serve you tonight."

He strode into my kitchen and started pulling out ingredients.

"Do you have any vegetable oil?" he asked. He needed it for the homemade bread.

"Let's see ... I have olive oil, coconut oil, peanut oil. Will those work?"

He shrugged. "We'll find out."

I opened the bottle of wine he brought, an elegant zin, and he perused my cupboards for cookware.

"You have pretty nice stuff!" he remarked.

I blushed. It was all my mom's hand-me-downs. I cooked, but it was essentially limited to stir-fries, sautéed chicken, and brussels sprouts. I didn't even know what my steamer was until Josh informed me.

While he prepared the steaks and locally grown chard, I readied my tiny kitchen nook with candles and silverware.

"Dinner is served! Although we're still a few minutes away on the bread." Josh dropped plates and slipped onto the bench. "If it's too rare, you can send it back to the kitchen."

I smiled. "I'm sure it'll be perfect."

But it was undercooked. Even in the faint glow of the candles, I could see the cow still mooing.

"Maybe just a little longer," I said gently. "It's not quite done."

He gracefully whisked the steaks away and spoke to me from the kitchen.

"But you see, this is actually even better, because now everything will be ready at the same time!"

He returned with the steaks and the bread. Well, it was sort of bread. It vaguely resembled a larger version of the dough porcupines we made at my grade school.

I smiled. "Everything looks great." *Okay, so it's not*

Glasserie, but what is? Besides, it's the imperfections that add character. Perfect is boring. I ripped off a piece of the loaf and dipped it in olive oil. "Not bad!"

The conversation started off lightly, with talk of our upcoming high school reunion, our families, how much Josh loved New Haven winters. I told him about wanting to move to New York, the possibility of subletting, about my neighbors and their new baby.

"How many kids do you want?" he asked. *Wait, hold on, did he just ask* me *how many kids I wanted? How many times have I dropped that bomb and watched it implode in my horrified suitor's face?*

"Two or three. Depends on how all this goes." I motioned to my midsection. "You?"

"Well, for a while I wanted a huge family." He smiled. "Like a whole soccer team of kids. It just seems like it would be so fun, you know? But now I'm not so sure."

I studied him. He was going to make a great father.

"So what happened with Taylor?" I finally addressed the elephant on my shoulder.

"We broke up a couple of weeks ago. The distance. She'd been wanting a break for a few months, but I didn't think we could survive it."

I nodded. I could tell it was still fresh.

"The same thing keeps happening to me in my relationships," he said quietly. "I think it's that I look really great on paper, and girls see that, so they don't want to lose me, but they don't actually want to commit."

I wanted to hug him. That had been me, three years ago.

"I think it's all timing," I said. "Can I tell you about this script idea I've been tossing around for a couple of years?"

He nodded.

"So it's this pair of high school friends, right? And the guy tells the girl senior year that if they're still single at twenty-seven, he's going to marry her. Well, on her twenty-seventh birthday, he shows up on her doorstep and proposes to her. And she says yes. He's everything she's ever wanted, right? It's perfect. But then they go ahead and do it and she starts to freak out and ruin it."

Josh's face fell. "Why?"

"Because she doesn't feel worthy of him," I continued. "She doesn't think she deserves someone that good, that nice; someone who loves her that much. So she leaves him. But then she has this process of self-discovery and finally believes she's enough. I haven't fully fleshed that part out yet, but they end up together."

I was crying. He rubbed my leg softly under the table.

"Anyways, it's not about you, Josh. You're amazing on paper and in real life." I smiled.

"So are you," he said.

I picked up the plates.

"Let's move this into the living room. It's more comfortable in there."

♥

We curled up on my suede love seat, my legs draped over him, our words jumping back and forth, tickling my ears and running down my spine. I had a brief moment of déjà vu, to the first night I'd hung out with Old James. We'd sat here in this same position, the same magnetic chemistry pulsing, the same sort of buildup to the inevitable kiss.

But it wasn't the same. History may repeat itself, but we have the opportunity to come at it differently. Because people do change. We do grow up. We do get wiser. And what we may not have been prepared for ten years ago, three years ago, heck, even forty days ago, we might be prepared for now.

I'm not saying that I was ready to marry Josh that night. Or that he was ready to marry me. For one, he had just gotten out of a very serious relationship, and I had just opened up my world to a whole bunch of incredible opportunities (great guys, New York, a writing career, a pole dancing movement). No, that kind of thing only happens in a movie. The movie I'm going to write.

But what I will say is that I was more prepared right then for what the future held than I ever had been before. In something of a paradox, through getting to know these forty different guys, I really got to know myself. And as it turns out, I'm pretty darn great.

The Morning After

You know that feeling after finals week has ended, and you've just finished twenty credits while working two part-time restaurant jobs and shooting a two-week industrial? Or what about when you've just come home from a whirlwind European tour, hitting five countries in a month, running on four hours a night? Or how about the morning after your birthday, when you drank one or four too many cocktails and now must somehow hold that cake down while standing on stage at an improv show? Well, that's what it felt like coming out of *40 Dates*.

A dating and blogging binge is a bit like a drinking binge. It's intoxicating and wild, dizzying and borderline psychotic. It's at some points the high of your life, dancing on top of a New York table with new besties, and at others the low, kneeling next to a toilet. And then in the end, when all is said and done, it leaves you with that most celebrated of post-awesome pastimes: a hangover.

The first couple of days after my date with Josh were a bit hazy. I finally caught up on some much-needed sleep, clocking eight hours here, nine there. I saw long-lost girlfriends, my parents, Benedict Cumberbatch (at a screening on my birthday, much better than a Tinder date). I went grocery shopping. Cracked open a book. Read the news. SoulCycled and pole danced. Did the dishes. Bought a new shirt ... In short, I missed dating.

It's not that I didn't need a break—I did. Or that I wasn't ready to further explore some of the great guys I'd met—I was. But it was tough to go from the crazy, exciting world of daily Tindering and blogging to the usual grind of my perfectly enjoyable normal life.

So *40 Dates & 40 Nights* was exhausting, and probably legitimately crazy, but it was also hands down one of the most worthwhile things I've ever done. Sure, I became a boy-crazy Tinder addict. And no, it didn't end with a wedding chapel in Vegas. But I did learn. A *lot*. And I changed. Or rather, I became more of the person I really am. Which was way better than finding a husband. Because let's be honest, how could I expect to meet my husband before I'd really met myself?

So. What exactly did I learn? I'll tell you. Not because I'm now some dating expert and think you should listen to me. Or because it's super profound and life-changing (I told you there would be no secrets to the universe revealed). But because I want to make sense of my own journey. A journey I'm still on.

OBVIOUS TINDER DATING WISDOM

1. IF YOU GET KNOCKED OFF THE POLE, GET BACK UP AND KEEP SWINGING.

This is more of an all-around life lesson, one we learn on the jungle gym, but it's easily one of the most important things this project taught me (or rather, reinforced for me). We are all in this game of life together, and sometimes it's super fun, or super sucky, or super thrilling, or super boring, but one thing it never is is worth quitting.

Before my Tinderbender, I was ready to give up. On men. On storytelling. On dancing. On myself. I was a heartbroken mess, vacillating between crying over depressing music and crying over depressing books. Sometimes I just cried over nothing.

Joining Tinder changed all that. A technological sponge and kick in the butt, it dried up my tears and got me back on the pole. Was it a little bumpy at first? Did I mess up here and there and get a few extra bruises? Sure, it's an inevitable part of the learning process. But imagine if I hadn't.

We're often so afraid of what will happen when we put ourselves out there that we hide our desires, our inner truth. *What if I'm no good? What if no one likes me? What if no one cares?* The fear of failure is so powerful it stops us in our tracks. But once we commit, and show up daily in our work, our relationships, our passions, amazing things happen.

And those bruises? Yes, they hurt. Some so badly you might need to take a few days off. But eventually they go away. And if you keep working on it, sooner or later you're going to be able to Superwoman (or Superman). And trust me, it is SO worth learning how to fly.

2. WHEN ONE DOOR CLOSES, ANOTHER ONE OPENS.

Again, this is *super* obvious. Something we've been hearing since the invention of doors (or since Alexander Graham Bell said it). But it took my breakup with James for me to really understand what this means. You see, James had closed a door, but I just stood there in front of it, waiting for it to open again. Doors were opening all around me, but I couldn't see them, because I was staring at my one and only true door.

Tinder showed me that there are indeed more doors. That maybe there isn't just One True Door, but multiple ones, until we choose to commit to Just One. And that this doesn't ruin fairy tales, but rather makes a happy ending more likely. After all, more doors equals more opportunities. One door equals one opportunity. Which sounds better to you?

3. Dating is fun!

I know people will fight me on this one, but I swear it is! Or at least, it can be. As long as you go into it with a healthy perspective. For instance, "I'm just going to go connect with other human beings, hear their stories, possibly learn a thing or two I didn't know about the world, and laugh. And even if it's *awful*, I'll still get to laugh with my friends after. Or with the Internet." That's the attitude I maintained, and I ended up with forty valuable dates.

On the other hand, an unhealthy perspective might look like this: "Ugh, this better be the guy I'm going to marry, because I'm so sick of all the douche bags out there who just want to hit it and quit it. Why does everybody suck so hard?" If you're seeing the world through a red lens, everything is going to be red. And if you don't like the color red, maybe you should swap that lens out for a blue one.

4. Rejection is a necessary part of the process.

Just like you're not going to book every role you audition for, you're not going to click with every single person you match with. And that's okay. In fact, it's more than okay; it's completely natural and necessary. Through each experience and relationship, we grow and learn more about who we are and what we want. It's like putting together a puzzle. You find a piece here, a piece there, ten pieces in LA, two in New York, and then one day they all fit together and voilà! It's a picture of wedding bells! How fun was that?

But how boring would that puzzle have been if you took it out of the box and it was already finished? So much of the enjoyment comes from the journey. (And don't worry, after the wedding bells puzzle, you're going to start a whole new puzzle. The fun just continues!)

Unfortunately, it can be difficult to see the fun in all those different individual puzzle pieces if we see them each as failures. Especially when we see a whole puzzle in somebody else, and they only see an individual piece in us. But just because we're not the whole puzzle to everybody we meet doesn't mean that we aren't a whole puzzle by ourselves.

I've really pushed this puzzle analogy to the edge, but I think you can see what I'm trying to say. Just because someone doesn't want a second date or a relationship or a vow of matrimony doesn't mean they think you suck or that you're a horrible person or unworthy of love. It's just not the right fit. All you can do is be the best version of you, and stop taking things so personally.

Inversely, don't feel guilty about turning someone down. Just because they like you or you had a great first date or you had sex with them doesn't mean you owe them anything. If they're missing an important piece, it's okay to move on to the next one. It doesn't make you a bad person, or a shallow one, or an unreasonable one. It just means you know what you want. This is especially important for women, because we've been conditioned to think that the guy chooses us. It's "boy chases girl," after all. But it's a woman's choice as well, and there's no need to apologize for wanting someone with a shared sense of humor, even if the rest of the boxes are ticked.

This feeling of guilt was one of the hardest things for me to overcome, but deeply necessary in my growth. Sascha said something to me right after I finished *40 Dates* that profoundly affected me: "By trying not to hurt someone's feelings and not being honest about your own, you're actually being manipulative." *Wow.* How many times had I gently continued to lead guys on for fear of hurting them? Or because I'd second-guessed my own feelings and been afraid to voice them? That same night I invited New James over and communicated that I only wanted to be friends. And guess what? He totally respected it, and we're still friends (at least on Facebook :P).

5. THERE SHOULD ONLY BE ONE RULE OF DATING: BE YOURSELF.

When I started *40 Dates*, I set up rules for myself, thinking that by following them I might solve the mysteries of dating. Well, I didn't. I broke every single one of them and ended up single. But during the course of my project, I did discover the one and only rule I should always follow: *be myself.* Because when I am comfortable in my own skin, when I own who I am and love who I am, then I'm going to attract the right partner for me. But if I'm pretending to be somebody I'm not, well, the other shoe will eventually drop, and in the meantime I'm going to stress the hell out about trying to maintain the facade.

Imagine if I had pretended to be a Serious Person Who Hates Partying in order to date Navid. First of all, it would have required a major purge of Facebook photos and a serious cleaning out of my closet (he would not like all those Katy Perry dresses). Second, at some point, I would probably have one too many cocktails at a holiday event and start swinging around a tentpole.

And finally, I *love* a crazy night out every once in a while in Vegas or the South of France—why would I give that up for someone? My Mr. Right will be there with me, spilling champagne on my dress and tearing up the dance floor. Then discussing the *New York Times*'s Sunday Review over a latte after our morning run, of course.